Client/Server Strategies

Implementations in the IBM Environment

Client/Server Strategies

Implementations in the IBM Environment

William Marion

Intertext Publications
McGraw-Hill, Inc.

New York San Francisco Washington, D.C. Auckland Bogotá
Caracas Lisbon London Madrid Mexico City Milan Montreal
New Delhi San Juan Singapore Sydney Tokyo Toronto

Library of Congress Catalog Card Number 93-77965

0 9 8 7 6 5 4 3 2 1

ISBN 0-07-040539-5

Intertext Publications/MultiScience, Inc.
One Lincoln Plaza
New York, NY 10023

McGraw-Hill Book Company
1221 Avenue of the Americas
New York, NY 10020

Contents

Preface

The promise of client/server computing has been accompanied by a lack of definitive information on the subject beyond that provided by the product literature of software vendors. As is the case with many new technologies, the rush to implement the technology often overshadows the need to adequately define and understand it. Client/server computing is no exception to this phenomenon. Managers seeking to reap the rewards of client /server computing have had few sources of objective information. Many articles written in professional journals are at a conceptual level and do not present comprehensive information on the subject. Often managers are looking for answers to questions such as: "Should I implement client/server in my organization?"— "What approach should I follow?"—"What resources will be needed to implement it?" Programmers are looking for a clear definition of what client/server computing is and how to implement it.

This book attempts to present a more complete view of the client/server application architecture. The first chapter introduces the technologies and business factors that have led to the growth of client/server computing. The second chapter presents the evolution of computing models from simple time-sharing through client/server computing. The following chapters introduce four basic implementation approaches. These approaches span the full spectrum of implementations, from basic applications integration to true client/server architecture. The approaches are presented in order of increasing technical sophistication and complexity. A discussion of the underlying technology along with the potential benefits and limitations of each approach is presented. Included are real-world examples of how that particular approach has been implemented. Chapter 7 presents the concept of enterprise–wide data access. Chapter 8 discusses planning for a client/server implementation. The final chapter looks at trends in the industry and the future of client/server computing.

This book is aimed at two levels of *information system* (IS) professionals. High-level information on implementation is presented for IS and business managers who may be involved in information systems planning and decision making. Programmers desiring to keep their skills current in an increasingly competitive job market are offered examples of how each of the client/server approaches can be implemented, several of which include samples of actual program code. While these examples provide some technical detail, they are intended only to introduce the concepts involved in the implementation of that particular approach. The reader can follow the text to the level of technical knowledge desired.

Managers and those interested in approaches and general concepts should read Chapters 1 and 2 and the introductory material in Chapters 3, 4, 5, and 6. Chapters 7, 8, and 9 would be useful to anyone planning or managing a client/server project. Programmers and those desiring a more detailed look at the underlying technology will be interested in the technical information and implementation case studies presented in Chapters 3, 4, 5, and 6.

While the computing industry seems to change almost daily, the author has endeavored to include the most up-to-date information available at the time. Specific products and manufacturers are mentioned for informational purposes only and no endorsement of any product or services is made. For more information on specific products, please contact the vendor.

I would like to thank Steve Barretta for his review of the IBM communications material in this book. To my wife Lori and my sons Ian and Neil, thanks for the support and time you gave me. Special thanks to my friend and mentor for this book, Alan R. Simon.

William Marion

Trademarks

AT, PC, XT, OS/2, AIX, MVS, CICS, TSO, PC3270, AS400, PROFS, OfficeVision, LAN Server, OS/2 Database Manager, APPN, APPC, DB2, RS6000, Information Warehouse, and IBM are registered trademarks of International Business Machines, Inc.

Attachmate,and Attachmate EXTRA 3270 are registered trademarks of Attachmate Corporation.

Windows 3.0, Windows 3.1, Windows NT, LAN Manager, SQL Server, and Windows for Workgroups are registered trademarks of Microsoft Corporation.

LOTUS, LOTUS 123, DataLens, and 123/M are registered trademarks of Lotus Development.

DEC, VAX, and VMS are registered trademarks of Digital Equipment Corporation.

EASEL and EASEL/2 are registered trademarks of Easel Corporation.

Mozart is a registered trademarks of Mozart Systems Inc.

Flashpoint is a registered trademarks of Viewpoint Systems.

Netware, Netware 4.0, and Unixware are registered trade marks of Novell Inc.

Paradox and dBase are registered trademarks of Borland International.

Data Ease is a registered trademarks of Data Ease Corporation.

1

The Move to Client/Server Computing

No other topic in the field of information systems has been more talked about in the 1990s than client/server computing. It has been presented as one of the most promising applications architectures of the future. Virtually every trade journal and industry publication has presented articles on client/server computing and its potential benefits. A recent survey of major corporations indicated that 36 percent had implemented client/server computing and an additional 15 percent were in the process of piloting applications.[1] As the technology matures, these numbers can be expected to increase. Vendors are scrambling to develop and market client/server products and services in this rapidly expanding market. Many corporations are basing strategic information system decisions on client/server computing. One vendor recently lost a multimillion-dollar outsourcing contract because of its inability to provide client/server solutions.[2]

A powerful force behind client/server computing has been the move by many organizations to "downsize" their computing operations. A 1992 study indicated that fewer than half of planned new corporate applications would be developed on mainframe platforms.[3] This move has been fueled by the development of powerful and relatively inexpensive midrange and microcomputer systems and the promise of cost savings through downsizing.

While downsizing may offer more power on the desktop for less cost, most organizations still have large investments in mainframe hardware, software, and data. Many downsizing strategies do not totally eliminate traditional mainframe systems, but rather attempt to select the most appropriate platform or mix of platforms for a business enterprise. Each type of platform has its own particular advantages. Mainframes tend to be best suited for the storage and management of large amounts of data while personal computers and local area networks are known for their flexibility and user-friendly interfaces. A downsizing strategy that employs client/server computing exploits the relative advantages of each type of platform while maximizing an organization's investment in current systems. Some experts believe that client-server computing could be half as expensive as minicomputer-based systems and one-third as expensive as mainframe computing.[4] Cost savings of this magnitude have captured the attention of IS professionals and business managers alike.

A number of factors have contributed to the development and growth of client/server computing. Several of the major factors include advances in technology, the economics of today's business environment, and the changing role of information systems in business organizations.

Advances in Technology

Client/server computing is based on several technologies which have developed during the first two decades of the information age. Among these technologies are personal computers and workstations, local area networks and data communications, database management software, and graphical user interfaces.

Personal Computers and Workstations

The growth of the personal computer since its introduction in 1981 has been nothing short of phenomenal. The original IBM PC/XT used the Intel 8088 microprocessor, which operated at a speed of 4.77 megahertz (MHz).[5] Modern microprocessors operate at speeds 10 to 20 times faster than the original 8088, and the next generation of microprocessors will soon be in the marketplace.[6] Today's personal computers are capable of processing speeds that rival mini and mainframe systems. Advances in storage match those made in processing power. The diskette drives of the first XT offered 160 kilobytes (KB) of storage. Today disk storage in the hundreds of megabytes (MB) is common on desktop PCs.

While the performance of personal computers has greatly increased, the costs have decreased dramatically. A typical configuration for the original IBM XT consisted of 64KB of memory, a single diskette drive, a color display adapter, and the IBM *Disk Operating System* (DOS) and was priced at $2,665. Today, systems are available with more than 50 times the performance of the original PC, 1,000 times the memory capacity (64MB), and 10,000 times the storage of the original PC (1.6 billion bytes or 1.6 gigabytes), for little more than the price of the original XT.

A recent addition to the "personal processing" scene has been the *Reduced Instruction Set Computing* (RISC) workstation. The RISC workstation is built around RISC processor technology pioneered by Motorola, while the PC is more commonly associated with the 80X86 family of processors by Intel Corporation. Currently, RISC microprocessors comprise between 4 and 5 percent of the microprocessor market; estimates are that will increase to 30 percent by 1995–96 and 50 percent by 1997.[7] RISC technology offers greatly improved processing speed and is often used in high-performance workstations for *computer-aided drafting* (CAD) and *computer-aided software engineering* (CASE). Both of these applications require numerous calculations and often incorporate graphic displays. Complex mathematical modeling for engineering and research can be quickly accomplished on RISC-based workstations. New RISC processors operate at speeds in the range of 100 MHz and yield between 35 and 57 *million instructions per second* (MIPS).[8] The workstation market is expected to grow rapidly in the next few years, and the number of installed RISC units is expected to rise to 1.9 million by 1995.[9]

While the power of PCs and workstations has increased dramatically since the emergence of the first XTs, the cost of these systems has continued to drop. Even more significant is the price per MIP in comparison to other platforms—such as mini or mainframe systems. This has led to "a migration of MIPS" from the more expensive centralized platforms to the desktop. It is estimated that by 1994, PC workstations will cost $100 per MIP, as compared to $15,000 per MIP for mainframes.[10] While offering better performance for the price, PCs and workstations offer organizations more flexibility in upgrading their computing hardware. With mini or mainframe systems, often the entire system must be upgraded to provide increased performance. The PC provides the ability to selectively upgrade processing power as needed. Engineers and designers may need more powerful workstations to utilize computer-aided design and drafting tools, while word processors can utilize less expensive systems. As new advances in hardware occur, the users who will best benefit from these innovations can be upgraded. Several new PC designs have incorporated plug-in processor cards.

Local Area Networks and Data Communications

The recent growth of the *local area network* (LAN) has been a major factor in the growth of client/server technology. The LAN provides a means to connect the new generation of powerful personal workstations. Not only can workstations be connected to each other, but they can also be connected to other LANs, midrange, or even mainframe systems. This ability to be connected to multiple data sources enables the creation of a "user-centered" environment, where the user has transparent access to whatever data is needed regardless of what platform it is located on. A recent study of major corporations indicated that 71 percent had already installed departmental LANs.[11] LAN operating systems are becoming a major portion of corporate IS capital expenditures, with purchases totaling more than $1.14 billion in 1990 and expectations for this figure to grow to more than $2.8 billion by 1995.[12]

Initially, the LAN market lacked standards; many systems used proprietary protocols that made it difficult to interconnect with other manufacturers' systems. The development of networking standards by the IEEE contributed to the growth of network interoperability. Network components are now as generic as "clone" parts, and hardware from multiple vendors is easily integrated. Network hardware has followed the same trend as PC hardware and has been steadily dropping in price while increasing in performance.

Recent promising advances in LAN technology include fiber optic, *infrared* (IR) and *radio frequency* (RF) transmission systems. Fiber optic technology offers high-speed, high-volume transmission while IR and RF systems offer wireless networks that can easily be installed and reconfigured. LANs are quickly becoming the corporate information distribution systems of the 1990s. In looking to the future, a 1992 study indicated that 26 to 35 percent of the organizations surveyed planned to use networked PCs and workstations as their primary hardware platforms for business applications, while 50 to 68 percent planned to use LANs and PCs as their primary office automation platforms.[13]

While the LAN serves as the vehicle to interconnect computing devices in a limited geographical area, advances in data communications technology have given rise to the WAN or wide area network. Wide area networks link local area networks separated by great distances. International LAN connectivity is now commonplace in the business world. Of the corporations responding to a recent study, 40 percent of those with LANs had implemented sitewide or campus networks and 31 percent had completed enterprise–wide networking.[14] This type of connectivity has been available for some time, and the cost of using this technology has now dropped to the point where it is affordable for even small firms.

Most carriers of telecommunications services now offer high-speed data links or other special services such as digital communication lines. For shorter distances, a combination of leased data lines and LAN bridges can provide LAN-to-LAN connectivity in a regional or metropolitan area. Other options include microwave and specialized *integrated services digital networks* (ISDN) provided by some telephone carriers. Growth in the use of laptop computers and cellular telephones has led to the development of cellular modem systems. Now users can be connected to their office from virtually any location.

In addition to providing communications between physically separated networks, advances in data communications have also provided links between differing network protocols and operating systems. Often networks are used to gain access to midrange or mainframe systems through the use of gateways. Gateways accomplish the necessary protocol conversions between LAN and mainframe communications systems. This allows the workstation to access the mainframe system as if it were a terminal attached to the mainframe. Figure 1.1 illustrates how a typical corporate network can be configured to provide connectivity throughout an organization.

Specialized applications gateways link client and server platforms together. An example of this is an SQL gateway between a LAN application and a mainframe database. In this case, the gateway would perform the necessary protocol conversions for the

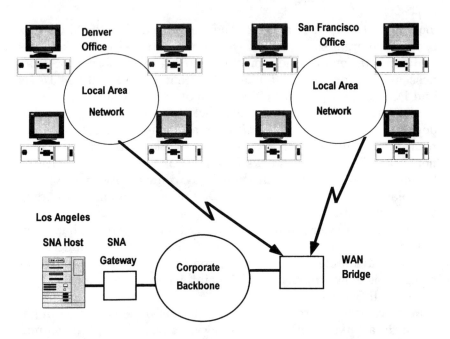

Figure 1.1 Corporate Wide Area Network

two platforms and would also act as the application's link between the two processes. This topic will be covered in more detail in later chapters.

Database Management Software

Advances in database management software have greatly increased the utility of corporate databases by simplifying access to data. Data that was once only accessible via expensive custom programs is now readily accessible to end users via fourth generation (4GL) tools. These tools provide simple, easy-to-use data access interfaces. Little specialized training is required, and often programmer involvement is not needed. The development of *structured query language* (SQL) has provided a standardized method for data access. SQL and 4GL data access tools allow users on client platforms such as PCs or workstations to develop queries or requests for data that will be processed on server platforms—such as network file servers, minicomputers, or even mainframes. The users need not learn the operating system or database management system on the server platform because the

SQL commands provide a generic means to request data between platforms. The benefits of using SQL include:[15]

- Reduced network traffic because only the required data is transmitted to the client.
- A common data access method across multiple platforms.
- A common data access method that is portable across applications.

While local area networks and other data communications systems provide the hardware connection between platforms, SQL and 4GL tools provide the software connection between platforms. Figure 1.2 shows how a 4GL could use SQL commands to access data stored in a corporate database. In this example, the user would request data on export sales for the month of July in an English-language syntax or through a graphical interface. The user interface of the 4GL would then translate the request into

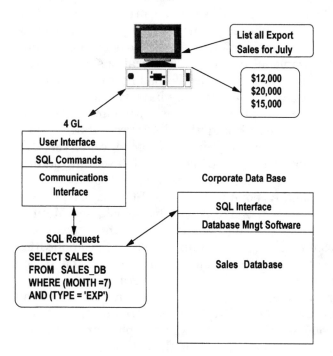

Figure 1.2   SQL Access to a Corporate Database Using a 4GL

an SQL request. The request when translated may read something like:

```
SELECT SALES FROM SALES_DB WHERE (MONTH = 7) AND (TYPE='EXP')
```

The request would then be directed to the host database or server by a communications interface. On arrival at the host database, the SQL commands would be executed against the database. When the data is retrieved, it is returned to the requesting client workstation. Most 4GLs have the capability to format retrieved data as well as perform calculations such as totals and subtotals. Prior to the advent of 4GLs, this request would have required a programmer to write a program to access the data requested by the user.

Graphical User Interfaces

Traditionally, as software has become more advanced, it has also become more difficult to use. To use new software, it was often necessary to invest a considerable amount of time and money in end-user training. Most applications were keyboard intensive and there was little commonality among applications. The rapid growth of *graphical user interfaces* (GUIs) has now not only made software systems more user friendly, they have also set standards for applications program interfacing. Two popular GUIs have been Windows from Microsoft and the OS/2 Presentation Manager from IBM. Windows has captured a large share of the GUI market with over 9 million copies of Windows 3.0 sold in the first two years since its introduction; the recent release of version 3.1 is expected to be equally popular.[16] For RISC and UNIX platforms, popular GUIs include X-Windows, Open Look, and Motif.

All of these products provide an end user with a "point and click" type environment. The user simply selects the application of choice from a set of graphical images or icons on the screen and the program is executed. Within the program the user may select options or input data by the use of pop-up menus, scroll boxes, or radio buttons. The GUI concept is based on the premise that people respond to and interact with graphic images much more easily and quickly than they do with text alone. A box with a red stop sign easily conveys the message "click here to stop execution."

The development of GUIs has also led to a standardized interface for applications. Basic application functions such as opening and closing files is the same in any GUI application. Users who learn one GUI application can usually make a quick transition to other GUI applications. It is estimated that the use of GUIs allows workers to attempt 23 percent more tasks and complete 35 percent more tasks than with character-based applications.[17]

Many GUI-based applications development tools are available. These tools allow developers or end users to build complete applications programs in a graphical environment without writing program code. Development time is greatly reduced and many applications can be developed by the end user without involving expensive applications programmers. Often development that took hours on character-based, mainframe systems can be accomplished in minutes with client/server, GUI applications development tools.[18]

While the technologies presented in this chapter are individually quite impressive, it is the combination of these technologies that has enabled the development of client/server computing. Figure 1.3 illustrates the mixture of enabling technologies that could

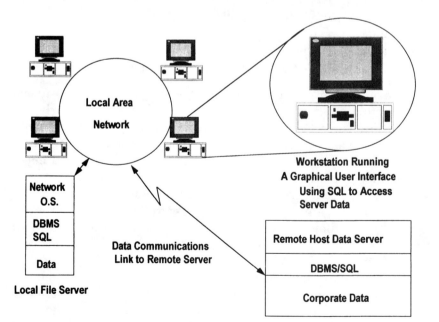

Figure 1.3   Enabling Technologies

be used to support a client/server application. In this example, a powerful workstation is used to run a GUI.

A typical scenario might involve users developing a spreadsheet application to analyze corporate sales. Through the GUI, the users would build a spreadsheet. The data for the users' department are located on a local file server and data for other divisions are located on a remote mainframe host system. The users are unaware of the location of the data and simply select desired data elements from a list of fields presented by the GUI. The list of fields presented to users is based on their system identification and their security privileges. After selecting the desired fields and locating them on the spreadsheet, users enter selection criteria for the data—for instance, "list only sales data for the current year." Transparent to the users, their request for data has been translated into SQL commands and sent via the LAN to the appropriate data repository. Sales data for their department is retrieved from the local database server. The request for corporate data has been forwarded via data communications links to the remote corporate mainframe database. Both requests are processed and returned to the client application. The users are required to master only the GUI and the particular application they are using—for example, a spreadsheet program.

The Economics of Today's Business Environment

The move to client/server computing has in large part been fueled by economic considerations. The late 1980s and particularly the early 1990s have been tough economic times for most organizations. The general slowdown in economic growth in the early 1990s combined with increasing competitiveness has forced many firms to look at ways to reduce cost while increasing productivity. This phenomenon has affected the IS function in many firms, particularly those in which IS performs primarily a support role. A poll of 114 major corporations in the United States indicated that approximately 50 percent of the firms surveyed would have reduced or flat IS budgets for 1992.[19] Many CIOs are being asked to do more with less. This is being accomplished through increased automation and reductions in IS staff. The few increases that were reported were in the areas of desktop computing and local area networking; decreases were noted in large centralized systems.[20]

There are several scenarios in which client/server computing can lead to cost reductions. The two most obvious are the replacement of existing systems and the development of new systems. Another area that may potentially yield a great deal of growth is that of new client/server applications developed on existing systems. Many organizations have large investments of time and money in existing systems. Often it is not possible or desirable to totally replace an existing system. In this type of situation, client/server computing can be used to maximize an organization's investment in current systems. As new applications or capabilities are desired, client/server computing can be coupled with existing systems to yield the advantages of this new architecture while extending the life of an existing system. This type of scenario may not be possible in all cases, but it may be a means for an organization to pilot client/server computing. The following example illustrates a situation in which client/server could be combined with an existing system:

> The XYZ Corporation currently utilizes an on-line financial management system on a mainframe computer. The application is written in COBOL and the data is stored in a DB2 relational database. The existing system receives input from various departments in the organization and produces several special-purpose reports. These reports detail the financial activities of the company and have been used to analyze the performance of the organization. Figure 1.4 is a high-level schematic of the system.

> The new Director of Finance wishes to have the ability to access information from the system and use it in financial forecasting models. By more accurately forecasting the company's cash needs, the director hopes to be able to make better investments for the company and earn a high rate of return on their excess cash. The finance model requires data on a daily basis, and often the Finance Director needs data for ad hoc reports and forecasts. The Director of Information Services wishes to help the Finance Department in their quest for information, but he estimates the cost of a mainframe-based, ad hoc reporting tool and a financial forecasting system to be too high. Additionally, the host system is heavily used and would most likely require an expensive upgrade to support such a new system. The firm would like to move in the direction of client/server computing but is not ready at this point to make major changes in existing systems or major investments in new systems.

Client/server computing can be the answer in this situation. The existing mainframe-based system has the data that the Fi-

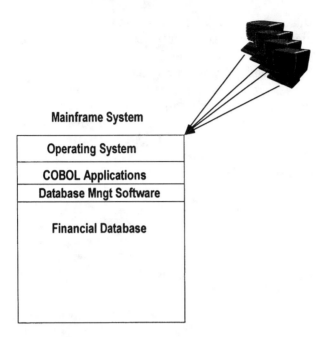

Mainframe System

Operating System
COBOL Applications
Database Mngt Software
Financial Database

Figure 1.4   Corporate Financial System

nance Director needs—it just doesn't have the capability to provide it in the desired form, nor does it have the needed modeling and forecasting tools. While it is possible to implement these features on the mainframe, it is very costly to do so. With client /server computing, the solution would be to marry a client system that features ad hoc reporting and financial modeling with a mainframe-based server that would extract data from the existing financial management system. Figure 1.5 shows how this could be accomplished using some of the technologies previously mentioned in this chapter. With the addition of an SQL interface to the existing mainframe database, it would be possible to extract data from the mainframe host and then pass that data to a LAN or PC-based client. At the client level, the desired analysis and forecasting tools could be implemented at a much lower cost than a similar implementation on the mainframe host.

The ability to access data and move it to the client platform provides the end user with a great deal of flexibility in designing applications. For ad hoc analysis, the client could import data into a spreadsheet program such as Lotus 1-2-3, which would allow the data to be manipulated as desired. Many popular spreadsheet programs now offer direct SQL links into external host

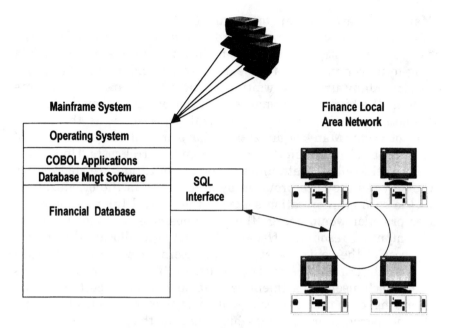

Figure 1.5   Corporate Financial System

databases. These links are often transparent to the end user and require little additional training. On the host side of this system, existing applications are unaffected and the addition of an SQL gateway would most probably utilize fewer resources than if the complete system were implemented on the host.

In this hypothetical example, client/server computing was used to maximize an organization's investment in current systems, while providing new capabilities at a low cost.

Two major economic factors that have contributed to the move to client/server computing are the cost of mainframe hardware and operations, and applications development cost on mainframe platforms.

Mainframe Hardware Expense

While the performance of PC and workstation hardware has increased and costs of these platforms has decreased, the same has not been as dramatically true for mainframe hardware. Due to recent economic and competitive pressures, many mainframe hardware vendors have been offering large discounts to encourage buyers to purchase new hardware or upgrade existing systems.[21]

Many firms are hesitant to commit to the investment of millions of dollars in new mainframe hardware given the volatility of the computer industry. An investment in a mainframe computer is a long-term commitment to the technology and to the hardware vendor. Many firms are waiting for new hardware developments such as the higher-performance RISC-based mainframe systems.

Another consideration with centralized systems is the allocation of costs. Many organizations have moved to the concept of "cost centers" in an effort to identify and control costs. Under this concept the subordinate units of the organization are charged for the services they are provided by other units in the organization. In the case of information systems, the central Information Services provider would charge the other business units for their use of computing resources. Usually the goal is to allocate the operating cost of the central system to all users based on actual usage or a predetermined percentage of usage. If the latter approach is used, each user department is responsible for a portion of the operating cost that represents its usage of the central system. When upgrades or additions are made to the central system to support new applications, often the result is higher overall operating expenses, which must be passed on to the user departments.

In one example, an organization implemented a new information system for one department that eventually required the upgrade of the central processor. These upgrades led to higher system charges for all user departments, even those whose system usage did not change. In an effort to control costs, some departments began to move applications to their own platforms. This way they could more closely control hardware costs and could make their own decisions on hardware upgrades or replacement.

One example of the potential cost savings that can be realized by downsizing to client/server architecture rather than investing in mainframe hardware is the Union Electric Company.[22] By downsizing engineering applications from a mainframe platform to UNIX workstations, the company saved $105,000 in mainframe upgrade costs; the increased utility of the system saved an additional $100,000 per year in plant maintenance and operating costs.[23]

A mainframe system is not only expensive to purchase, it is also expensive to support. Often a large IS staff is required to support a mainframe system. Expensive and often time-consuming training is required for systems programmers, operators, and other support staff. Since staff salaries are often one of the larger items in an organization's budget, many firms are looking for ways to reduce IS staff size. Downsizing by reducing IS staffing is a means to accomplish cost savings. For example, a major entertainment company converted to a PC network and reduced its MIS staff from 50 to 8 employees.[24] Additionally, mainframes often require special facilities that are temperature and climate controlled. Providing and supporting these facilities add to the operating cost of a mainframe. A study of 100 major MIS shops in the United States showed an average annual operations cost of $14,300 per mainframe workstation.[25] This compares with an estimated annual cost of between $6,000 and $7,000 for a networked PC.[26]

Applications Development Costs

Applications development on mainframe or even midrange platforms is substantially higher when compared to LAN systems. Estimates are that PC LAN applications cost from 60 to 80 percent less than a comparable mainframe application and 50 to 75 percent less than a minicomputer application.[27] The Los Angeles branch of the Industrial Bank of Japan offers an example of the cost comparison between applications development on a midrange and a LAN-based system.[28] The branch office had been using an old mainframe system for all data processing. In addition to the mainframe system, the bank also used a midrange DEC VAX system and had installed a PC LAN. Due to high maintenance costs and applications limitations on the mainframe, the branch was looking to use other platforms to support the personnel system and manage client liability records. The options were to develop a relational database for these applications on either the VAX or the LAN. The Los Angeles branch opted for development on the LAN and completed the project for $40,000. The New York branch of the bank was looking to automate the same processes and had estimated the cost of developing the applications on the VAX at from $250,000 to $500,000.[29]

This example illustrates the potential cost saving in applications development that can be realized on downsized platforms. As the use of applications development tools becomes more widespread, the potential cost savings could be even greater. Often with mainframe applications development, there are great backlogs for new applications development. One study showed that 75 percent of large mainframe shops had applications backlogs of one year, and 36 percent of that number have backlogs of up to two years.[30] These lengthy delays in applications development can be costly considering the lost revenue or cost savings from new applications. Delays in implementing new systems can also put firms at a competitive disadvantage with firms that are able to respond quickly to the marketplace.

The Changing Role of Information Systems

As technology moves processing power and applications development tools to the user department level, fundamental changes are promoted in the role of the central IS function. The traditional IS functions are more and more being decentralized and delegated to the user departments. This is occurring not only due to technological changes, but is also due to organizational changes that are occurring in the business world. Major corporations are finding that "less is better." Small, lean business units are more adaptable to changes in the business environment and are correspondingly more competitive. Three major factors contributing to the changing role of IS are: moves to departmental computing, the development of user-centered environments, and increasing end-user sophistication.

Moves to Departmental Computing

As processing power moves to the desktop, along with it goes many of the roles and responsibilities traditionally associated with centralized information processing. Many organizations are taking steps to distribute existing IS expertise to the user departments or are developing departmental IS staffs. This move has been prompted by a general trend to decentralize authority and responsibility in corporations.[31] This approach gives departments their own technical resources to devote to automation projects that best fit their needs. As priorities and business needs change, the department can quickly move its applications development staff to new projects.

Businesses are not locked into information systems and can change or develop systems as needed to remain competitive. Programmers and analysts in this type of organizational structure have the advantage of being able to become more knowledgeable about the business operations they support. This greatly reduces the developer's "learning curve" and allows the programmer/analyst to more closely identify with the user's needs and goals. This type of organization prevents the central IS department from making project priority decisions for the entire organization.

How does client/server computing support this type of organizational change? Typically, client/server applications or downsized applications require less development time and ongoing support. Previously cited examples demonstrate this. With centralized mainframe systems, it would be impractical, not to mention expensive, for individual departments to maintain their own applications development staff. With client/server and other downsizing strategies, it is possible to support applications development with a small staff.

Centralized versus Decentralized

With decentralization also comes the potential for the evolution of incompatible "islands of technology." If individual business units were left totally to their own devices to develop, support, and manage information systems, there would of course be great problems in attempting to develop integrated enterprise–wide information systems. Regardless of how much autonomy a business unit has, it still needs to share information with other business units in the overall organization. That is why some experts believe that the role of central IS in the future will be to formulate and define standards and provide consulting services to other business units in the organization.[32] By acting in this role, the IS function can assure compatibility between the various information systems that may evolve in the overall organization.

Most likely, central IS will no longer be the primary developer of applications programs. This function would be carried out by the user departments with central IS setting standards. In some organizations, it is foreseeable that the central IS department will retain responsibility for the operation of "corporate" resources such as central data servers or communications networks. Figures 1.6 and 1.7 contrast the differences in the organizational structure between a centralized and a decentralized firm.

In the centralized organization, the IS department would be responsible for such functions as applications development, maintenance, and enhancement; operation of the hardware platform and

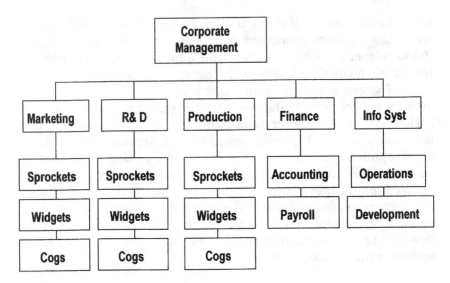

Figure 1.6   Centralized Information System

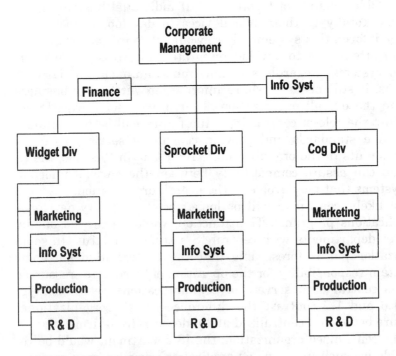

Figure 1.7   Decentralized Information System

operating system; and day-to-day production support. In this type of structure the automation expertise is centralized in one unit of the organization. Any other unit in the firm must request the services of the central IS department. This may lead to priority decisions, which can cause the extensive application development backlogs previously mentioned.

In the decentralized organization, the central IS department is in more of a consultation and standard-setting role. The majority of the automation expertise is distributed to the individual business units. The business units are now responsible for many of the tasks previously performed by the central IS department. New technologies have provided individual departments with the processing power they need, and new applications development tools have provided the capability to accomplish programming at the departmental level.

One organization that pursued a strategy of decentralized IS with centralized coordination and support is the 3M Corporation.[33] As a large firm with numerous divisions and product lines, 3M found that it was unable to provide timely, cost-effective IS support with a centralized IS. To become more competitive and responsive, 3M has established separate IS functions in each of the firm's divisions. The divisional IS staffs are able to respond much more quickly to the specialized needs of the individual divisions and are able to develop greater expertise on divisional systems. The central IS function acts to coordinate efforts between the various divisional IS departments.

3M is currently implementing client/server computing. A major function of the central IS group is to ensure interoperability between divisional and corporate systems. The divisional IS groups are able to develop systems that they feel would best meet their particular needs; however, the overall goal is to provide an enterprise–wide, information-sharing capability. To make this type of decentralized/centralized organization work, 3M has regular meetings in which divisional and corporate IS managers discuss major projects and planned developments.

Development of the User-Centered Environment

As information systems evolved in organizations, they frequently developed independently of other systems. Often separate hardware platforms were acquired for specialized applications. It was and often is still not uncommon to find several terminals on one desk, each for access to a separate application on a separate platform. This required expensive redundant telecommunications systems, not to mention the duplication in computing platforms. Integration of applications or data was best accomplished with pencil and paper. Users were faced with the prospect of learning several different operating systems and applications. Situations such as these are best described as "platform–centered" in that the users of the system are required to conform to the specific requirements of the computer they are using.

A combination of technologies, some of which were previously mentioned, has led to the development of a "user-centered" approach to developing information systems. In a user-centered environment, the systems to which the user is connected conform to the needs of the user. A user-centered environment can be implemented to varying degrees. By simply connecting all platforms to a single interface device (terminal, PC, or workstation) some of the redundancy is eliminated. Users are still, however, faced with learning each of the systems they are connected to. The addition of a GUI provides the user with a common interface and some capability to integrate data from different platforms via the "cut and paste" features common to most GUIs. To complete the picture, add an enterprise–wide data access scheme based on SQL and a common user application such as a spreadsheet. The user now has access to all of the data in the organization regardless of its host platform or its physical location. Data located on the user's workstation is as easily accessed as data located on a network file server down the hall, a mini system across the country, or a mainframe around the world. The user now becomes the center of the information system. All data access is done via a common interface and the user simply learns one application.

This type of environment is dependent on a number of enabling technologies, some of which were described earlier in the chapter. Advances in workstation hardware have provided the processing capability necessary to run GUIs. LANs and data communications technology have provided the means to connect workstations to local as well as physically distant data sources. SQL–based applications have provided the capability to programmatically access data independent of its native database structure.

Figures 1.8 and 1.9 illustrate the conceptual differences between a platform-centered environment and a user-centered environment.

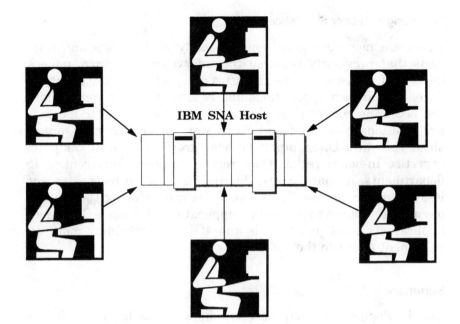

Figure 1.8   Platform-Centered Environment

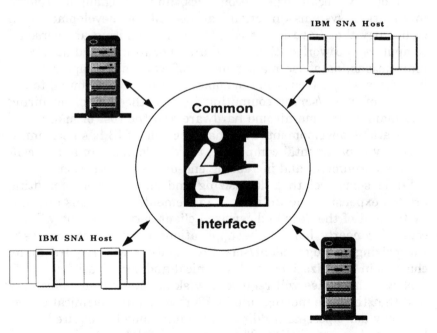

Figure 1.9   User-Centered Environment

Increasing End-User Sophistication

Users are now able to accomplish many of the tasks and functions that previously required the intervention of programmers. GUIs and 4GL tools have given user departments the ability to develop their own applications and reports. Basic computer skills are becoming common; employment advertisements for most office positions now ask for skills in word processing and spreadsheet software. Often organizations "grow" their own computer expertise in-house rather than rely on support from central IS departments. In many cases, this results in more responsive and less expensive service. Tools like GUIs are reducing the amount of end-user training required on applications software. GUI-based applications development tools and 4GLs are providing more development power to the end user.

Summary

The development of client/server computing has been driven by a number of factors. Three major factors have been the development of new technologies, economics, and the changing role of information systems in organizations. Major developments in technology that have led to client/server computing are personal computers and workstations, local area networking and data communications, database management software, and graphical user interfaces. Major trends in economics that have contributed to the growth of client/server computing include the cost of acquiring and maintaining mainframe hardware and the cost of mainframe applications development. The changing role of IS has been influenced by departmental computing, the development of a user-centered environment, and increasing end-user sophistication.

While some feel that downsizing and client/server computing are too expensive and difficult to implement, predictions are that by the end of the decade downsized client/server systems will account for nearly half of the applications of major companies.[34] Downsizing through client/server computing will require many changes in organizations, both technical and organizational.

New technologies will require new skills. Many companies may find that they are moving into areas that require technical expertise they don't possess. Additional training may be required at all levels in the organization. The traditional roles and relationships of units within the organization may change. The responsibility for information systems is moving from central IS departments to the user departments. Departments that previously have had limited involvement in the development of applications systems will now be responsible for their own systems and applications.

End Notes

1. Dwight B. Davis, "Building Up Steam for '93," *Datamation*, June 1, 1992, p. 44.

2. Bruce Caldwell, "Swapping Outsourcers," *Information Week*, May 11, 1992, p. 12.

3. Davis, op. cit., p. 41.

4. Quoted in Tim Mead, "The Attraction Is Price," *Datamation*, March 15, 1990, p. 49.

5. "Work-Group Computing Report," *EDGE*, August 19, 1991, p. 1.

6. Jim Seymour, Julie Cohen, M. Keith Thompson, Jon Zilber, and Don Crabb, "PLATFORMS: How the PC Stacks Up," *PC Magazine* May 12, 1992, p. 113.

7. *Computergram International*, March 19, 1992.

8. Cate Corcoran, "Next Wave of RISC Relies on Power," *INFOWORLD*, March 2, 1992, pp. 29–30.

9. "RISC Workstations Emerge As Leader," *Computer Reseller News*, October 21, 1991, p. 24.

10. "Downsizing—Where Do LANs Fit into the '90s Computing Puzzle?" *LAN TIMES*, May 20, 1991, p. 75.

11. Davis, op. cit., p. 44.

12. Jane Morrissey, "LAN Operating Systems on Upswing, IDC Predicts," *PC Week*, November 18, 1991, p. 183.

13. Davis, op. cit., p. 46.

14. Davis, op. cit., p. 46.

15. Setrah Khoshafian, Arvola Chan, Anna Wong, and Harry K. T. Wong, *A Guide to Developing Client/Server SQL Applications* (San Mateo: Morgan Kaufman Publishers, 1992), p. 10.

16. Tim Parker, "Reflections on Windows (the Microsoft Graphical User Interface Has a Sound Market Future)," *Datasystems*, March 1992, p. 26(3).

17. John Kador, "Downsizing Is Ready for Prime Time (Companies Cut Costs, Improve Quality by Converting to Networked Microcomputers)," *MIDRANGE Systems*, May 12, 1992, p. 50.

18. Damian Rinaldi, "Client/Server Economics: Balancing the Equation: Care and Feeding of Client/Server May Cost More Than Development," *Software Magazine*, January 1992, p. 79(4).

19. Scott Lieb and Peter Krass, "1992: The Squeeze Is On," *Information Week*, March 9, 1992, p. 34.

20. Ibid., p. 45.

21. Robert Moran and John Soat, "Have I Got a Deal for You," *Information Week*, February 24, 1992, pp. 52–54.

22. Mark Schlack, "UNIX on the LAN Eases Mainframe Load; Large Engineering Simulations Can Be Moved to LANs by Using UNIX Workstations As Computer Servers, Cutting Costly Mainframe MIPS," *Datamation*, February 15, 1992, p. 58.

23. Ibid.

24. Andrei M. Chivvis, "Downsizing: The Business Decision," *LAN TIMES*, May 20, 1991, pp. 76–77.

25. David Ferris, "Figuring the Real Cost of Operating a PC Network," *LAN TIMES*, May 20, 1991, p. 52.

26. Ibid.

27. Chivvis, op. cit., pp. 76–77.

28. Karyl Scot, "Enterprise Computing," Editorial Supplement, *INFOWORLD*, February 10, 1992, p. S63.

29. Ibid.

30. Davis, op. cit., p. 51.

31. Mead, op. cit., p. 49.

32. Mead, op. cit., p. 50.

33. John Pepper, "Decentralize? Centralize? Yes!" *Information Week*, June 29, 1992, p. 34.

34. Kador, op. cit., p. 50.

2

Client/Server Computing

Even though client/server computing is one of the most talked about subjects in the computing industry, there still is some question as to what exactly client/server computing is. A 1991 survey of Fortune 500 business and IS executives revealed that 60 percent were planning to move to client/server computing. Even more interesting is that 74 percent said they thought that the industry has done a poor job of explaining what client/server computing is.[1] Client/server computing often conveys images of downsizing and replacing mainframe systems with LAN-based servers and workstations. To further cloud the issue are the concepts of cooperative processing and distributed processing. Few today agree on what client/server computing is. In this chapter, we will attempt to define client/server computing and follow its evolution through the use of several computing models. Finally, four basic client/server implementation approaches will be introduced.

Distributed Processing and Cooperative Processing

To clarify the definition of client/server computing, let us first define two more general data processing concepts. The first concept is that of distributed processing. Distributed processing usually involves the implementation of related software across two or more data processing centers. This infers some type of geographic separation of processing. According to Crepeau and Weitzel,[2] distributed data processing

> "can be defined as a set of geographically distributed data processing resources and activities that operate in a coordinated fashion to support one or more organizational activities."

This definition does not differentiate the capabilities of the various platforms involved, nor does it specify how the processing functions are divided among the platforms. Distributed processing became a viable option as alternatives to centralized processing became available. Rather than shipping data to a centralized data center for processing, distributed processing became a means to place processing power where it was needed. Advances in telecommunications provided links between distributed systems, allowing them to communicate when necessary. The ability to use multiple systems provides a ready backup should one system fail. A major point of distributed processing is that each node can operate independently and has all the computing resources necessary to support an application. Basically, in a distributed environment computing tasks that were once accomplished by a single centralized system are distributed to a number of smaller self-contained systems.

Cooperative processing, while similar to distributed processing in some aspects, has one major characteristic that differentiates it from distributed processing. Cooperative processing is defined as a computing architecture that enables applications to be divided across multiple platforms.[3] The key point to emphasize in this definition is that the computing process is distributed across multiple platforms. This contrasts with distributed processing in that the complete computing process is distributed among several platforms. In cooperative processing, a single computing process uses several connected platforms, while with distributed processing, a single computing process runs independently on multiple platforms. The goal of cooperative processing is to allocate the separate elements of the computing process to the platforms that are best suited for each computing element.

Figures 2.1 and 2.2 illustrate the difference between distributed processing and centralized processing. Figure 2.2 shows an example of an inventory control system that has been decentral-

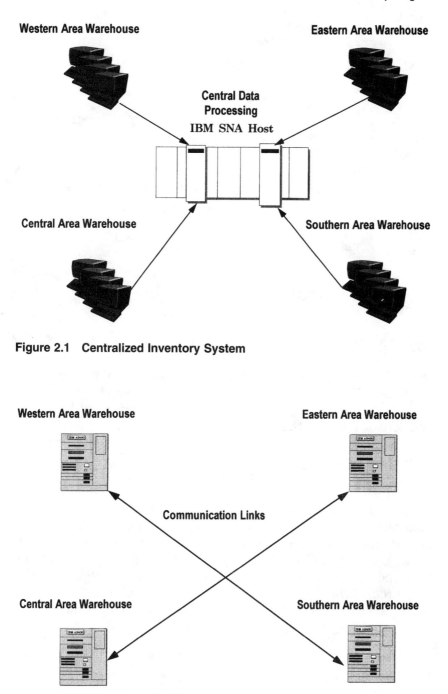

Western Area Warehouse

Eastern Area Warehouse

**Central Data
Processing**

IBM SNA Host

Central Area Warehouse

Southern Area Warehouse

Figure 2.1   Centralized Inventory System

Western Area Warehouse

Eastern Area Warehouse

Communication Links

Central Area Warehouse

Southern Area Warehouse

Figure 2.2   Distributed Inventory System

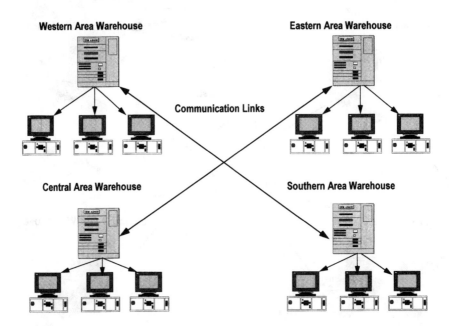

Figure 2.3   Cooperative Processing Order Entry

ized from the single centralized system shown in Figure 2.1 to multiple processing platforms located at regional warehouses. Each of these distributed platforms has the necessary hardware and software to run the inventory control system. The distributed systems are linked so that data can be transferred between systems if needed.

Figure 2.3 shows how cooperative processing could be implemented with distributed systems. In this example, an order entry system has been devised that accesses stock availability from the distributed systems. The process of entering an order and checking for stock in inventory is divided between the PC and the midrange host. The PC would obtain inventory information from the host and accept input of customer information to prepare a shipping order. When the order is complete, the PC would then pass the order to the host for processing. This division of processing leads us to the client/server architecture.

Client/Server Computing

Client/server computing can best be defined by defining what a client is, what a server is, and what the relationship between the two is. In the broadest sense, client/server computing takes a computing process and splits it into two parts. One part of the processing is completed by the client, the other by the server. Let us examine the role of these two in detail.

The Client

The client is usually the "front-line" processor that is operated by the end user and is generally the originator of the computing process. Most of the processing will occur on the client; processing that is not completed on the client processor is delegated to the server. Often clients are PCs or workstations but can be mini or midrange computer systems. The computing processes assigned to the client are those that are best suited to that particular platform. For example, a PC is much more capable of supporting a GUI than a mainframe terminal. Additionally, the processes that are most economically performed on the client should be placed there. Calculation-intensive operations, such as spreadsheets, may be less costly to perform on a client workstation where MIPS are much less expensive than on other platforms.

The Server

The second component of client/server computing is the server. The role of the server is to provide processing and/or information to the client. Typically the server provides data to a client; however, the server may need to perform some processing to produce the desired data. For example, if a client requested sales data for a particular region, the server may need to perform some processing to extract the data from the overall corporate database and format it as requested by the client. As with the client, the processes that are best suited and most economical for the server should be placed on it. Most often, servers are the repositories of data and are, in comparison to the client, more efficient at managing and retrieving data. This usually implies that the server would have external storage devices connected to it and would operate some type of database management system.

Client and Server

For this division of labor to succeed, there must be some type of integration between the client and the server. Most often the two are linked via a LAN or other data communications system. The major requirement is that the two components be able to freely transfer information. This flow of information is most often portrayed as a one-way flow, with the client requesting data and the server returning data. It is also possible that the client may provide data to the server to be processed and incorporated into the server's database.

Consider the example of a client/server airline reservation system. The client used by the ticket agent would request information on flights to a specific location on a specific date. The request would be passed to the server, which would extract the information from the flight reservation database and return that information to the client. The client would then process the flight information with other data such as ground transportation and prepare a proposed itinerary. After the ticket agent presented the information to the customer and the customer decided on a flight, the client would pass the reservation back to the server for processing. The server would then add the new reservation to the database. Figure 2.4 shows an example of client/server configuration on a LAN.

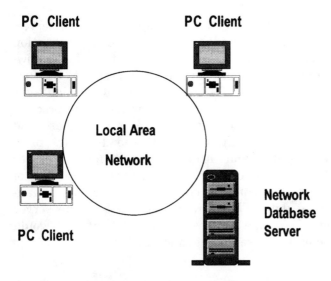

Figure 2.4   Example Client/Server Configuration

The PC clients are connected via the LAN to a network database server. The role of the server is to provide data to the PC clients. The basic tenet of the client/server architecture is that the computing process is divided between two connected hardware platforms. To more closely study the relationship between client and server, it will be necessary to examine the basic elements that make up the computing process. Once we have defined the basic elements, we will use these elements to build a few simple computing process models.

The Computing Process

Let us first define the basic elements of a computing process. These elements are separate functions that interact with each other to accomplish a computing task. Just as an orchestra is composed of many different instruments all functioning together to produce a symphony, a computing process is composed of different elements working in conjunction with each other to accomplish a common task. Six basic elements are shown in Figure 2.5.

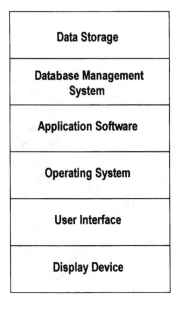

Figure 2.5   Elements of the Computing Process

Data Storage

Often, retrieving a certain piece of data is the primary purpose of the application program. The function of the data storage element is to provide a means to store data and allow a higher-level process to access the data. Data storage is primarily involved with the data storage media, the storage control system, and interfaces to higher-level systems. Typical data storage media include magnetic disks, tapes, or optical disks. Recently the performance of optical storage has increased while the cost of such systems has decreased. Often optical storage is used in conjunction with image-processing applications.

The storage control system consists of the logic required to physically access the data of the storage media. On magnetic disks, the storage control system controls a read/write head that must be physically moved to the proper location to access data on the disk. Once the data is accessed, it must be passed back to the process that requested it. The disk control system must manage the flow of both incoming and outgoing data. Often there are backlogs of data as the disk I/O speed is slower in comparison to the speed of other computing processes. Storage control systems may use a buffer or cache to minimize the impact of these backlogs.

Database Management System

The *database management system* (DBMS) is the element that allows the data to be organized so that it can be easily accessed by applications programs. The DBMS manages the logical organization of data, and the data storage system manages the physical organization of data. This is important when it is necessary to access data from an application program. Within an application program the user or programmer knows that they want to access the inventory record for part "XYZ." The DBMS is able to determine where record "XYZ" is located and in turn passes that request to the data storage unit. This allows the applications program to deal with the data at a higher level and eliminates the need for the application program to deal with the hardware-specific complexities of accessing the storage device directly.

DBMSs are also capable of managing complex relationships among data files. It is possible to join or relate several physical databases in a single logical database or view. This allows the end user or applications program access to related data although the data may reside in separate physical databases. Figure 2.6 shows the concept of a view or virtual database and related databases.

The related databases are separate databases linked by a common data element. In this example, the employee number is used to link the three employee databases. With the virtual database or view, a higher-level logical definition of the data has been designed so that a data record appears as one logical record while in reality it is made up of several physical records. This is often done in enterprise–wide data access schemes to simplify ad hoc data reporting and retrieval for end users.

DBMSs also allow the selective retrieval of data. The database can be searched for data that meets specific selection criteria. For example, the employee database in Figure 2.6 could be searched for all employees who earn more than $50,000. Without a view or single logical database, the task of searching and combining data from multiple databases becomes much more complex. The con-

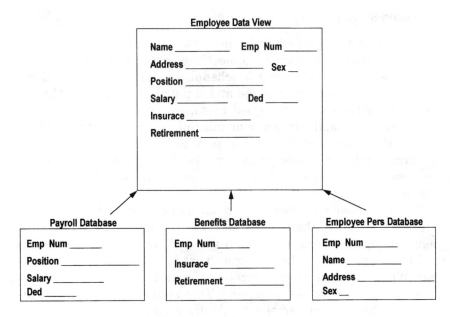

Employee Data View

Name _____   Emp Num _____
Address _____   Sex __
Position _____
Salary _____   Ded _____
Insurace _____
Retiremnent _____

Payroll Database

Emp Num _____
Position _____
Salary _____
Ded _____

Benefits Database

Emp Num _____
Insurace _____
Retiremnent _____

Employee Pers Database

Emp Num _____
Name _____
Address _____
Sex __

Figure 2.6   Virtual Database

cept of SQL that was introduced in Chapter 1 is based on the ability to search and access data through a DBMS.

Applications Software

The applications software is the element that allows the user or programmer to accomplish a specific task. This could take the form of a program written in a high-level language such as CO-BOL or C, or it could take the form of a general-purpose application package such as Lotus 1-2-3. Applications written in programming languages tend to be special purpose and are usually reserved for larger, more complex systems.

General-purpose packages typically provide a capability that can be tailored by an end user to meet specific needs. Lotus 1-2-3 is an example of a common general-purpose applications package. End users can perform spreadsheet calculations, reporting, and develop graphics through the use of on-screen menus. Interfaces are available that can transparently link general-purpose packages to external data sources such as SQL databases.

Operating System

The operating system controls the resources of the computer system and allocates resources to meet the requests of the user. The operating system controls job scheduling and priorities, and access to devices such as storage and input/output devices. The operating system can be designed to support a single user such as DOS on a personal computer or multiple users such as UNIX or MVS. Multiuser operating systems allow more than one user or program to use a single processor.[4] In this type of environment, processing speed is usually constrained by the speed of the storage devices.

The processor operates at a much higher speed than the data storage devices. Rather than wait for a response from a data storage device, the operating system will put the current process on hold and execute another program that is waiting for the processor. When the first process receives the data it needs, it is put in a queue to wait for the processor. This swapping of programs allows for the efficient use of a single processor.

The new PC-based operating systems, while supporting only one user, offer multitasking capabilities. With applications such as Windows or with the OS/2 operating system, a single user may have multiple programs operating at one time, all serviced by a single microprocessor. For example, a user could be downloading data from a remote mainframe database with one program while simultaneously running a word processing program. Depending on the operating system and the microprocessor hardware, the programs could either be running simultaneously or sharing a single microprocessor. The sharing of a single processor by multiple applications is referred to as "time slicing," as each process receives a share or slice of processor time. The switching between each application is accomplished at a speed which makes it appear to the user that the programs are running simultaneously.

User Interface

The user interface allows the end user to communicate with the applications program. This interface could be a character-based menu or a GUI. Often the type of interface is dependent on the underlying applications programming language. The more traditional programming languages, such as COBOL, generally support character-based interaction with a user. The user would select an operation from a menu or type in a request and would receive character-based output on a display screen or as a printout.

With the advent of GUIs, applications programs were able to receive requests from users and present information in a graphical form. A user could select an icon that represented corporate sales figures and be presented with a three-dimensional chart of sales data. Graphical representations of data are often much easier to comprehend than text reports. While graphical interfaces are found primarily with newer Windows and OS/2 applications packages, several types of GUIs are available that can interface with existing character-based mainframe applications. These GUIs utilize an *applications programming interface* (API) to link a GUI with an existing application. These types of interfaces will be discussed in more detail in Chapter 4.

Display Device

The display device is the physical hardware that allows the operator to communicate with the user interface. This could take the form of a computer terminal, a PC, or a workstation. The display device determines what type of user interface can be

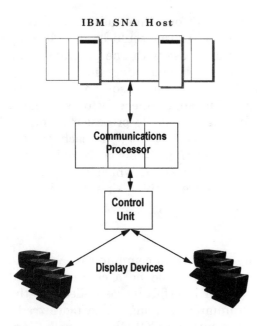

Figure 2.7   Typical IBM Mainframe Configuration

used. Graphical interfaces require the use of PCs or workstations that can run GUI software and support input devices such as mice and touch screens. Character-based applications usually require only a "dumb terminal" or a device capable of emulating a terminal.

The term "dumb terminal" is often used to indicate that the terminal does not possess any processing capability. The terminal simply passes keystrokes to another computing device and in turn displays data returned to it. Often these terminals are connected to communications devices that support multiple terminals, and these communications devices are in turn connected to a communications processor. The communications processor manages all the display devices and the interface between the communications network and the central processor. Figure 2.7 shows a typical configuration for an IBM mainframe computer system.

Computing Models

Now that we have defined the basic elements of a computing process, let us explore how these elements can be used to build three simple computing models. These models will then be used to follow the evolution of client/server computing. The three models that will be examined are time-sharing, resource-sharing, and client/server.

Time-Sharing

The earliest computer systems consisted of a central processor with attached terminals. All of the processing functions were completed by the central processor. This is referred to as a time-sharing model in that each of the attached terminals or users shared processing time on a central processor. Figure 2.8 shows how the basic computing elements that were defined earlier would be configured in a time-sharing model. This is typical of the configurations found in mainframe and midrange computer systems. The data storage, database management, applications software, operating system, and user interface elements would all be located on the central processor. The display device would be the only independent element in this model.

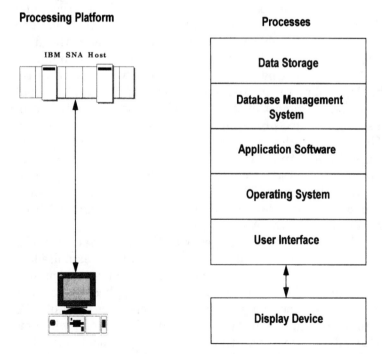

Figure 2.8   Time-Sharing Model

The time-sharing model does possess certain advantages.[5] Mainframe systems generally are configured with vast amounts of high-speed data storage. Since the applications programs and data are centrally located and controlled, applications security and data integrity are easily enforced.[6] Backup and recovery procedures for mainframe systems are usually very comprehensive, and system availability is normally quite high.

As mentioned in Chapter 1, there are disadvantages to mainframe-based systems. One of the primary disadvantages is the high cost of mainframe systems when compared to other platforms. From an applications standpoint, mainframe applications generally lack the user-friendly interfaces found with PCs or workstation-based applications. Changes or modifications to programs are often time consuming and expensive, requiring the intervention of programmers.

Resource-Sharing

With the development of more powerful personal computers and workstations, it became possible to move some of the processing that was occurring on centralized platforms to the desktop. The resource-sharing model shown in Figure 2.9 illustrates the division of basic computing elements between a personal computer and a data source—in this case, a LAN file server. The term resource-sharing refers to an architecture in which the individual workstations perform most of the computing processes with a central data storage device providing access to data and network devices.[7] The display device, user interface, operating system, application software, and the database management software are all resident on the personal computer. The data storage element resides on the file server. This is a major shift from the time-sharing model in that most of the elements have migrated from the central platform to the workstation.

This model offers some advantages over the time-sharing model in that the power and flexibility of the PC can be exploited to provide a more user-friendly interface. General-purpose application packages allow the end users to tailor an application to their specific needs. The increasing power and decreasing cost of PCs make resource-sharing an attractive option. This model, while offering some advantages over the time-sharing model, also has some disadvantages. Since the application programs and the DBMS reside on the workstation, large amounts of data must be

Processing Platform

Processes

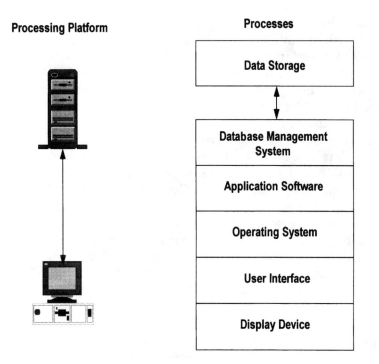

Figure 2.9   Resource-Sharing Model

transferred from the data server to the workstation.[8] This can become a problem with large databases and with remote sites. Large databases frequently accessed can generate a great deal of network traffic, which may impact overall network performance. For remote locations, it may be difficult and expensive to establish high-speed data communication links capable of handling the required volume of data. Ensuring data integrity also becomes more difficult, since the control of the DBMS has been delegated to the workstation level.

Client/Server

The client/server model is a combination of the time-sharing and resource-sharing models and exploits the relative advantages of each.[9] Client/server accomplishes this by dividing the basic computing elements among the platforms that are best suited for each element. Figure 2.10 shows the division of computing elements in a client/server architecture. The display device, user in-

terface, operating system, and applications software are all located on the client platform. The database management software
and data storage system are located on the host platform.

In this configuration, the power of the desktop PC can be used
to drive a GUI, the operating system, and the applications program. The tasks of data storage and retrieval are delegated to the
data server, which could be a network file server, midrange system, or even a mainframe database. The need to transfer large
amounts of data from the server to the client is eliminated because the DBMS is located on the data server and can extract
and transfer only the required data. Centralization of the DBMS
and the data permit better data security and integrity. With this
architecture, the separation of the DBMS and data storage from
the other computing elements allows for more flexibility in applications development. New applications can be developed independent of the underlying databases and would not require any
new programming on the data server.

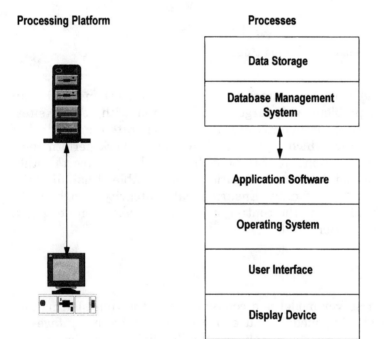

Figure 2.10   Client/Server Model

Implementation Approaches

Client/server computing actually covers a broad spectrum of implementation approaches. These approaches can range from simple data transfer to complex peer-to-peer applications integration. The basic architecture remains the same—a client receives data provided by a host. The major difference in these approaches is the complexity of the relationship between the client and the server. In this book we will examine four client/server implementation approaches. Each of these approaches splits the computing process between platforms, but each approach represents a differing level of complexity in the client/server relationship. This relationship can be quite simple or quite complex. The four approaches to be presented are simple file transfer, applications programming interfaces, Windows and OS/2 client/server products, and peer-to-peer communications. Although these approaches will be presented in more detail in the following chapters, let us briefly describe each.

Simple File Transfer

This is the least complex approach, both in terms of the technology required and the relationship between the client and the server. The basic concept in simple file transfer is that a server or host possesses data needed by a client. This data is by some means extracted and passed to the client, where it is further processed. The relationship between client and server is, quite simply, the data that is passed between them. The client and server may be independent applications running on different platforms, but they retain a basic user–provider relationship. While there are some limitations to this approach, there are some situations in which it is highly effective.

Applications Programming Interfaces

The *applications programming interface* (API) is a more technically complex approach that allows a client/server relationship to be developed between an existing host application and a PC client. The client/server relationship in an API is based on an application-to-application interface. This approach can be quite effective in situations where existing host applications provide the basic functionality needed. The existing host application can be given a more user-friendly interface as well as be integrated into PC applications.

Windows and OS/2 Client/Server Products

Windows and OS/2 provide an excellent GUI-based operating system for running and developing client/server applications. In addition to supporting GUIs, these products allow multitasking, which is sometimes required in client/server applications. These products support a true client/server relationship in that the DBMS software and data storage are usually located on some type of database server while the client application and GUI run on a client platform. Many of these products support this relationship across multiple platforms, allowing the development of a user-centered environment such as that described in Chapter 1. In addition to specific client/server applications, Windows and OS/2 provide a means to integrate data between applications.

Peer-to-Peer Communication

IBM has developed a new architecture that allows peer-to-peer communications between systems and applications. This expands the basic client/server relationship into a two-way relationship in which either system can operate as a client, a server, or both. Peer-to-peer communication can occur between platforms of equal capability or between platforms of vastly differing processing power. The peer-to-peer relationship allows applications and systems to interact on an equal basis.

In the following chapters, each of the approaches described above will be presented in more detail. The approaches are presented in order of increasing complexity. Each approach is presented and explained in terms of the computing process model introduced in this chapter. The relative advantages and disadvantages of each approach are presented along with criteria for determining what situations would be appropriate for that particular approach. Examples are provided of how each approach could be implemented.

Summary

While client/server computing is a topic of great interest in the computing industry, there is no clear definition of what exactly it is. Two related concepts are distributed processing and cooperative processing. With distributed processing, a single computing process is run independently on multiple interconnected hosts. With cooperative processing, a single computing process is divided among multiple platforms, each accomplishing the processing tasks it is best suited for. In client/server computing, the computing process is divided between a client and a server.

The computing process that is divided between the client and the server consists of the following elements: data storage, database management, applications software, operating system, user interface, and display device. These elements can be used to describe three basic computing models: time-sharing, resource-sharing, and client/server. In time-sharing, all elements with the exception of the display device are resident on a central host. With resource-sharing, a majority of the processing elements are shifted to a workstation or personal computer with only data storage residing on a data server. In the client/server model, the display device, user interface, operating system, and application software are located on the client while the DBMS and data storage reside on the host or server. There are several approaches to implementing client/server computing including: simple file transfer, applications programming interfaces, Windows and OS/2 client/server products, and peer-to-peer communications.

End Notes

1. Barbara DePompa, "More Power at Your Fingertips," *Information Week*, December 30, 1991, p. 22.

2. Raymond G. Crepeau and John R. Weitzel, "A Manager's Guide to Distributed Data Processing," *Journal of Systems Management*, September 1989, p. 17(5).

3. Robert Francis, "The PC Perspective Cooperative Processing (Part 2 of 3)," *Datamation*, September 15, 1989, p. 63(3).

4. James Bradley, *Introduction to Database Management*, (New York: Holt, Rinehart and Winston, 1987), p. 16.

5. *Client / Server Computing: An Overview of Client / Server Technology in the Distributed Computing Environment.* (Redmond: Microsoft Corporation, 1991), p. 5.

6. Ibid.

7. Ibid.

8. Ibid.

9. Ibid.

3

Simple File Transfer

Simple file transfer is the least complex of the client/server implementation approaches. With this approach, data from a server platform is transferred to a client platform. This approach is often employed to transfer data from mainframe platforms to individual PCs or LAN servers. Once the data has been transferred to the client platform, it can be manipulated using inexpensive PC or workstation applications packages. This approach is a relatively inexpensive means to maximize the value of existing data and systems. Capabilities such as 4GL ad hoc reporting can be implemented on a PC or LAN at a much lower cost than on a mainframe. By utilizing this approach new capabilities can be implemented on the platform that provide the best cost/performance ratio. While PC and LAN-based systems are less expensive to acquire and operate, there are some operations—such as data storage and retrieval—that are performed much more efficiently on other platforms such as mainframes.

In terms of the computing processes model presented in Chapter 2, simple file transfer separates the data storage, DBMS, and operating system into two duplicate systems. Figure 3.1 illustrates how simple file transfer can be described in relation to the conceptual client/server model. The operating system, data stor-

Processing Platform   Processes

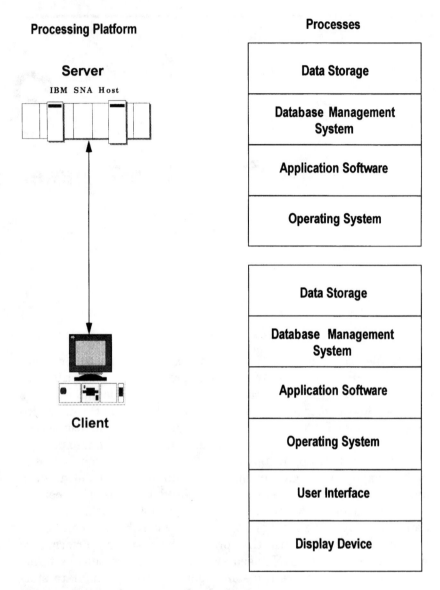

Figure 3.1   Simple File Transfer Conceptual Model

age, and DBMS reside on the mainframe client host. The PC/LAN client uses its own operating system, data storage, and DBMS in addition to the applications program, user interface, and display device. This duplication would seem to negate the client/server relationship; however, this relationship is maintained because the mainframe server is the primary source for data. The server would in all likelihood have other applications programs resident in it that would produce and maintain the data. The client is dependent on the host for data. The duplicate processes on the client are solely a "temporary" storage location for data. The client is incapable of producing its own data. This is analogous to a VCR on a television set. The VCR is only capable of recording information from the television for use at a later time. In the same fashion, the data storage and DBMS processes of a simple file transfer client/server implementation hold the data for use by the application program only until it is replaced by new data from the host server. Mainframes are often the clear performance leader when it comes to manipulating large amounts of data. Many systems are optimized for I/O-intensive processing. Advances in PC/workstation hardware architecture and the development of specialized LAN data servers are closing the I/O gap.

In this chapter, we will first discuss the general configuration required for simple file transfer. Simple file transfer software will then be presented, followed by a discussion of considerations for implementation of the file transfer approach. At the end of the chapter, examples of client/server implementations using simple file transfer are presented.

Hardware Requirements

Three main hardware components are required for simple file transfer: a PC or workstation capable of storing data, a terminal emulation device, and a physical connection to the host system. Let us examine each of those components in detail.

PC/Workstation

The PC/workstation must be capable of receiving and storing data. It is not possible to download data to a "dumb" terminal since that terminal has no capability to store data. The data storage device can reside on the PC or on a device connected to the PC, such as a LAN file server. In using an attached data storage device, the PC would receive the data from the host server and then pass the data via the LAN to the file server. The data could then be used by other workstations on the LAN. A PC or workstation is also required to run the terminal emulation software and the file transfer software. Both of these items will be discussed in detail later in the chapter.

Terminal Emulation

For the PC/workstation to communicate with the host, it must emulate the characteristics of a host terminal device. Terminal emulators display the host screen and translate workstation keyboard input into a form understandable by the host. This is most often accomplished with the use of a terminal emulation card and emulation software. The emulation card is a PC card that provides the hardware connection to the host; the emulation software handles the display and keyboard translation. A number of emulation cards for IBM systems are available today, including the IBM 3270 adapter, DCA IRMA adaptor, and the Attachmate Extra 3270 adapter. Most adapters have the capability to interface with any one of the various types of IBM communications protocols.

For workstations connected to a LAN, an alternative to the use of an emulation card is the use of a LAN gateway. A gateway provides connectivity between different platforms. Multiple work-

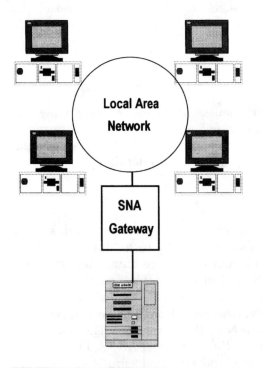

SNA Host

Figure 3.2   LAN Gateway to an SNA Host

stations can use a single gateway. For workstations on a LAN, a gateway is often a less expensive option than installing emulation cards in all PCs requiring connection to a mainframe host. In a gateway configuration, the network adapter card in the PC in combination with the gateway serves the same function as the emulator card. Figure 3.2 shows a typical LAN gateway configuration.

The second component of a terminal emulation package is the emulation software. As previously described, the emulation software allows the PC to function as if it were a terminal device. Often the keyboard arrangement of PCs differs from those of terminals. The emulation software redefines the PC keyboard so that it has a layout and functionality similar to that of a terminal. The emulation program is a PC application that must be loaded prior to starting terminal operation. Often a "hot key" is used to allow rapid switching between PC and mainframe sessions. Each logical connection to the host is referred to as a session.[1] The emulation software can be configured to support multiple host sessions and printer sessions to allow host printing on an attached PC printer. Emulation software is available for the DOS, Windows, and OS/2 operating systems.

Host Connection

For the emulation device to communicate with the host it must be physically connected to the host by some means. Before defining the types of connections that may be used with simple file transfer, let us take a moment to briefly examine IBM's *Systems Network Architecture* (SNA). In most computing environments, there are a large number of devices that need to communicate with either each other or some type of host platform. Within an IBM environment, SNA provides a set of rules for controlling the transfer of information between devices. It uses a layered protocol structure for network communications.[2]

Figure 3.3 shows an example of an SNA network. In this example it is easy to see the hierarchical structure of SNA. The communications controller manages communications between the host platform and a number of cluster controllers. The cluster controllers provide a means to group together a number of devices and consolidate their traffic for transmission to the communications controller. This eliminates the need for a physical connection from each device to the communications controller. This is

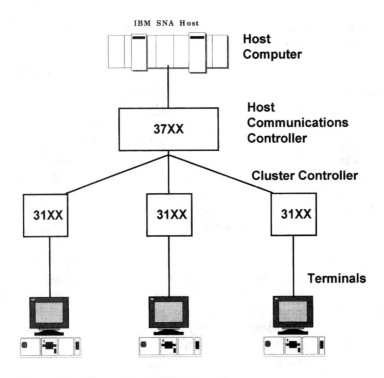

IBM SNA Host

**Host
Computer**

37XX

**Host
Communications
Controller**

Cluster Controller

31XX   **31XX**   **31XX**

Terminals

Figure 3.3   Hierarchical SNA Network

particularly useful when connecting a number of remote devices to a host via leased telephone lines. Rather than requiring a separate line for each terminal device, a group of terminals can be connected to a cluster controller and that controller can then be connected to the communications controller by a single communications line.

Within an SNA network, two types of devices exist—physical units and logical units.[3] Physical units, or PUs, represent the actual physical devices on the network. Logical units, or LUs, are the logical ports, connected as defined within the network. For example, in Figure 3.4 the connection between the cluster controllers and the communications controller would be defined by physical units. The sessions of individual terminals connected to the cluster controllers would be defined by logical units. Terminals that support multiple host sessions would have more than one logical unit assigned to them. Multiple logical units may exist over a single physical connection. Within SNA, there are several types of logical units. Figure 3.5 lists some of the common types.[4]

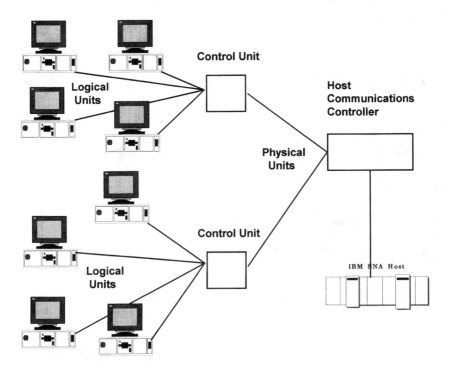

Figure 3.4 Logical versus Physical Units

Several types of physical connections can be established between a terminal device and an IBM host. All provide the same basic functionality, but use slightly different hardware configurations. The four configurations that we will consider are distributed function terminals, LAN attachment, synchronous data-link communication attachment (SDLC), and asynchronous data-link control attachment.[5]

Distributed Function Terminals The *distributed function terminal* (DFT) attachment provides a means to connect a terminal device to an SNA network.[6] Figure 3.6 shows a typical DFT configuration.

The terminal in this configuration is connected directly to a control unit. The function of the control unit or cluster controller is to act as a hub or single point of connection for a number of terminals. These devices are normally from the IBM 31XX or 32XX hardware series. The control unit is then connected to a host communications controller, sometimes referred to as a front-end processor. The communications controller manages communi-

LU2
Logical Unit type for a single display device using the 3270 data stream
LU3
Logical Unit type for a single printer using the 3270 data stream
LU6.2
Logical Unit type that supports sessions between two applications in a distributed environment

Figure 3.5   Common Logical Unit Types

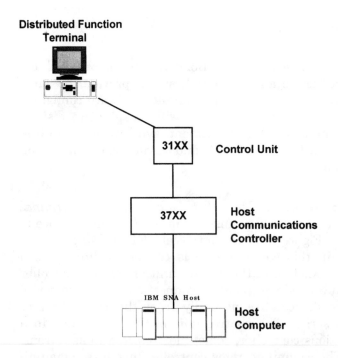

Distributed Function Terminal

31XX   Control Unit

37XX   Host Communications Controller

IBM SNA Host

Host Computer

Figure 3.6   Distributed Function Terminal Configuration

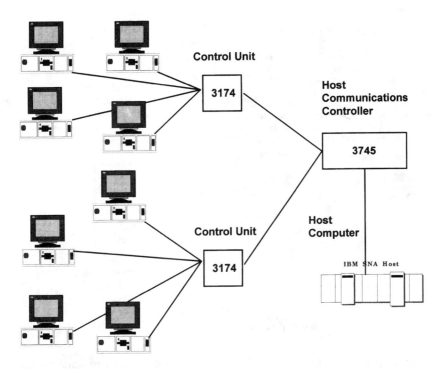

Figure 3.7   Typical DFT Configuration

cations among control units, other communication devices, and the host. In an IBM environment, communications controllers are usually from the 37XX series or other compatible hardware. Figure 3.7 shows a typical DFT configuration with multiple terminals and control units attached to a communications controller.

In an SNA network, a DFT connection supports a logical connection referred to as an LU2-type connection.[7] An LU2, or Logical Unit 2, provides communications with a single terminal using the IBM SNA 3270 data stream.

LAN Attachment   As was discussed earlier in the chapter, a LAN gateway may be used to provide terminal emulation to workstations connected to the LAN. Figure 3.8 shows a typical LAN gateway configuration. A single gateway is capable of supporting sessions for multiple workstations.[8] LAN gateways to IBM SNA environments are available for most LAN operating systems.

Synchronous Data-Link Communication Attachment   SDLC attachments are used to connect terminal devices over dedicated nonswitched

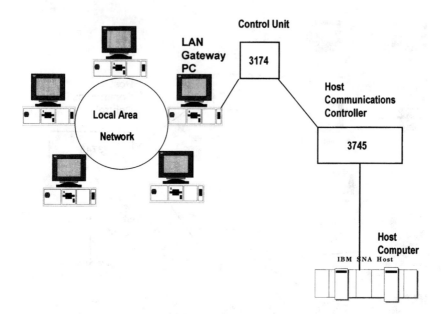

Figure 3.8   Typical LAN Gateway Configuration

or switched communications links.[9] This type of configuration can be used to connect remote devices to a central host system. Modems and communications lines are used to connect the terminal to the host communications controller.

Asynchronous Data-Link Control Attachment   Asynchronous, sometimes referred to as start–stop, provides the same type of connection as an SDLC connection; however, it uses asynchronous modems and switched communications lines.[10] Asynchronous modems are less costly than synchronous modems, but their transmission speed is usually lower than that of synchronous modems.[11] Figure 3.9 illustrates an SDLC and an asynchronous connection.

File Transfer Software

Once the physical connection to the host has been established and the terminal emulation software is loaded, the file transfer software can be used. This software uses the LU2-type connection established by the emulation software to transfer data between the PC and the host. The file transfer package consists of two components: the PC software and the host transfer program. These two components interact to send and receive files in an

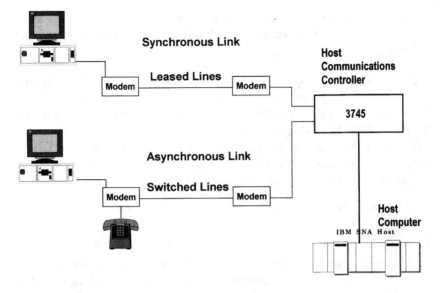

Figure 3.9   Synchronous and Asynchronous Communications

IBM environment. The IBM host program is generally the IND$FILE program.[12] Versions of the IND$FILE program are available for various IBM host operating systems. Third-party vendors of terminal emulation and file transfer software often provide their own proprietary host and PC software.

The programs employed by the PC are the SEND.EXE and RECEIVE.EXE programs.[13] Figure 3.10 shows the relationship between the various file transfer components. Let us examine the SEND and RECEIVE programs in more detail.

Sending Files

The SEND command is used to transfer data from the PC to the host. The basic syntax for the IBM SEND command is

```
SEND <PC-FILE NAME> <DATASET NAME> <OPTIONS>
```

where

PC-FILE NAME is the full path and file name of the PC file to send.

DATASET NAME is the name of the host dataset to which the PC file will be transferred.

OPTIONS include such items as ASCII character conversion, append to existing dataset, and options for dataset type and format.

The syntax and options may vary slightly depending on the host operation system and the PC send–receive software. Most third-party terminal emulation software will function with the IBM IND$FILE host component. As previously mentioned, some third-party emulators supply an alternative to the IND$FILE program to be used with their PC file transfer software.

The process to transfer a PC file to a host would be as follows:

1. The emulation software is loaded and a host session established.
2. A log-on to the host operating system is completed.
3. The user "hot keys" or switches from the host session to a PC session. At the DOS prompt, the SEND command is entered.

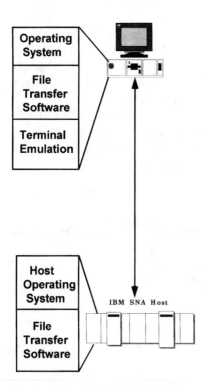

Figure 3.10   File Transfer Components

Some emulation packages have special function keys that will invoke the PC file transfer programs directly from the host session. This eliminates the need to "hot key" or jump back to a DOS prompt.

4. Once the file transfer is complete, the user has the option to sign off or continue working with the host.

The SEND command may be entered at the DOS prompt or included in a DOS batch file. A batch file simplifies the process if the host dataset names are lengthy or if multiple files are being transferred. The following example shows how a DOS batch file could be constructed to send the PC file PAYROLL.DAT in the PC directory C:\PAY to the host dataset PROD.PAYROLL.INPUT.

```
@ ECHO OFF
PC3270
CLS
ECHO "PRESS ALT-ESC TO SWITCH TO THE HOST SESSION"
ECHO "WHEN YOU HAVE SIGNED ON TO THE HOST, PRESS ALT-ESC
     TO RETURN TO THIS SCREEN."
ECHO "PRESS ANY KEY TO START THE FILE TRANSFER."
PAUSE
CLS
SEND C:\PAY\PAYROLL.DAT PROD.PAYROLL.INPUT ASCII CRLF
CLS
ECHO "FILE TRANSFER COMPLETE"
ECHO "PRESS ALT-ESC TO RETURN TO"
ECHO "THE HOST SESSION"
```

The first line of the batch file prevents the DOS commands from being displayed on the screen as they are executed. The next line loads the IBM emulation software with the command PC3270. The next four lines clear the screen and display instructions for use. With the IBM PC3270 emulation software, by pressing the ALT and ESC keys, the user can switch from the PC session to the mainframe session. Once in the mainframe session, the user logs on to the host. After completing the log-on procedure, the user again presses the ALT and ESC keys to return to the PC session and continue execution of the batch file. The PAUSE statement causes execution of the batch file to halt until the user presses any key. Once a key is pressed, the CLS statement clears the screen and the SEND command is executed.

The options ASCII and CRLF are added to the SEND command to specify ASCII to EBCDIC character translation. The CRLF option indicates that individual records in the PC data file are delimited by the carriage return and line feed codes. Additional options are possible, depending on the particular PC and host transfer software used. While this is a general example, it provides an illustration of how a batch file can be built to simplify a file transfer.

Receiving Files

The RECEIVE command is used to transfer files from the host to the PC. The syntax for the basic IBM RECEIVE command is

```
RECEIVE <PC-FILE NAME> <DATASET NAME> <OPTIONS>
```

where

PC-FILE NAME is the full path and name of the file to be received.

DATASET NAME is the name of the host dataset to be transferred to the PC.

OPTIONS include such items as EBCDIC to ASCII conversion and the addition of carriage return and line feed codes to the end of each record.

As with the SEND command, the syntax and options may vary depending on the host operating system and the file transfer software used. The process to receive a file is basically the same as that used to send a file. The steps would be

1. Load the emulation software and establish a host session.
2. Log-on to the host operating system.
3. "Hot key" to the PC session and invoke the RECEIVE command.
4. When the file transfer is complete, switch back to the host session and sign off.

Again the SEND and RECEIVE commands may be entered at the DOS prompt or be included in the batch files. In the following example, the host dataset PROD.EMPLOYEE.DATA is transferred to the file EMPLOYEE.TXT on a network file server.

```
@ECHO OFF
PC3270
CLS
ECHO "PRESS ALT-ESC TO SWITCH TO THE HOST SESSION"
ECHO "WHEN YOU HAVE SIGNED ON TO THE HOST, PRESS ALT-ESC
     TO RETURN TO THIS SCREEN."
ECHO "PRESS ANY KEY TO START THE DOWNLOAD."
PAUSE
RECEIVE G:\DATA\EMPLOYEE.TXT PROD.EMPLOYEE.DATA ASCII CRLF
CLS
ECHO "FILE TRANSFER COMPLETE."
ECHO "PRESS ALT-ESC TO RETURN TO THE HOST SESSION."
```

This batch file is basically the same as the Send File example described previously in the chapter. The major differences are the use of the RECEIVE command, the use of a network drive, and path for receiving the PC file. In this case, C:\DATA\EM-PLOYEE.TXT identifies a file stored on a network file server. Generally, file transfer software will function with all local and network addressable drives. Prior to initiating the download batch file, the network log-in would need to be accomplished.

Implementation Considerations

While simple file transfer is relatively uncomplicated and inexpensive, it has several limitations to be considered.

- Host Data Files

  Simple file transfer can be used only with "flat" or sequential files. If the data resides on the host in a relational database, it would need to be exported to a flat file prior to being downloaded. This may require additional programming on the host. The host data source may also contain more data than desired or, conversely, not all the desired data. In the case of the data source containing unwanted data, it may be necessary to extract only the desired data prior to downloading. This is often done to reduce the size of the download file and to save storage on the client system as well as reduce transmission time. If the data sought by the client does not reside in a single file on the host, a download file may need to be produced by the host or the individual files downloaded to the client and then combined. The approach taken will depend on the amount of data and the complexity of the programming involved. It may, in some cases, be more cost effective to download multiple files and process them with less expensive client MIPS.

- Scheduling

  Depending on the size of the files to be transferred and the speed of the communications links, the file transfer could be a lengthy process. This may impact operations on the client side of the process. For example, if data is downloaded to a LAN file server for use by multiple clients, it may be impractical to suspend operations during normal business hours while new data is downloaded and processed. The download process may need to be scheduled for nonbusiness hours. File transfer, using the basic SEND and RECEIVE commands, is an attended process. This sometimes complicates scheduling transfers during nonbusiness hours.

- Frequency

  Given that the file transfer process may be lengthy and interrupt operations, it would be impractical to implement simple file transfer in an environment where it is necessary to obtain updated host data on a frequent basis. A simple file transfer approach would be appropriate in a situation where updated host data is needed only on a daily or less frequent basis. The host data may be updated more frequently or in some cases continuously. However, the client would download it only daily. An example would be an *Executive Information System* (EIS) that accessed corporate sales data for management reporting and analysis. The sales database would be updated throughout the day as orders were received. The client EIS application, however, would only download data early each morning to reflect the previous day's sales activity. In this example, the client application does not need real-time access to server data. Client/server systems that support real-time data access will be discussed in later chapters.

- Security

  A major concern with file transfer, particularly in a mainframe environment, is security. Mainframes are known for comprehensive system security. Often the security authorization required for file transfer raises concerns with system security and data integrity. To transfer files, a user normally requires security access to the operating system, the host file transfer program, and the desired host dataset. Downloading data may present a risk to the confidentiality of host data. Once data is transferred to a client platform, it is not necessarily protected with the same degree of security as it was on the host.

Uploading data to a host platform can potentially present data integrity security risks. When uploading data, it is possible to overwrite existing data or upload invalid data either intentionally or unintentionally. In one case, a company inadvertently uploaded an incorrect PC data file to a banking electronic funds transfer system. This error proved not only embarrassing but costly, as each transaction had to be reversed by the bank.

- Automated File Transfer

Given the scheduling and security concerns presented in this chapter, the use of automated file transfer software may be worth consideration. These packages allow unattended, prescheduled file transfer. Most packages allow for the transfer process to be initiated either by the client or the server. To minimize security risks, file transfers can be controlled by the host. In this type of configuration, the host starts the transfer at a predetermined time. The PC component usually is in the form of a *terminate-and-stay-resident* (TSR) program, which waits for the host to initiate the transfer process. The transfer can occur in either direction, with the host sending files to or receiving files from the client. Automated file transfer packages are particularly useful in situations where large amounts of data are transferred during nonbusiness hours. Software distribution and client file backup can also be accomplished with these packages.

The second implementation case at the end of the chapter shows how an automated file transfer package can be used.

Situations Appropriate for This Approach

While simple file transfer is somewhat limited, it is still effective when implemented in appropriate situations. Simple file transfer is inexpensive and relatively easy to implement. The following criteria can be used to determine which situations would be appropriate for simple file transfer.

1. Client application requires infrequent access to updated server data.

   Simple file transfer is best implemented in a situation where the client is supplied data in an "overnight" or less frequent schedule.

2. Host data is easily accessible.

   For this approach to be practical, the host data must be in a form that is easily downloaded to the client and processed. The amount of programming effort to produce a host dataset should be considered.

3. The client application has ability to process the host data file.

   The client application must have the ability to import and process the host data. The format of the download file should be compatible with the file types supported by the client application.

Given the above criteria and a thorough understanding of the client application, it should be possible to determine if simple file transfer is a suitable approach. The following examples show how simple file transfer approaches have been effectively implemented. The first case study uses the SEND/RECEIVE file transfer programs described earlier in the chapter. The second case study uses an automated file transfer program.

Implementation Case Study #1

Payroll Personnel Download

A moderate-size municipal government recently installed a packaged human resources/personnel/payroll system on their IBM mainframe. The system tracked employee data and benefit information, and processed the bi-weekly payroll for approximately 6000 employees. Data was stored in a relational database and was accessible only through the applications programs and the standard reports supplied with the application. Custom reports required additional programming effort. Management reporting and reporting required by external agencies created a long reporting backlog. To alleviate the reporting backlog, a client/server application using simple file transfer was implemented.

The mainframe application allows on-line updates to be made to the employee database. Bi–weekly information is entered from employee time cards and a payroll is run. Employee earnings and deduction information are updated during payroll processing. A flat file is then created from the employee database. This file contains employee personal data and payroll data. The file is downloaded by several departments to LAN file servers. The file is then imported to a database accessed by a fourth generation reporting tool. End users use this tool to easily and quickly develop reports. Turn–around on reports has dropped from weeks to hours, and report preparation costs have been greatly reduced.

Simple file transfer was an effective approach in this situation because of the following:

- Due to the bi–weekly payroll processing, there was little need for the client application to access data on a more frequent basis. Employee personal information was updated more frequently; however, the client application could wait until the next payroll processing cycle to acquire the updated information.

- The host data was easily accessible. Selected data elements from the host database were easily extracted and written to a flat file. As end-user requirements changed, the addition of data elements to the download file was easily accomplished.

- The client application was well suited to import the host data. The database offered a great deal of flexibility in importing data. Its ease of use made the application particularly useful to managers and end users. In most cases, no programmer involvement was required in report preparation.

Implementation Case Study #2

Banking Automated File Transfer

A banking organization with many geographically separated branches needed to distribute updated interest rate and bank service fee information on a daily basis. To provide better customer service, the bank wished to integrate this information into PC-based applications.

The bank's computing environment consisted of a mainframe computer with remote connections to the PCs in the branches.

Using terminal emulation software, the PCs were used to access account information on the mainframe, as well as run PC applications. While file transfer software was available with the terminal emulation software, it was deemed too awkward to use.

In this situation, the bank chose to implement a client/server simple file transfer approach that used automated file transfer software. This software consisted of a PC component and a mainframe component. The PC component was a TSR program that waited until a predetermined time and then connected to the host computer. The host computer would then transfer the latest interest rates and fee information to the PC. This information was then used by the PC applications program. The transfer was scheduled to occur nightly, providing updated information for the start of each business day.

This approach was effective because:

- The client PC applications required updated data on a nightly basis. Normal operations were not interrupted to download the data. An important factor was that the interest rate was updated only daily.

- Given the small amount of data downloaded, it was not difficult for the client application to process the data. Little processing was necessary short of using the downloaded information as input to loan payment calculation programs.

- Given the environment of the PC with terminal emulation connected to a remote host, there were few other options. Simple file transfer offered a means to use the existing communications network rather than installing an expensive wide area network.

These two examples illustrate how a simple file transfer approach can be implemented. This approach is best suited in cases where an infrequent update to the server data is acceptable. Some situations require more frequent access to source data. The following chapters discuss approaches that employ a more real-time relationship between the client and the server.

Summary

In this chapter simple file transfer was introduced. This approach involves the transfer of data from a host server to a client workstation or LAN. The client application then accesses and processes the data. Although the client duplicates several of the computing processes of the host, the basic client/server relationship still exists. To use a file transfer approach, the client workstation must be connected to the host system and be capable of emulating a host display device. Several different types of physical connections can be established between the workstation and the host. Connection from a workstation to a host is normally accomplished via a terminal emulation card or a LAN gateway. The latter offers cost savings for LAN workstations.

In addition to the physical connection, the workstation requires emulation software to allow it to function as a host terminal. The emulation software supports software that can send files to or receive files from the host. The file transfer process consists of loading the terminal emulation software, establishing a host session and completing a log-on, switching to a DOS or PC session, and issuing the file transfer commands. DOS batch files can be used to simplify the process.

While simple file transfer is relatively uncomplicated and inexpensive to implement, it does have several limitations. First, the desired data must reside on the host in a form that is easily downloaded. This normally requires a "flat file" format. Scheduling of the file transfer process may be a consideration, given the possibility of lengthy transfers and interruption of the client application.

The frequency of updates is a consideration with this approach. Simple file transfer works best in situations where access to real-time data is not required. Data security may also be a consideration when this approach is used. Automated file transfer packages can alleviate some of these concerns. Simple file transfer is appropriate in situations where the client application requires infrequent access to updated server data, where the host data is easily accessible, and where the client application has the capability to further process the host data.

End Notes

1. *IBM Personal Communications/3270 User's Guide*, 1989, pp. 2–10.

2. Alan R. Simon, *Enterprise Computing* (New York: Bantam Books, 1992), p. 222.

3. Ibid.

4. *IBM Personal Communications/3270 Customization and Installation Guide*, 1989, p. X-6.

5. Ibid., pp. 3–19.

6. Ibid., pp. 3–19.

7. Ibid., pp. 3–20.

8. Ibid., pp. 3–25.

9. Ibid., pp. 3–26.

10. Ibid., pp. 3–28.

11. *Data Communications Concepts* (Baton Rouge: Communications Research Group, Inc., 1989), pp. 3–8.

12. *IBM Personal Communications/3270 User's Guide*, 1989, p. 3-1.

13. Ibid.

4

Applications Programming Interface

In the previous chapter we examined how a simple file transfer approach could be implemented in an environment in which the client application required infrequent access to updated server data. In some situations, however, the client application may require frequent access to current server data.

Consider the example of an airline reservation system. While a simple file transfer approach may be appropriate for a client/ server application that does end-of-day reporting, it is not at all suited for an on-line reservation application. One approach that can be used in this situation is the *Applications Programming Interface* (API). APIs are often used to bridge PC/LAN client applications and mainframe/midrange applications. This approach usually requires no modification to existing host applications. By using an API-based client/server approach, firms can maximize their investment in existing host applications and data.

API applications are relatively inexpensive to develop and implement. Often an API-based approach is selected as a first step in moving to more complex client/server strategies, such as IBM's LU6.2.[1] Some of the advantages of using APIs are that they require no modification of existing host applications and can be accomplished without specialized programming expertise. Peer-to-peer computing and other more advanced architectures often require extensive modification of existing applications and specialized programming skills.[2]

In this chapter we will first examine what an API is and how an API can be described in terms of our conceptual processing model. Next, we will look at IBM's *High-Level Language Applications Programming Interface* (HLLAPI) and how it can be used to develop client/server applications. Two API development tools will then be examined. Finally, the selection criteria for an API approach will be presented, followed by API implementation examples.

Applications Programming Interface Defined

An API, as its name states, is an applications interface. The purpose of this interface is generally to link a client application to a server application. Often APIs are used to give a client/server "front end" to existing mainframe applications. The client application may be a PC application program or simply a GUI for the host application. Providing a GUI front end for an existing mainframe application has many benefits. First, it maximizes the firm's current investment in existing hardware and applications software. A GUI based on an API is far less expensive than completely replacing an existing system. Second, a GUI can incorporate existing host application logic. Rather than passing invalid data to the host, the GUI can check the data and transfer only acceptable data. In this case, data validation is being performed on the client, with less expensive MIPS, rather than on the host with its relatively more expensive MIPS. The processing of the application is divided between the client and the server, with each performing the processes that it is best suited for. Figure 4.1 shows conceptually how an API is used to link client and server applications.

The API links the client application to the host via the terminal emulation software. The host application communicates to the client application as if it were a terminal user and is unaware that it is actually connected to a client application. The client user may be unaware of the existence of the host application. The client user is "removed" from the host application by the API and the application program. Often the client end user interacts with the client interface and never sees the host application. For example, Figure 4.2 shows a typical mainframe application screen.[3]

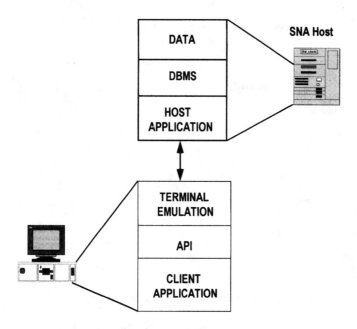

Figure 4.1 Applications Programming Interface

The data entry fields are far from easy to understand and an underlying knowledge of the data is required to use the application. In addition to the data entry fields, the user must understand the use of the "F" or function keys to navigate from screen to screen within the application. The user must also understand the use of several specialized system keys as well as the system log-on and log-off procedures.

Contrast the screen in Figure 4.2 with the screen shown in Figure 4.3.[4] This screen shows how an API can be used to link a GUI-based client application with a host server application. In this example, the client application is designed to allow a user to enter, edit, or view employee information on a mainframe personnel system. Notice how items such as position and pay rate can be selected by a scroll bar. This compares to the screen in Figure 4.2. To enter position and pay rate, the user must have some knowledge of the permissible values for these fields. With the API client, the user selects from a list of valid responses. The client GUI can also validate manually entered data such as social security number and birth date. Rather than pressing function keys, the user simply uses the mouse to click on the appropriate box for

Example Mainframe Application

```
HR0ARC01----------------- JOB APPLICANT RECORD KEEPER ---------------------
JOB CLASS TABLE
REQUIRED FIELDS ----------------------------------------------------------
ADDS
JOB CLASS, TITLE, SALARY, ACAD RANK, DATE
DELETES
JOB CLASS, TITLE, SALARY, ACAD RANK
ITEM NO.1 ----------------------------------------------------------------
LAST NAME Mozart                        FIRST NAME Wolfgang              MI
A/D   JOB CLASS A233    TITLE
RATE IND   SALARY MINIMUM 25000    MAXIMUM           GRADE G12 PAY SCALE F
STND HOUR 40        FLSA X    EEO CAT X     EEO SUB
EXP LVL 4     WORK COMP VARIABLE   EMP GRP Z   BARG UNIT
JOB STAT        START DATE 10-11-90           ACAD RANK MFA    TEN ELG X
ITEM NO.2 ----------------------------------------------------------------
A/D   JOB CLASS         TITLE
PRIOR JOB CLASS
REPORT GROUP1        REPORT GROUP2        REPORT GROUP3
IDENTIFICATION -----------------------------------------------------------
OPERATOR CODE 3002X      DATE 11/01/90
PROCESS ------------------------------------------------------------------
HUMAN RESOURCES
QUIT      TRAN IDENT APP12 CODE
ERR1033-JOB CLASS DOES NOT MATCH TITLE      ERR1036-INVALID EMP GRP
4B?                                         P
```

Figure 4.2   Example Mainframe Application

Example API GUI Screen

Figure 4.3   Example API GUI Screen

the operation to be performed. Navigating throughout the application can be done via menu bars and even the log-on and log-off processes can be automated. A simple GUI such as the one described here offers the following benefits:

- The easy-to-use GUI reduces operator training time.

- Data is validated before it reaches the host. Host processing time is reduced and fewer errors are introduced into the database.

Often the use of client GUIs with existing host applications is referred to as cooperative processing. The host and the PC "cooperatively" complete the processing task. The PC client has application software that provides a user interface, data entry, and data validation. The host or server runs the underlying applications software as well as the database management software. In terms of the conceptual computing processes model introduced in Chapter 2, the division between client and server in this approach would occur with the applications software.

Figure 4.4 shows the conceptual model for an API-based client /server relationship. Notice that both the client and the server have applications software. In some situations, an API can be used to combine data from multiple hosts as well as data contained on the client platform. In this situation, the client would also process its own database management software and data storage. Figure 4.5 illustrates this type of arrangement. Now let us look at IBM's API in more detail.

HLLAPI

IBM's *High-Level Language Application Programming Interface* (HLLAPI) is a programming interface that allows applications programs written in high-level programming languages to interface with a mainframe 3270 session.[5] The basic concept behind HLLAPI is that it allows the 3270 display screen to be mapped and data read from it or written to it.

Figure 4.6 shows a typical 3270 display screen. The screen consists of a display that is normally 25 rows from top to bottom and 80 columns from left to right. Given this row and column grid, it is possible to identify any position on the display screen. The first 24 rows are referred to as the presentation space. This is the display area for the applications program. It is through this

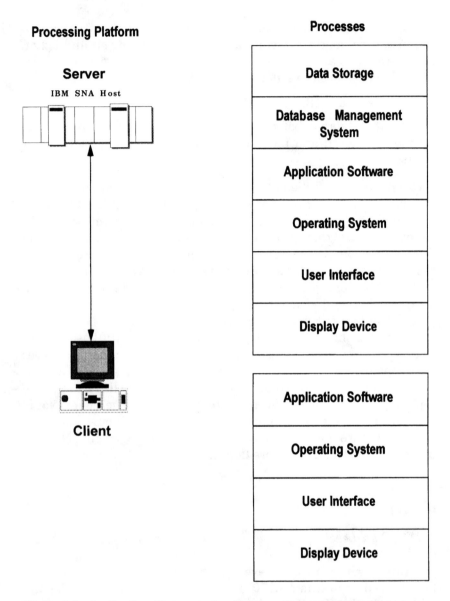

Processing Platform

Server

IBM SNA Host

Client

Processes

Data Storage
Database   Management System
Application Software
Operating System
User Interface
Display Device

Application Software
Operating System
User Interface
Display Device

Figure 4.4   Application Programming Interface Conceptual Model

mapped 3270 screen that the client application interacts with the host application.

With a 24-row by 80-column screen, there are 1,920 (24 × 80) charter cells in the presentation space. Line 25 is referred to as the *operator information area* (OIA) and displays information on

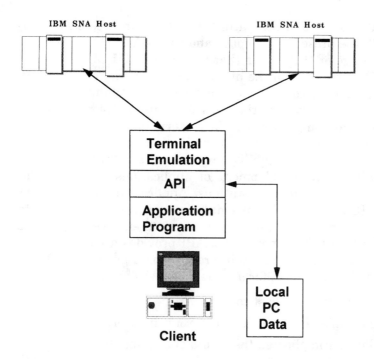

Figure 4.5   Use of an API to Combine Multiple Data Sources

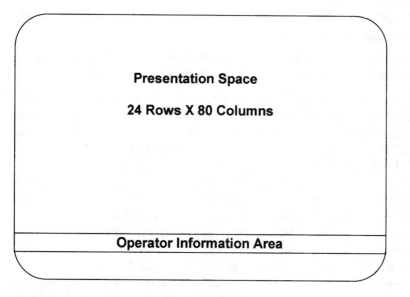

Figure 4.6   3270 Display Screen

the current session and its status.[6] HLLAPI can access information in both the presentation space and the OIA.

An advantage of HLLAPI is that it uses an IBM LU2-type connection. If you recall from the discussion of terminal emulation in Chapter 3, an LU2 connection is a basic 3270 "dumb" terminal connection. This eliminates the need for more complex communications hardware and software. Most terminal emulation packages support HLLAPI. The combination of an LU2-type connection and interoperability with several 3270 emulation packages allows the development of applications that are relatively portable between workstations. Applications developed for PCs using IBM 3270 terminal emulation can easily be ported to other workstations using third-party terminal emulation software or a LAN gateway. In general, HLLAPI provides a means for PC and mainframe applications to interact using a generic 3270 session. HLLAPI can be used for a variety of tasks such as:[7]

- Automating repetitive host tasks.
- Masking complex host applications from the user.
- Consolidating complicated tasks into one simple task.
- Simplifying existing host applications.
- Providing unattended operations through a programmed series of instructions.
- Creating a composite application that combines input from the host and the workstation.
- Developing cooperative processing applications that divide processing between the host (server) and the PC (client).

HLLAPI is an applications program interface, but not a programming language itself. HLLAPI functions must be called from a high-level programming language. Languages that may be used with HLLAPI include BASIC, C, COBOL, IBM Macro Assembler, and Pascal.[8] Within the applications program, a call is made to HLLAPI to execute a special function. Depending on the function, additional parameters are either passed to or received from HLLAPI. Figure 4.7 shows some of the HLLAPI functions.[9]

Using these functions, it is possible to read information from the presentation space, search the presentation space, or enter data in fields on the host display. The HLLAPI examples cited earlier in the chapter served as graphical front ends for host applications. The following example shows how HLLAPI can be

Function Number	Description
1	Establish connection to the presentation space
2	Disconnect from presentation space
3	Send keystroke to mainframe
4	Wait until mainframe is ready for input
5	Copy presentation space to a string
6	Search presentation space for specified data
7	Find cursor location
8	Copy all or part of presentation space to a string
9	Set session parameters
10	Query number and type of sessions
11	Lock out keyboard input
12	Unlock keyboard
13	Copy OIA to a string
14	Query field attribute
15	Copy a string to the presentation space
17	Allocate memory
18	Wait for a specified period of time
21	Reset HLLAPI
24	Determine if host display has been updated
30	Search field for specified data
31	Find field position
32	Find field length
33	Copy string to field

Figure 4.7   HLLAPI Functions

used to automate a file transfer process and mask a user from host transfer process.

Figure 4.8 shows a C program written to automate the transfer of a data file from a PC to a host. You may recall from Chapter 3, one of the limitations of a simple file transfer approach is the complexity of the transfer process and the requirement for the process to be attended. This program simplifies the process by prompting the user for all required inputs and masking the host screens from the operator. The user "sees" only one PC interface

Function Number	Description
34	Copy string to field
35	Define presentation space
36	Switch presentation space
37	Display cursor
38	Display presentation space
39	Delete presentation space
50	Filter keystrokes
51	Get keystroke
52	Get keystroke status
53	End keystroke filter
90	Send file
91	Receive file
92	Invoke DOS program
93	DOS redirect
99	Convert position to row and column

Figure 4.7   HLLAPI Functions *(continued)*

screen during the entire process. Behind the C program, HLLAPI connects to the underlying 3270 session, logs on to the host, initiates the file transfer, and then logs off the host. With the addition of a timer routine, this program could be used to perform an unattended file transfer at a predetermined time. Let us look at how HLLAPI is used in this program in more detail. (*Note:* While helpful, a knowledge of C is not required for the following explanation of the example program.)

The first section of the example program in Figure 4.8 defines the C libraries to be included during the compilation process. The next three sections define the variables, subroutines, and HLLAPI parameters used in the program. The main section of the program displays an entry screen and prompts the user for the name of the PC file to be transferred and the name of the host dataset to send the file to. Next, the user is prompted for the host ID and password. A call is made to the reset_system routine, which sets the API function to 21 (reset HLLAPI), and then calls HLLAPI. This call reinitializes the API and restores all default settings. The general process is to set the HLLAPI parameters (API_FUNC; API_STRING; API_LEN; API_RETC) to the desired

```
/****************************************************************/
/*                  HLLAPI File Transfer Program              */
/*                                                            */
/************** C Libraries to Be Included ******************/
#include          <stdio.h>
#include          <stdlib.h>
#include          <conio.h>
#include          <string.h>
#include          <dos.h>
#include          <ctype.h>
#include          <time.h>

/*************** Define Character Variables ****************/
char PC_FILE_NAME[60];
char DATASET_NAME[60];

/****************** Define Subroutines ********************/
void connect_host();
void pause(int API_LEN);
void search_pres(char *API_STRING,int API_RETC);
void reset_system();
void send_key(char *API_STRING);
void wait();
void error_routine();
void frame();
void exit_pgm();
void logon();

/****************** Define HLLAPI Parameters ***************/
int API_FUNC, API_LEN, API_RETC, X, MAIL_POS, POS_COUNTER,
API_LEN_OUT;
char API_STRING[255], MAIL_STRING[1512];
char USER_ID[8], PASS_WORD[8], ANSWER;

/*********************Main Logic Routine ******************/
main()
{
  frame();
  gotoxy(10,2);
  cputs("          Automated File Transfer Program");
  gotoxy(2,8);

/****************************************************/
/*      Enter Name of PC File to Upload        */
/****************************************************/
  cputs("Enter PC File Name:");
  gotoxy(22,8);
  gets(PC_FILE_NAME);
```

Figure 4.8   HLLAPI File Transfer Program

```
/*****************************************************/
/*    Enter Name of Host Dataset to Upload To     */
/*****************************************************/
  gotoxy(2,9);
  cputs("Enter Dataset Name:");
  gotoxy(23,9);
  gets(DATASET_NAME);


/*****************************************************/
/*          Get Host User ID and Password          */
/*****************************************************/
  gotoxy(27,10);
  cputs("Enter User ID:");
  gotoxy(41,10);
  gets(USER_ID);
  strncat(USER_ID,"@E",2);
  gotoxy(27,11);
  cputs("Enter Password:");
  gotoxy(43,11);
  textattr(0);
  cputs("          ");
  gotoxy(43,11);
  gets(PASS_WORD);
  textcolor(15);
  textbackground(1);

/************* Connect to Host and Log-on *****************/
  reset_system();
  connect_host();
  logon();
  gotoxy(10,15);
  printf("Starting File Transfer\n");


/*****************************************************/
/* Move PC File Name, Dataset Name and Transfer */
/*         Options to HLLAPI String              */
/*****************************************************/
  strcpy(API_STRING,PC_FILE_NAME);
  strcat(API_STRING," ");
  strcat(API_STRING,DATASET_NAME);
  strcat(API_STRING," ASCII CRLF LRECL(432) BLKSIZE(432) RECFM(F)");


/*****************************************************/
/*        Set HLLAPI Function to SEND File        */
/*****************************************************/
  API_FUNC=90;
  API_LEN=strlen(API_STRING);
  API_RETC=3;
```

Figure 4.8   HLLAPI File Transfer Program *(continued)*

```
/**************************************************/
/*          Call HLLAPI SEND File         */
/**************************************************/
  HLLC(&API_FUNC,API_STRING,&API_LEN,&API_RETC);

  frame();
  gotoxy(10,16);
  printf("File Transfer Complete, Please Wait, Logging Off
Mainframe");

/**************************************************/
/*              Log-Off Host             */
/**************************************************/
  wait();
  pause(20);
  send_key("LOGOFF@E");
  wait();
  pause(20);
  exit_pgm();
  return (0);


  }
/******************************************************************/

/***********Establish Connection to Host System **************/
void connect_host()
{
  API_FUNC=1;
  strcpy(API_STRING, "A");
  API_LEN=1;
  HLLC(&API_FUNC, API_STRING, &API_LEN, &API_RETC);
  if (API_RETC !=0)
     {
     error_routine();
     }
}
/******************************************************************/

/*************Wait for a Specified Amount of Time ***********/
void pause(int API_LEN)
{
  API_FUNC=18;
  HLLC(&API_FUNC, API_STRING, &API_LEN, &API_RETC);
}
/******************************************************************/

/*********************Reset HLLAPI *******************/
void reset_system()
```

Figure 4.8   HLLAPI File Transfer Program *(continued)*

```
{
  API_FUNC=21;
  HLLC(&API_FUNC, API_STRING, &API_LEN, &API_RETC);
}
/****************************************************************/

/*************Character(s) to Presentation Space **************/
void send_key(char *API_STRING)
{
  API_FUNC=3;
  API_LEN=strlen(API_STRING);
  API_RETC=0;
  HLLC(&API_FUNC, API_STRING, &API_LEN, &API_RETC);
  if(API_RETC!=0)
  {
  error_routine();
  }
}
/****************************************************************/

/**************Wait until Mainframe Ready for Input *********/
void wait()
{
  API_FUNC=4;
  HLLC(&API_FUNC, API_STRING, &API_LEN, &API_RETC);
}
/****************************************************************/

/*****************Search Presentation Space *****************/
void search_pres(char *API_STRING,int API_RETC)
{
  API_FUNC = 6;
  API_LEN = strlen(API_STRING);
  HLLC(&API_FUNC,API_STRING,&API_LEN,&API_RETC);
}
/****************************************************************/

/**********************Log-on Script ********************/
void logon()
{
  gotoxy(10,12);
  cputs("Logging on to Host System......Please Wait");
  gotoxy(10,13);
  cputs("Accessing Mainframe");

/**************************************************/
/*    Wait for Letters CICS to Appear on Screen   */
/**************************************************/
```

Figure 4.8   HLLAPI File Transfer Program *(continued)*

```
  strcpy(API_STRING,"CICS");
  API_LEN = 0;
  while (API_LEN == 0)
  {
  search_pres(API_STRING,1);
  }
  wait();
  pause(20);

/****************************************************/
/*    Send Command TSO/ENTER to Host            */
/****************************************************/
send_key("TSO ");
  wait();
  pause(20);

/****************************************************/
/*    Send User ID to Host                      */
/****************************************************/
  gotoxy(10,14);
  cputs("Processing User ID and Password\r\n");
  wait();
  send_key(USER_ID);
  wait();
  pause(20);


  strcpy(API_STRING,"TSO/E  LOGON");
  API_LEN = 0;
  while (API_LEN == 0)
  {
  search_pres(API_STRING,1);
  }
  wait();
  pause(20);

/****************************************************/
/*    Send Password to Host                     */
/****************************************************/
  send_key(PASS_WORD);

/****************************************************/
/*    Tab to Account Field and Send Acct Number  */
/****************************************************/

  send_key("@N");
  send_key("@N");
  send_key("240d167t@E");
```

Figure 4.8   HLLAPI File Transfer Program *(continued)*

```
 }
/****************************************************************/

/******************Create Window Frame ********************/
void frame()
{
  clrscr();
  textmode(3);
  textbackground(1);
  textcolor(15);
  clrscr();
  gotoxy(1,1);

puts(" ╔══════════════════════════════════════
═══════════╗ ");
  for (X = 2; X < 23; ++X)
  {
      gotoxy(1,X);
      puts(" ║ ");
      gotoxy(80,X);
      puts(" ║ ");
  }
  gotoxy(1,23);

puts(" ╚══════════════════════════════════════
═══════════╝ ");
  gotoxy(1,7);

puts(" ╠══════════════════════════════════════
═══════════╣ ");
  gotoxy(0,0);

}
/****************************************************************/

/************************Exit Program ********************/
void exit_pgm()
{
  API_FUNC = 2;
  HLLC(&API_FUNC,API_STRING,&API_LEN,&API_RETC);
  if (API_RETC !=0)
     {
     cputs("Warning  ...  Could not disconnect from Host\r\n");
     }
  gotoxy(15,20);
```

Figure 4.8   HLLAPI File Transfer Program *(continued)*

```
   cputs("File Transfer Program Complete");
   gotoxy(15,21);
   cputs("Press any key to Exit");
   getch();
   clrscr();
   exit(0);
}
/****************************************************************/


/*********************Error Routine ************************/
void error_routine()
{
   clrscr();
   textcolor(0);
   textbackground(12);
   gotoxy(25,12);
   cputs("A Communications Error Has Occurred");
   gotoxy(25,13);
   cputs("Check Mainframe Hardware Connections");
   exit_pgm();
}
/****************************************************************/
```

Figure 4.8   HLLAPI File Transfer Program *(continued)*

values and then call HLLAPI. Complete explanations of each function and the purpose of each parameter can be found in the IBM HLLAPI Programming Reference.[10] After the system is reset, control is returned to the main routine and then the connect_host subroutine is called. This routine "connects" the C applications program to the 3270 session via the HLLAPI interface. If an error code is returned from the HLLAPI call, an error routine is executed. Once connection to the 3270 session is accomplished, the log_on routine is called to complete the log-on to the host. After displaying a message to the user, the routine stays in a loop that calls a HLLAPI function that searches the presentation space for the character string "CICS." This character string indicates that the 3270 session is displaying the system log-in screen. Next, the WAIT and PAUSE routines are called to ensure that the host session is ready to receive input. The WAIT routine waits until the host is ready to receive input and the PAUSE routine waits for a specific amount of time. Because the PC application is capable of sending keystrokes faster than the 3270 session can receive them, it is necessary to check that the host is ready and allow a brief period of time for it to "catch up" to the PC application.

When the host is ready, the keystrokes "TSO" and "Enter" are sent to the presentation space. The program then sends the user ID and again loops, searching the presentation space for the string "TSO/E Logon." This indicates that the host is now on the TSO log-on screen. The user's password is sent to the presentation space, followed by two tab keys that position the cursor on the user account field. The account number is sent followed by an enter key. All commands are sent to the presentation space by use of the send_key subroutine. This subroutine sends the string and then checks for a return code. If an error occurs, an error routine is called. After the log-on is completed, the main routine sets the file transfer parameters and sets the HLLAPI function parameter to 90 to initiate the send file call. HLLAPI is called and the file is transferred. The log-off command is sent to the host and the exit_pgm routine is called. This routine disconnects from the 3270 session and terminates the program.

As you can see from this example, it is relatively easy for a programmer to develop an application that uses HLLAPI to interface a PC application with a host application. For instance, the example program could easily be modified to serve as an order entry program that would collect order information and then upload it to the host on a periodic basis. A PC interface that utilized GUI components such as pushbuttons, scroll bars, and pop-up menus could be developed as part of the order entry system. If on-line updates to the host system were desired, the program could be designed to log-on to the host application, call up the host order entry screen, and pass data as the user entered it in the PC application. All of this could be done without the end user interacting directly with the host application.

While HLLAPI is a very powerful and flexible tool, it does have some disadvantages. The major disadvantage is that the applications programs can become quite lengthy and complex. The example program dealt with only three host screens and a limited number of data entry fields. Imagine trying to develop an HLLAPI-based system for a host application that had several hundred screens, all with multiple data fields on each screen. While possible, it would be quite a task.

Another disadvantage to HLLAPI is its dependence on the structure of the host screens. Since an HLLAPI application is mapped to the location of the data fields on the presentation space, any changes to the host screens will most likely require changes to the PC application. In one organization, the applications programmers had developed several HLLAPI APIs for host applications that automated the log-on process and accessed host applications. One weekend the systems programmers changed the format of the system log-on screens and, as you might have expected, on Monday morning none of the HLLAPI applications worked and all required quick modification. While a change management program may have removed the surprise factor in this example, it still would not have eliminated the need to revise the HLLAPI applications.

API Development Tools

To overcome some of the difficulties in building applications with HLLAPI, several companies offer application development tools for creating GUIs for client/server or cooperative processing applications. These tools automate the task of mapping the 3270 screen and offer a full set of graphic objects such as scroll boxes, pushbuttons, and pull-down menus. Some of the major product offerings in this field include EASEL from Easel Corporation, Mozart from Mozart Systems, and Flashpoint from Viewpoint Systems. The application shown earlier in Figure 4.4 was developed using the Mozart product. These tools all offer a graphical applications development environment.

Complete applications may be developed graphically with little or no manually generated code. The process of mapping the 3270 presentation space is accomplished in a graphical environment, greatly simplifying the task of identifying the location of fields on the 3270 display screen. Should the underlying host application screens change, modifications can quickly and easily be made to the interface. These tools allow the combination of host applications and other data sources such as PC files or databases. Most of these development tools offer "portability" among operating systems. Applications developed for DOS or Windows environments can be ported to OS/2 or UNIX with little difficulty. Many of the Windows-based development tools support Windows features such as *dynamic data exchange* (DDE) and *dynamic link libraries* (DLL). Some of the more advanced development tools such as Mozart provide access to SQL databases in addition to existing host applications.[11]

Implementation Considerations

While APIs offer a means to develop a client/server architecture that utilizes existing applications, there are several factors to be considered:

- Suitability of Host Application

  Since the API is built on top of the host application, the underlying application must accomplish the functions required by the end user. For example, a host order entry system would probably not be an appropriate application to build an API-based accounts receivable system on. The underlying application must contain the required data and be capable of performing the required processing on the host. Some processing and data may be offloaded to the client, depending on the requirements of the system. An example of this would be a loan information system. The API would access host interest rate information, then combine data on the amount and term from the client to present a payment schedule on the screen. In this case the underlying host application is only providing interest rate information; the client application is designed to accept information from a user, access the host via the API, complete loan calculations, and display the results.

- Development Cost

  HLLAPI-based programs tend to be very programmer intensive. Applications with a large number of screens may take a great deal of time to program. Additionally, maintenance may become a consideration as frequent changes to the underlying host application will require changes to the client application. API development tools greatly simplify the development and maintenance tasks but are sometimes expensive.

- Hardware Requirements

  An API-based application normally requires a PC with 3270 emulation. For IBM AS/400 and System 3X computers, 5250 emulation support is required. Depending on the development tool used, additional hardware and software may be required to support Windows or OS/2.

Situations Appropriate for This Approach

Although an API approach does have some limitations, it offers a relatively quick and inexpensive means to implement client/server computing. Its major appeal is that it uses existing host applications and can be implemented with little or no modification to the existing host application. The investment in existing applications and data is maximized. The following criteria can be used to determine which situations would be appropriate for an API approach.

- Existing Host Application

  The underlying host application must contain the required data and be capable of performing processing if required. The function of the API is to provide a GUI to the host application or combine the host application with a PC application or data.

- Need for Updated Information

  The API provides access to on-line information on the host. This may be required if information is frequently updated or is part of an on-line system.

- Mixture of Host and Client Users

  Since this approach does not require the modification of the host application, it would be well suited for an environment in which both PC clients and "dumb" terminals accessed the same host application.

While API implementations depend heavily on existing host applications, they can provide effective solutions in some situations. The above criteria can be used to determine the suitability of an API approach. The following examples show how APIs have been successfully implemented. The first case study uses an HLLAPI API, and the second case illustrates how an applications development tool can be used to build an API application.

Implementation Case Study #3

Electronic Mail API

OfficeVision is an IBM software product designed to provide electronic mail, workgroup scheduling, and applications integration. It is a follow-on to IBM's very successful PROFS or Professional

Office System. The OfficeVision family of products offers software for IBM mainframe systems, midrange AS/400, and OS/2 local area networks. The mainframe product supports 3270-type terminals or PCs with 3270 terminal emulation. The user interface consists of menu items that are selected by entering the number of the desired option or by pressing one of the 3270 function keys.

An organization purchased the mainframe OfficeVision product to provide electronic mail and scheduling to its mainframe users. The system was piloted with the Information Systems Department and was generally successful. When the system was expanded to other departments, nontechnical users found the product difficult to use. The IS staff was familiar with mainframe applications and using a 3270 terminal. Users from other departments were mostly administrators and clerical staff who infrequently used the mainframe. To provide a more user-friendly interface, and to automate the log-on process, an HLLAPI API was developed for OfficeVision.

An excerpt of the code is shown in Figure 4.9. The program provides a PC-type interface with pop-up menus and automates the log-on procedure. During the log-on process, the user is prompted for the user ID and password. Using the HLLAPI interface, a 3270 session is established and the log-on completed. The OfficeVision application is invoked after the log-on is completed. The check_mail routine checks to see if the user has mail waiting in the in-basket and displays a message along with sounding a beep on the PC speaker. This is a feature not found on the mainframe application that was requested by the end users. PC pop-up and bar menus are used rather than the menus and function keys required by the underlying host application. Various HLLAPI features are used to search the presentation space for data. Electronic mail messages and calendar information are presented via the PC interface to the user. The API "removes" users from the host application and allows them to use the functions of the underlying host application without ever actually seeing any of the host screens.

In this situation, this approach was effective because:

- The underlying host application possessed the required functionality. An electronic mail and scheduling capability was needed and the host application provided those functions.
- The host application was basically stable. Since the OfficeVision product had a limited number of screens that rarely

```
/******************************************************************/
/*              HLLAPI OfficeVision Interface                   */
/******************************************************************/

#include          <stdio.h>
#include          <stdlib.h>
#include          <conio.h>
#include          <string.h>
#include          <dos.h>
#include          <ctype.h>

void connect_host();
void pause(int API_LEN);
void search_pres(char *API_STRING,int API_RETC);
void reset_system();
void send_key(char *API_STRING);
void wait();
void error_routine();
void frame();
void check_mail();
void view_mail();
void file_mail();
void delete_mail();
void main_menu();
void bar_menu();
void logon();
void in_basket();
void note();
void file_cabinet();
void list_apps();
void make_appt();
void exit_pgm();

/*  HLAPPI PARAMETERS */
int API_FUNC, API_LEN, API_RETC, X, MAIL_POS, POS_COUNTER,
API_LEN_OUT;
char API_STRING[255], MAIL_STRING[1512];
char USER_ID[8], PASS_WORD[8], ANSWER;
char *MAIL, MAIL_FLAG = 'M', BASKET_ENTRY = '/';
char *INBASKET = "WIB@E";
char *VIEW = "V@E";
char *FILE_MAIL_ITEM = "FIL@E";
char *DELETE = "DEL@E";

/***********************Main Menu***********************/
main()
{
```

Figure 4.9   HLLAPI OfficeVision Interface

```
    frame();
    reset_system();
    connect_host();
    logon();
    frame();
    check_mail();
    main_menu();
    return (0);

 }
/****************************************************************/

/*********Establish Connection to Host System ***************/
void connect_host()
{
  API_FUNC=1;
  strcpy(API_STRING, "A");
  API_LEN=1;
  HLLC(&API_FUNC, API_STRING, &API_LEN, &API_RETC);
  if (API_RETC !=0)
    {
    error_routine();
    }
}
/****************************************************************/

/****************Wait for a Specified Amount of Time ********/
void pause(int API_LEN)
{
  API_FUNC=18;
  HLLC(&API_FUNC, API_STRING, &API_LEN, &API_RETC);
}
/****************************************************************/

/********************Reset HLLAPI**************************/
void reset_system()
{
  API_FUNC=21;
  HLLC(&API_FUNC, API_STRING, &API_LEN, &API_RETC);
}
/****************************************************************/

/**********Send Character(s) to Presentation Space***********/
void send_key(char *API_STRING)
{
  API_FUNC=3;
  API_LEN=strlen(API_STRING);
  API_RETC=0;
```

Figure 4.9   HLLAPI OfficeVision Interface *(continued)*

```
HLLC(&API_FUNC, API_STRING, &API_LEN, &API_RETC);
if(API_RETC!=0)
{
error_routine();
}
}
/*************************************************************/

/*************Wait until Mainframe Ready for Input ***********/
void wait()
{
  API_FUNC=4;
  HLLC(&API_FUNC, API_STRING, &API_LEN, &API_RETC);
}
/*************************************************************/

/*****************Search Presentation Space *****************/
void search_pres(char *API_STRING,int API_RETC)
{
  API_FUNC = 6;
  API_LEN = strlen(API_STRING);
  HLLC(&API_FUNC,API_STRING,&API_LEN,&API_RETC);
}
/*********************Log-On Script ***********************/
void logon()
{
  gotoxy(17,3);
  cputs("Logging on to Host System......Please Wait");
  gotoxy(25,5);
  cputs("Accessing Mainframe");
  strcpy(API_STRING,"CICS");
  API_LEN = 0;
  while (API_LEN == 0)
  {
  search_pres(API_STRING,1);
  }
  wait();
  pause(20);
  send_key("CICS@E");
  wait();
  pause(20);
  strcpy(API_STRING,"USERID:");
  API_LEN = 0;
  while (API_LEN == 0)
  {
  search_pres(API_STRING,1);
  }
  gotoxy(27,7);
```

Figure 4.9   HLLAPI OfficeVision Interface *(continued)*

```
  cputs("Enter User ID:");
  gotoxy(41,7);
  gets(USER_ID);
  strncat(USER_ID,"@N",2);
  gotoxy(27,9);
  cputs("Enter Password:");
  gotoxy(43,9);
  textattr(0);
  cputs("           ");
  gotoxy(43,9);
  gets(PASS_WORD);
  textcolor(15);
  textbackground(1);
  strncat(PASS_WORD,"@E",2);
  gotoxy(27,11);
  cputs("Processing User ID and Password\r\n");
  wait();
  send_key(USER_ID);
  send_key(PASS_WORD);
  wait();
  pause(20);
  gotoxy(27,13);
  cputs("Accessing OfficeVision");
  strcpy(API_STRING,"SIGN-ON");
  API_LEN = 0;
  while (API_LEN == 0)
  {
  search_pres(API_STRING,1);
  }
  send_key("OV@E");
  wait();
  pause(20);
}
/******************************************************************/

/******************Create Window Frame ********************/
void frame()
{
  clrscr();
  textmode(3);
  textbackground(1);
  textcolor(15);
  clrscr();
/*  window(1,1,80,25); */
  gotoxy(1,1);

puts(" ┌═══════════════════════════
════════════┐ ");
```

Figure 4.9   HLLAPI OfficeVision Interface *(continued)*

```
    for (X = 2; X < 23; ++X)
    {
        gotoxy(1,X);
        puts(" ‖ ");
        gotoxy(80,X);
        puts(" ‖ ");
    }
    gotoxy(1,23);

puts(" └─────────────────────────────────
─────────────┘ ");
    gotoxy(0,0);


}
/******************************************************************/

/***************Check for New Mail Flag ********************/
void check_mail()
{
    API_FUNC = 8;
    API_LEN = 1;
    API_RETC = 1839;
    HLLC(&API_FUNC,API_STRING,&API_LEN,&API_RETC);
    MAIL = strchr(API_STRING,MAIL_FLAG);
    gotoxy(27,22);
    if (MAIL)
        {
        sound(1000);
        delay(500);
        nosound();
        textcolor(143);
        cputs("Mail is waiting in your In-Basket");
        textcolor(15);
        }
      else
        {
        cputs("                                        ");
        }
}
/******************************************************************/

/*********************Create Main Menu********************/
void main_menu()
{
    gotoxy(30,05);
    cputs("Main Menu");
    gotoxy(25,7);
    cputs("1. Check In-Basket");
```

Figure 4.9   HLLAPI OfficeVision Interface *(continued)*

```
gotoxy(25,8);
cputs("2. Send Note");
gotoxy(25,9);
cputs("3. File Cabinet");
gotoxy(25,10);
cputs("4. List Appointments");
gotoxy(25,11);
cputs("5. Make Appointments");
gotoxy(25,12);
cputs("6. Exit ");
gotoxy(27,14);
cputs("Enter Choice:");
gotoxy(40,14);
ANSWER = getche();
switch (ANSWER)  {
case '1':
 in_basket();
  break;
case '2':
  note();
  break;
case '3':
  file_cabinet();
  break;
case '4':
  list_apps();
  break;
case '5':
  make_appt();
  break;
case '6':
  exit_pgm();
  break;
default:
  main_menu();
  }
}
/****************************************************************/

/******************List In-Basket Items*********************/
void in_basket()
{
 frame();
 gotoxy(20,2);
 cputs("One Moment Please......Accessing Mail");
 wait();
 send_key(INBASKET);
 wait();
```

Figure 4.9   HLLAPI OfficeVision Interface *(continued)*

```
pause(20);
gotoxy(2,2);
cputs("     Received            From       Document Name
Subject                 P");
POS_COUNTER = 408;
X = 3;

while (POS_COUNTER < 1529)
{
   /*  GET FIELD          */
   API_FUNC = 8;
   API_LEN = 72;
   API_RETC = POS_COUNTER;
   HLLC(&API_FUNC,API_STRING,&API_LEN,&API_RETC);

   /* IF BLANK FIELD, EXIT */
   MAIL = strchr(API_STRING,BASKET_ENTRY);
   if (MAIL)
   {

      gotoxy(5,X);
      X = X + 1;
      cputs(API_STRING);
      POS_COUNTER = POS_COUNTER + 80;
   }
   else
   {
   break;
   }
}
bar_menu();
MAIL_POS = 3;
while (ANSWER != 'E')
{
gotoxy(3,MAIL_POS);
ANSWER = toupper(getche());
switch (ANSWER)
  {
  case 'D':
    delete_mail();
  case 'V':
    view_mail();
  case 'F' :
    file_mail();
  default:
    MAIL_POS = MAIL_POS + 1;
    if (MAIL_POS > X)
    {
```

Figure 4.9   HLLAPI OfficeVision Interface *(continued)*

```
      X=3;
      }
      }
   }
   main_menu();
}
/****************************************************************/

/*********************View Mail in In-Basket******************/
void view_mail()
{
    frame();
    gotoxy(20,2);
    cputs("One Moment Please......Accessing Mail");
    wait();
    send_key(VIEW);
    wait();
    pause(20);
    API_FUNC = 8;
    API_LEN = 1512;
    API_RETC = 1;
    HLLC(&API_FUNC,MAIL_STRING,&API_LEN,&API_RETC);
    gotoxy(1,1);
    clrscr();
    cputs(MAIL_STRING);
    bar_menu();
    getche();
    clrscr();
}
/****************************************************************/

/*********************File Mail in In-Basket******************/
void file_mail()
{
 gotoxy(15,24);
 cputs("Filing Mail Item");
 wait();
 send_key(FILE_MAIL_ITEM);
 wait();
 pause(20);
 send_key("@E");
 pause(20);
 gotoxy(15,24);
 cputs("Item Successfully Filed");
 gotoxy(5,MAIL_POS);
 cputs("Filed    ");
}
/****************************************************************/
```

Figure 4.9   HLLAPI OfficeVision Interface *(continued)*

```
/***********************Send Note ************************/
void note()
{
}
/*************************************************************/


/**********************Access File Cabinet *****************/
void file_cabinet()
{
}
/*************************************************************/


/***********************List Appointments******************/
void list_apps()
{
}
/*************************************************************/


/*********************Make Personal Appointments***********/
void make_appt()
{
}
/*************************************************************/



/**************************Exit Program*********************/
void exit_pgm()
{
  API_FUNC = 2;
  HLLC(&API_FUNC,API_STRING,&API_LEN,&API_RETC);
  if (API_RETC !=0)
     {
     cputs("Warning  ...  Could not disconnect from Host\r\n");
     }
  gotoxy(15,20);
  cputs("Use Hot Key (Shift/Shift) to Access Mainframe Session");
  gotoxy(15,21);
  cputs("Press any key to Exit Logon Program");
  getch();
  clrscr();
  exit(0);
}
/*************************************************************/
```

Figure 4.9   HLLAPI OfficeVision Interface *(continued)*

```
/*******************Error Routine****************************/
void error_routine()
{
  clrscr();
  textcolor(0);
  textbackground(12);
  gotoxy(25,12);
  cputs("A Communications Error Has Occurred");
  gotoxy(25,13);
  cputs("Check Mainframe Hardware Connections");
  exit_pgm();
}
/*************************************************************/


/*******************File Option Bar Menu ******************/
void bar_menu ()
{
    gotoxy(2,25);
  textcolor(12);
  cputs("V");
  gotoxy(7,25);
  cputs("F");
  gotoxy(12,25);
  cputs("D");
  textcolor(15);
  gotoxy(3,25);
  cputs("iew");
  gotoxy(8,25);
  cputs("ile");
  gotoxy(13,25);
  cputs("elete");
}
/*************************************************************/


/*********************Delete Mail Item ******************/
void delete_mail()
{
gotoxy(15,24);
 cputs("Deleting Mail Item");
 wait();
 send_key(DELETE);
 pause(20);
 gotoxy(15,24);
 cputs("Item Successfully Deleted");
 gotoxy(5,MAIL_POS);
 cputs("Deleted ");
}
/*************************************************************/
```

Figure 4.9   HLLAPI OfficeVision Interface *(continued)*

changed, the API did not require frequent modification. The host screens and functions were relatively fixed.

- The host application served both 3270 and API users. The underlying host application was used to link users of the API and basic 3270 sessions. Technical users familiar with mainframe applications could use the base host application, while nontechnical users could use the same host application with a more user-friendly API interface.

Implementation Case Study #4

Mozart API Development Tool

Conoco, Inc., a leader in the energy and petroleum industry, wanted to make its mainframe applications easier to use.[12] However, the company was wary of the risks involved in altering its mission-critical mainframe applications. Rather than rewriting the host-based applications, Conoco decided to seek out a tool that would provide a front-end graphical user interface for its existing host software. This would not only increase productivity, but also enable Conoco to extend the useful life of its host applications, thereby protecting the substantial investment already made in mainframe software.

Mozart, an API development tool from Mozart Systems Corporation, was selected for use. The first project Conoco's developers undertook with Mozart was the construction of a front end for GOLD, Conoco's Gas On-Line Data application. The GOLD application runs on an IBM mainframe and is used for the approval and review of gas contracts. Its users, natural gas accountants with varying degrees of computing experience, found the GOLD application cumbersome and difficult to manage.

Conoco's normal development methodology consists of a five-step process: a requirements/feasibility study, design, development (coding and testing), parallel running, and implementation. Mozart's graphical development environment enabled the project to be completed more than a month ahead of schedule.

With the Mozart application in place, users were able to exchange information from multiple screens through a single Mozart screen. With Mozart, Conoco was able to automate the log-on process and simplify navigation through screens. Conoco's development effort was made easier through Mozart's developer assists, the most important of which was Mozart's .MFS Mapper.

With the .MFS Mapper, developers were able to import mainframe screen definitions directly into Mozart, eliminating the need to rename variable names on the Mozart screen. This development technique eliminated the need for a screen capture, which saved development time and effort.

Mozart also improved the user interface by providing intuitive, CUA-compliant screens featuring objects such as action bars, pushbuttons, radio buttons, drop-down fields, and list boxes, all of which simplified the user interface to the mainframe. In addition, Mozart provided local validation and on-line context-sensitive help, which virtually eliminated errors by the user. The end result of the project was a 50 to 60 percent time savings in gas contract approval.

In this situation, this approach was effective because:

- The underlying host application possessed the required functionality. The GOLD application, while effective, was cumbersome for nontechnical end users.

- The host application was basically stable. The firm wished not to alter its existing applications. In the event of modifications to the host applications, the API design tools selected provided means to update the API front-end application.

These two case studies illustrate how an API approach can be successfully implemented. The primary ingredient to a successful API implementation is the underlying host application. In Chapter 5 we will examine how a client/server architecture can be implemented without benefit of an existing host application.

Summary

In some situations, the client application may require frequent access to updated host server information. An approach that can be used to accomplish this is the *Applications Programming Interface* (API). APIs are used to link client applications with existing host applications. This approach usually requires no modification to existing host applications and can be used to extend the life of existing host applications as well as a first step in implementing more complex client/server strategies.

API's require little in terms of specialized programming skills. Often they are used to provide a graphical front end to existing host applications and remove the end user from the complexities of using a mainframe application. Cooperative processing can be achieved by offloading some tasks such as data validation and editing to the client API, where they can be performed by a less expensive processing platform. GUI objects such as scroll bars and pop-up menus can be incorporated in APIs to provide a more user-friendly interface.

An API works in conjunction with the terminal emulation software and maps the display screen so that specific fields can be read or written to by the applications program. In terms of the computing processes model, an API approach divides the processing between the client and server at the applications program level. Both client and server run applications programs that cooperatively accomplish the overall computing task.

APIs can be written using IBM's *High-Level Language Applications Programming Interface* (HLLAPI). HLLAPI uses an LU2-type connection and can be called from high-level languages such as BASIC, C, and COBOL. Tasks that HLLAPI can be used for include automation of repetitive tasks, masking complex host applications, consolidation of tasks, providing unattended operations, and developing cooperative processing applications. HLLAPI interfaces can become cumbersome and difficult to maintain if there are a large number of mainframe screens or if the underlying host application changes frequently. An alternative is to use an API development tool that provides a graphical development environment and screen-mapping utilities.

An API approach would be appropriate in situations where the existing host application meets the basic functional requirements, there is a need for updated or on-line information, and there is a mixture of host and API users.

End Notes

1. Leila Davis, "Peering at the LU6.2 Choice," *Datamation*, February 1, 1990, p. 50.

2. Ibid., p. 52.

3. Provided courtesy of Mozart Systems Corporation, Burlingame, California.

4. Ibid.

5. Mike Fichtelman, "Don't Worry, Use HLLAPI," *Byte, IBM Special Edition*, Fall 1990, p. 208.

6. *IBM Personal Communications/3270 EHLLAPI Programming Reference*, May 1989, p. E-1.

7. Ibid., pp. 1-1, 1-2.

8. Ibid., p. 3-3.

9. Fichtelman, op. cit., p. 210.

10. Fichtelman, op. cit., Section G.

11. *MOZART-Facts and Features,* Mozart Systems Corporation, Burlingame, California.

12. Case study provided courtesy of Mozart Systems Corporation, Burlingame, California.

5

Windows and OS/2 Client/Server Products

One of the major enabling technologies behind the growth of client/server computing has been the GUI. The two leading GUIs in the client/server marketplace are Microsoft Windows and IBM OS/2. Both Microsoft and IBM are aggressively targeting their products for the client/server market. While neither OS/2 nor Windows alone support client/server computing, both can be used in conjunction with other products, notably server databases, to build client/server applications. Windows and OS/2 simply provide the GUI environment in which to develop and run client/server applications. While other GUIs are available, most client/server vendors are primarily providing products for these two GUIs.

Client/server products for Windows and OS/2 generally, conform to the true client/server model. In terms of the conceptual model presented in Chapter 2, the data storage and database management systems reside on the server, and the applications software, operating system, user interface, and display device reside on the client. Figure 5.1 illustrates the division of computing processes typically found with Windows and OS/2 client/server applications.

The division between client and server can occur between a PC client and a LAN database server, or between a PC client and a midrange or mainframe database server. In either case the conceptual division is the same; the only difference is in the connectivity between the client and its server. Connectivity will be discussed in more detail later in the chapter. By dividing the computing processes as shown in Figure 5.1, the relative advantages of each platform are maximized.

The operating system and user interface are the primary processes that use the features of Windows and OS/2. Both processes provide a GUI as well as multitasking. IBM's OS/2 is a true operating system while Windows 3.X is a GUI that runs on top of an existing DOS operating system. Windows NT, released in 1993,[1] is in itself an operating system and does not require an underlying operating system. Both Windows and OS/2 allow multitasking or multiple processes to be running concurrently. Additionally, data may be linked or exchanged between applications. These features and their implications for client/server applications will be discussed in more detail later in the chapter.

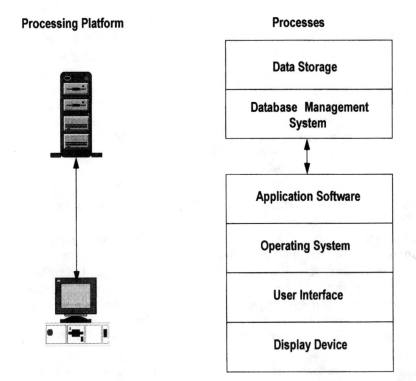

Figure 5.1   Client/Server Model

In this chapter, we will examine the hardware and software configurations for Windows and OS/2 client/server implementations. First, the general hardware requirements for client and server platforms will be discussed. Next, software for the client and server will be covered. Selection criteria for a Windows–OS/2 implementation approach will be presented, followed by an implementation example.

Client/Server Hardware

Client Platform

In most situations, the client platform in an IBM environment consists of a personal computer. Most GUIs require a 386 or higher processor and large amounts of RAM. In the IBM PS/2 product line, this would equate to a PS/2 model 70 or higher, or an equivalent "clone" PC. Depending on the GUI and operating system used, RAM memory of eight or more megabytes may be required. Less powerful PCs can be used, but performance may not be acceptable. Additional requirements would include a display device and a pointing device such as a mouse. To communicate with the server platform, the client will require a network adapter card or a host emulation card.

Server Platform

Generally, the hardware configuration for a client/server application requires that the client and server be connected by some type of high-speed data communications link. Most often, the server is a database server attached to a LAN. In some situations, the server may be a database on another platform such as a mainframe or midrange system. In the case of the latter, a gateway is used to connect the LAN clients to the host database. Let us now look at both types of server platforms.

LAN Database Server With a LAN database server, the hardware typically consists of a high-performance network file server either directly or indirectly attached to the same LAN as the client. Figure 5.2 shows both a directly attached and a remote database server.

In this example, the marketing server is directly connected or locally attached to the same LAN as the marketing client. The

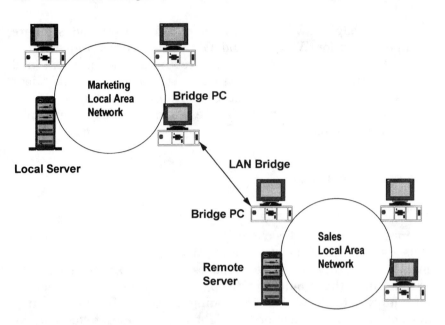

Figure 5.2   Local and Remote Network Servers

sales database server is remotely connected to the marketing LAN via a bridge connection. The remote connection does not prevent a marketing client from accessing information on the sales database server. Depending on the actual physical connection between the two LANs, performance may be a concern. The server may be a dedicated database server or it may be the same server used for other network applications. Again, depending on the particular application, the size of the database, and the number of users, performance may dictate a dedicated server.

Several vendors offer LAN servers that are optimized to function as database servers. Typically these servers have high-speed processors; large amounts of RAM memory for disk caching; high-performance network adapter cards; and high-capacity, high-speed disk storage. Often on mission-critical systems, disk storage is mirrored or duplexed to provide a measure of fault tolerance to the data storage system. For situations that require completely fault tolerant systems, servers are available that have redundant processors as well as data storage.

High-performance network cards, such as IBM's Micro Channel token ring adapter and the 32-Bit EISA network adapter cards from various vendors, are used to prevent network "bottlenecks" by transferring data as quickly as possible between the server

Server

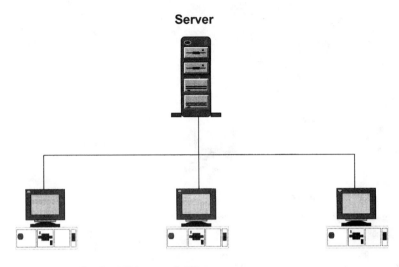

Figure 5.3   Typical Ethernet LAN

and the network. The use of multiple network cards and other network devices such as bridges can help to improve performance by reducing traffic on the local area network.[2] This is particularly true on Ethernet systems that use the IEEE 802-3 *Carrier Sense, Multiple Access/Collision Detection* (CSMA/CD) standard.[3] Ethernet provides a network "party line," which is available when not in use by another station. As the number of users and network traffic increases, Ethernet LANs may experience performance degradation if they are not properly configured and managed. Figure 5.3 illustrates a typical Ethernet system.

IBM's 802.5 token ring topology provides a network environment with deterministic network access in that each station in turn is provided an opportunity for exclusive use of the network.[4] A network "token" travels around the ring and is available to each station on the LAN. A station wishing to use the LAN retrieves the token and attaches data to it for its trip around the ring to its intended destination. Figure 5.4 shows a conceptual diagram of a token ring local area network.

Database Gateway   A database gateway provides a means to access data on a mainframe or midrange host server.[5] This may be desirable if a host system contains data needed by the client applications. The use of a gateway is in some respects similar to the simple file transfer approach presented in Chapter 3. The major differentiation is that only the specific data required by the client

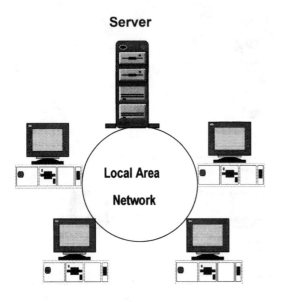

Figure 5.4   Typical Token Ring LAN

application is retrieved from the server and transferred to the client. This overcomes some of the limitations of simple file transfer and allows the development of client/server applications based on existing host databases. In terms of the hardware configuration, a database gateway is similar to the LAN gateways described in Chapter 3. Figure 5.5 illustrates a typical database gateway.

The gateway is usually connected to a local area network via a network adapter card. Host connectivity is provided by an SDLC or token ring adapter.[6] The host adapter card connects to either a cluster controller or directly to a communications controller. The communications controller is connected to the host. The gateway itself is often a high-end PC.

Client/Server Software

The software configuration of a client/server application consists of a client component and a host component. The client component typically executes on the workstation while the host component runs on either the LAN server or, in the case of a database gateway, on the gateway and the host server. A single client application may access server applications on multiple hosts or gateways. The server software may be used by multiple client ap-

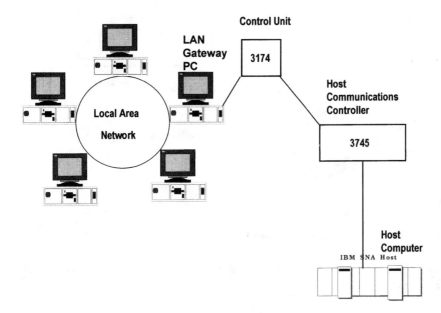

Figure 5.5   Typical LAN Gateway Configuration

plications. Let us now examine the client and server software components in more detail.

Client Software

The client software is responsible for the processes shown in Figure 5.6. The display device and user interface are often dictated by the type of workstation hardware employed. To take advantage of a GUI, a high-resolution monitor, a keyboard, and some type of pointing device such as a mouse and the software to support them would be required.

An innovative combination of display device and input device is the touch screen. These screens display information and options graphically, and the user interacts with the application by touching an area of the screen. This provides an easy-to-use interface for end users. Touch-screen applications have been developed for uses such as department store credit card inquiry, order entry, and public access to information on government services. While the touch screen provides an interesting combination of display device and user interface, most client/server applications today rely on a PC-type monitor as a display device and some type of software to provide a user interface. The two predominant user

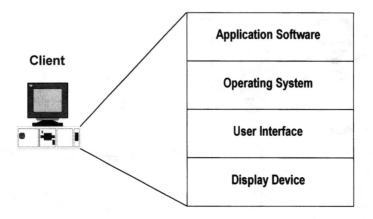

Figure 5.6   Basic Client Software Elements

interfaces in the IBM environment are the Microsoft Windows and IBM OS/2.

Graphical User Interfaces

Microsoft Windows   As mentioned in Chapter 2, Microsoft Windows has captured a large percentage of the GUI market. Designed to run on top of the DOS operating system, Windows provides a full-featured GUI environment. A large number of "off-the-shelf" applications programs are available for Windows and range from word processing to spreadsheets and presentation graphics. The advantages of using a GUI have been discussed earlier in the text, but let it suffice to say that graphical interfaces offer many advantages over character-based interfaces. A majority of client/server application developers produce products for Windows. In addition to the GUI, Windows offers the following advantages for client/server implementations:

- Multitasking

  Windows allows multiple applications to be running concurrently.[7] This is useful when it is necessary to run multiple client programs. For example, a communications program running in one window may be accessing data from a host server while an applications program that uses the data, such as a spreadsheet, runs in another window.

- Memory Management

  DOS-based applications are generally limited to 640KB of memory. Windows provides memory management that allows applications to access memory in excess of the 640KB DOS limitation.[8] Virtual memory allows applications to utilize more memory than is physically available.[9]

- Data Linking

  Windows allows data in various applications to be linked so that as data in one application is changed or updated, it is automatically updated in all other applications that use that data. Data is linked between applications through the use of *Dynamic Data Exchange* (DDE) and *Object Linking and Embedding* (OLE).[10] The DDE link establishes a conversation or a communications link between a server program that contains the data and a client program that needs the data. This client /server relationship exists within the Windows environment and is conceptually the same as the relationship that exists in client/server applications such as those described in this book. The DDE solely allows the exchange of data between applications; it does not support specialized data such as digitized speech. Object linking and embedding allows data to be exchanged between applications and retains a link between the data and the applications program from which it came.[11] With OLE it is possible to link not only data but also applications within a Windows environment. Additionally, Windows supports a "cut and paste" data transfer between applications.

While Windows has captured much of the GUI market, it does have several limitations. Chief among these limitations is the fact that Windows must run on top of an underlying DOS operating system. To overcome this reliance on the aging DOS operating system, Microsoft has developed Windows NT, which is an operating system combined with a GUI. Windows NT will provide a 32-bit operating system with built-in networking capabilities.[12]

OS/2 OS/2 is IBM's combination user interface and operating system. Unlike Windows 3X, OS/2 does not require an underlying operating system. Originally developed as an IBM/Microsoft product, OS/2 now seems to be in direct competition with Windows in the GUI market.[13] For a time, the products were marketed as complementing each other rather than competing with each other. Windows was targeted at the low-end personal computer market while OS/2 was intended for use with high-end corporate client/server workstations. As each product began to move into the other's intended territory, the convenient division of the market failed. IBM began to package OS/2 on its own low-end PCs and offered OS/2 to clone vendors to bundle with their PCs. The phenomenal success of Windows has led to the development of numerous third-party Windows products and the adoption of Windows as the corporate platform of choice. While OS/2 currently offers more as an operating system than Windows, the introduction of Windows NT will bring the two products even closer together in capabilities and will further intensify the competition between the two products.

OS/2 provides a complete PC operating system based on a graphical user interface. It was designed to provide multitasking, scheduling, disk management, and memory management—all within a GUI.[14] As with Windows, the major reasons for developing client/server applications with OS/2 are its GUI and multitasking capabilities. The GUI is similar to that found in Windows and, being an IBM product, conforms to the IBM Systems Application Architecture and Common User Access standards. The multitasking capabilities allow multiple applications to be running concurrently and take full advantage of the capabilities of the 80386/486 processors.[15] The major detraction of OS/2 is its need for large amounts of RAM and disk storage. As advances in PC hardware produce more power at a lower cost, these concerns will most likely become inconsequential.

Other Products   Although Windows and OS/2 comprise the largest share of the client/server GUI markets, there are other GUIs to consider. Most notable are the UNIX-based products. These products provide a graphical user interface similar to those provided by Windows and OS/2. While not a major player in the client /server market at this time, the continued growth of UNIX and AIX, the IBM version of UNIX, may lead to more growth in the UNIX GUI client market.

Client Operating System Software

The operating system software for the client component consists of the client *operating system* (OS) and, in the case of a LAN-based client/server application, the *network operating system* (NOS). Let us examine each in more detail.

Client Operating System   The client operating system may be a separate operating system such as DOS or may be combined with the GUI as is the case with OS/2. The basic functions of an operating system were described in Chapter 2. To quickly review, an operating system is responsible for managing the disk storage system, scheduling of the processor, and memory management. With most client/server applications, the client OS is independent of the server operating system. With Windows 3X the underlying operating system is most often DOS 3X, 4X, or 5.0. Each succeeding version of DOS offered more features, but was still constrained by the "640KB" memory limitation.

To fully utilize the capabilities of the 386/486/X86 microprocessors, a 32-bit operating system such as OS/2 or Windows NT is required. Current 16-bit operating systems are capable of addressing multiple 64KB blocks of memory as compared to the 2-gigabyte addressing capability of 32-bit operating systems.[16]

Network Operating System   In addition to its own operating system, a client on a LAN-based system must also run a portion of the *network operating system* (NOS). The NOS provides a software connection between the operating system and the network. Figure 5.7 shows how the NOS relates to the client operating system. The client NOS, sometimes referred to as the workstation or workstation shell software, allows applications programs to access the network through the client operating system.

Network devices and storage are addressed as if they were physically attached to the client PC. In the case of a network file server, the client would access a logical drive that had been assigned to the network disk drive. Figure 5.8 shows the physical and logical drives for a network client. Logical drive assignments

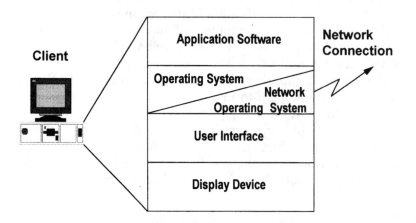

Figure 5.7   LAN Client Software Elements

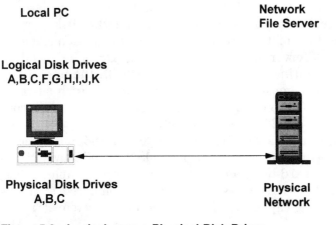

Figure 5.8   Logical versus Physical Disk Drives

to multiple file servers can be established allowing the client to access data on remote servers as easily as it would on its own local storage.

The client NOS is also responsible for managing the client's connection to the network. Depending on the network topology, this could involve "listening" for an opportunity to use the network as with Ethernet or, with token ring, checking for a token to pass a request to the network. The client portion of the NOS usually consists of some type of device driver that allows the operating system to communicate with the network card and the NOS client software. The NOS client software allows the operating system to interact with the network operating system. Major network operating systems include NetWare from Novell, IBM's LAN Server, and the Microsoft LAN Manager. In terms of market share, Novell is the largest supplier of network operating systems. A recent survey predicted that Novell would hold 65 percent of the market in 1992.[17] Microsoft and IBM make up the bulk of the remaining market share. The predominance of Novell has led software developers to produce products compatible with Novell. While Novell itself has produced a few client/server products, most of the client/server products available have been developed by independent third parties or in partnerships between Novell and applications developers.[18] The role of the server NOS will be discussed in more detail later in this chapter.

Client Applications Software   The client applications software is the component that receives the request from the user via the GUI, creates a database request, and then passes that request via the client operating system and NOS to the server. The client application can take several forms. The major types of client applications are SQL client additions to existing PC applications, client /server application development systems, and high-level language client applications.

SQL Client Additions SQL client additions allow existing PC applications packages to use a client/server architecture. The functionality of the application is not changed—rather it now has the ability to request and extract data from a server. These products are often purchased as an add-on or option to the original PC application. An example of this type of product would be DataLens for 1-2-3 from Lotus Development.[19] DataLens is an add-on for Lotus 1-2-3/3.2 and Lotus 1-2-3/Windows. It provides spreadsheet users a means to extract data from an external data server such as a mainframe host. The user is able to complete the request and execute it entirely within the 1-2-3 application using Lotus-type commands and syntax. Client additions such as these provide a client/server architecture without requiring extensive development of the client application. Little additional user training is required. Figure 5.9 is a conceptual diagram of a client addition to an existing PC application.

Add-ons are available for specialized applications packages such as Lotus and for PC databases such as Paradox, Data Ease, and dBASE.[20] The PC database products generally use SQL to access server data. The server components of these applications will be discussed later in the chapter.

Client/Server Applications Development Software In addition to the add-on products, vendors of client/server products offer numerous applications development packages. These packages allow complete applications to be developed without the use of a high-level programming language. Objects such as scroll bars and pushbuttons can be selected and associated with input fields and program options. Programming logic can be assigned to objects to provide input validation and editing. These products are most often available for the Windows and OS/2 environments.

If applications are being developed for a number of different processing platforms, portability is a definite consideration. Portability is the ability to take an application developed for one platform or environment and transfer that application to a different platform or environment without recoding the application and

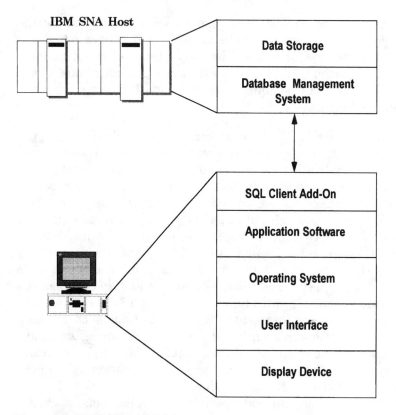

Figure 5.9   SQL Client Add-Ons

without any loss in functionality. An example of this would be the development of an application on an IBM PC under Windows and then the transfer of that application to an Apple Macintosh.

Portability among platforms and operating systems can save development time and provide standardized applications throughout an organization. An example of an applications development environment that offers portability is the ORACLE Tools line of products from Oracle Corporation. Oracle offers a full line of client/server development tools that are portable to over 80 different hardware platforms and operating systems.[21] These tools range from high-level CASE tools to client applications development tools. Some of the major vendors of applications development tools include Oracle, Sybase, and Gupta. These vendors offer complete client/server environments that include server database management systems in addition to client applications development software. Server database management software will be discussed in more detail later in this chapter.

In addition to the applications development software offered by vendors of DBMSs, client applications development software is available from third-party vendors that can be used with database servers from Oracle, Microsoft, Sybase, and Gupta. Many of these products are capable of accessing data from multiple server databases. The growth of server database systems, such as those from the vendors listed above, has created several de facto industry standards for databases. By offering features not found with the DBMS vendors' client software and access to multiple vendors DBMSs, these "fourth-party" vendors have created a marketplace for "client only" applications software. Some of the major product offerings in this market are Forest & Trees by Channel Computing, Flashpoint by Viewpoint Systems, Mozart by Mozart Systems, and EASEL/2 by Easel Corporation.

Of particular interest in the IBM environment are Flashpoint and EASEL/2. Flashpoint by Viewpoint Systems is a Windows-based visual applications development tool.[22] It can access data from Microsoft SQL server or SQL base from Gupta. Additionally, it can access host databases via IBM 3270 or 5250 terminal emulation. This allows data to be captured from existing host applications in the same manner as the API approach described in Chapter 4. Flashpoint offers portability to OS/2 for mixed Windows and OS/2 environments.[23] EASEL/2 from Easel Corporation runs under OS/2 and offers a graphical development tool that conforms to IBM SAA and *Common User Access* (CUA) guidelines.[24] Data can be accessed from Microsoft/Sybase SQL server databases by SQL commands generated by the EASEL/2 application or by direct SQL statements programmed into the application. As with Viewpoint, EASEL/2 supports IBM 3270 and 5250 terminal emulation, allowing data from existing host applications to be incorporated into the client application.[25] EASEL/2 supports IBM's *Advanced Program-to-Program Communications* (APPC). APPC can be used to communicate on a peer-to-peer basis with applications residing on other platforms. More information on APPC is presented in Chapter 6. While offering a number of interface options in the IBM environment, EASEL/2 supports the VT100 asynchronous communications protocol. This allows the client application to communicate with "open" systems as well as proprietary IBM systems.

High-Level Language Client Applications   Another option is to use a high-level programming language to develop client applications. This is accomplished by embedding SQL commands in the applications code. These SQL commands would then access and receive data from a server database. While offering the most flexibility, this option is also the most complex and potentially the most costly. Programming expertise is required for the programming language, SQL, and the GUI. Many high-level languages do not directly support GUIs. Often the long development time and high costs make this option unattractive.

Server Software

The server software is responsible for the processes shown in Figure 5.10. Server software receives requests from the client, processes the requests, and, if required, returns data to the client. The data storage process is generally a function of the underlying operating system of the server platform and deals with the physical storage of data on some type of storage device. The database management system handles the logical organization of the data and interfaces with the server operating system to access the data storage devices.

Servers can be either a LAN database server or a host database accessed via a database gateway. While the client software component is basically the same in either case, the server software is very different. With a LAN-based data server, both client and server exist on basically equivalent platforms and generally use a common network operating system. In the case of a LAN client and a host database server, the client and server exist on different hardware platforms and use platform-specific software. Let us consider each situation separately.

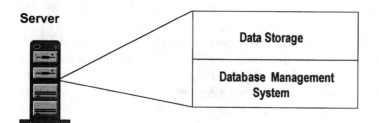

Server

Data Storage

Database Management System

Figure 5.10   Server Processes

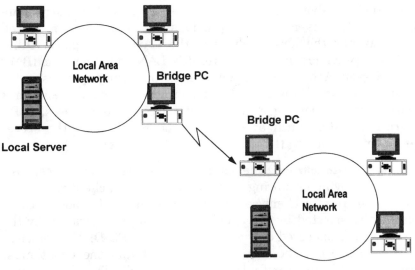

Figure 5.11   Local versus Remote Database Server

LAN Database Server Software   In the case of a LAN database server, the server resides on a LAN to which the client has connectivity. It may be that the client and server are on the same LAN, or are on connected LANs. (See Chapter 2 for more information on LANs and data communications.) Figure 5.11 shows an example of each type of configuration.

The data server will normally have at least the network operating system and the server DBMS running on it. Software for communications or network printing may also run on the database server. The database server may be configured as either a dedicated or nondedicated server. A dedicated server provides only one function, that being to run the server DBMS software. A nondedicated server may perform other functions in addition to running the server DBMS. The determination of dedicated versus nondedicated depends on the capacity of the server, the requirements of the DBMS, and the client load. In high-volume situations, a dedicated server may be desirable or even required.

Server Network Operating System   The network operating system provides software connectivity between the server DBMS software and the LAN. The LAN OS manages basic operating system functions such as disk management, scheduling, and memory management. As was mentioned previously in this chapter, Novell currently has the largest share of the LAN marketplace. Other LAN OS providers include Microsoft's LAN Manager and IBM's LAN Server. A full comparison of LAN operating systems is beyond the scope of this book, but all provide the same basic functions when supporting a server database. In some cases, a PC operating system such as OS/2 may be required by the server DBMS in addition to the network operating system.

Server Database Software   The server database software is responsible for retrieving or storing data in response to a client request. A major feature of a client/server DBMS is that only those records specifically selected by the client application are retrieved by the server and transferred to the client. A typical PC DBMS transfers all the data from the server to the client and the client must process the file until it finds the data it needs. The client/server architecture greatly reduces the amount of traffic transferred over the network and lessens the processing load for the client.

Numerous DBMS products are available for LAN database servers. Most are based on SQL as a data retrieval mechanism. (See Chapter 2 for a more complete explanation of SQL.) Some DBMSs are designed to work specifically with their own client software while others provide a more generic SQL database that may be accessed by any one of a number of SQL-based client applications packages. Figure 5.12 shows the relationship between the network operating system and the server DBMS.

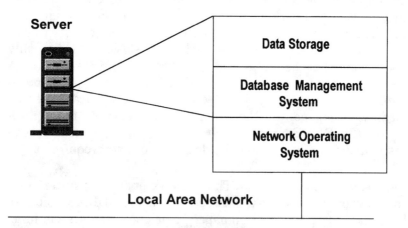

Figure 5.12   Server Network Operating System

In the case of Novell networks, many DBMS packages run a *network loadable module* (NLM). NLMs can be dynamically loaded and unloaded without interfering with the operation of the network operating system.[26] This is particularly useful on nondedicated database servers. The DBMS can be loaded and "brought down" without interrupting the operation of other applications on the file server.

With IBM's OS/2 database manager, the operating system contains its own database management system.[27] The OS/2 database manager, along with the network communications software, is controlled by the OS/2 operating system loaded on the file server. In an OS/2 LAN Server environment, the OS/2 operating system combines the functions of the server operating system and the DBMS. Let us now briefly look at some of the LAN database server software currently available.

The following section presents a brief overview of four popular SQL database server products. A general description of each product will be given followed by a discussion of the operating systems, network operating systems, and languages supported by each product.

IBM OS/2 Extended Services Database Manager

Description   The OS/2 Extended Services Database Manager is an optional component of the OS/2 operating system.[28] When used in conjunction with the Extended Services Communications Manager, the Database Manager provides an ANSI Level I—compliant SQL database server.[29] In addition to ANSI Level I compliance, Database Manager also conforms to ANSI Addendum-1 and supports many additional SQL commands. OS/2 Database Manager under IBM's LAN Server operates in a slightly different configuration than a database server on a Novell network. Figure 5.13 illustrates an OS/2 Extended Services Database running under OS/2 and utilizing LAN Server.

The OS/2 operating system controls both the database manager and the communications manager. For comparison, a Novell NetWare 3.X configuration is shown in Figure 5.14. The Novell NetWare operating system allows a database server NLM or other NLMs to be loaded and run on top of the Novell operating system. The database NLM is not controlled by NetWare—it simply uses NetWare as a means to communicate with the network. In an OS/2 environment, the OS/2 operating system directly controls the database manager and the communications manager and co-

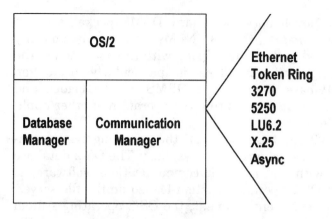

Figure 5.13   OS/2 Database Server

ordinates the activities of both. The OS/2 Database Manager provides SAA SQL compatibility with the high-level data definition and data manipulation language of IBM host database management systems such as DB2 and SQL/DS.[30] The *SQL Query Management Facility* (SQLQMF) provides a means to download and import data from host DB2 and SQL/DS databases to OS/2 database manager tables. The database server can be configured to allow OS/2, DOS, and Windows client workstations to access Database Manager databases.

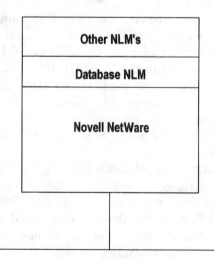

Figure 5.14   Netware Database Server

Operating Systems   The OS/2 Database Manager was designed specifically to run as a component of the OS/2 operating system, which limits its ability to run under any other operating systems.[31] An alternative to using other platforms and operating systems would be to use the multiple protocol support of the OS/2 Communications Manager to provide connectivity to non-OS/2 systems.

Network Support   OS/2 Database Manager is again specifically designed for an OS/2 IBM LAN Server environment but is also compatible with Microsoft's LAN Manager and Novell NetWare.[32] In a Novell environment, a separate database server running under OS/2 and the NetWare Requester for OS/2 is required. Figure 5.15 shows configurations for both LAN Server and Novell NetWare.

Language Support   Database Manager can support SQL statements embedded in C, FORTRAN, COBOL, and Pascal.[33] The Database Manager also supports Query Manager, a graphical SQL query interface that runs under Presentation Manager, the OS/2 GUI. Other third-party client products such as Info Alliance from Software Publishing Corporation can access OS/2 Database Manager databases.

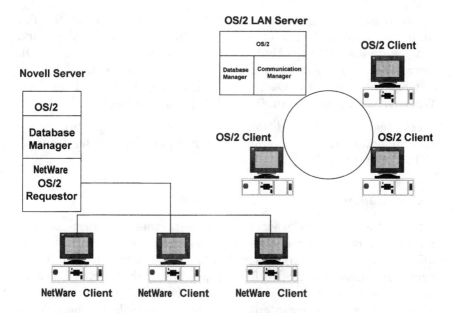

Figure 5.15   LAN Server and Novell Database Servers

Microsoft SQL Server

Description   Like OS/2 Database Manager, Microsoft SQL Server is designed to run under the OS/2 operating system. It is designed to act as a "back-end" server for client/server applications. It does not possess its own client applications development tools; however, many third-party software developers either provide SQL Server add-ons for their applications or allow direct SQL Server calls from within their software to SQL Server. Among the major software developers supporting SQL Server are Borland International, Data Ease, Information Builders, Lotus Development, and Symantec Corporation.[34] While not totally conforming to ANSI Level 1 or 2, SQL Server does provide a basic functionality similar to the ANSI standards and does support many of the additional common SQL commands.[35] SQL Server supports multiple client applications running under DOS, Windows, or OS/2. Data can be shared with the Sybase SQL family of products running under UNIX and VMS. By the use of a database gateway, mainframe DB2 data can be accessed by SQL Server.[36]

Operating Systems   Although designed to run in an OS/2 environment, SQL Server will also run under UNIX and VMS.[37] Sybase markets versions of SQL Server for DEC, VAX, Sun, HP, and other minicomputer platforms.

Network Support   SQL Server is compatible with Microsoft LAN Manager, IBM LAN Server, 3Com 3+Open, Novell NetWare, and other network software that offer compatibility with OS/2.[38] SQL Server runs on Novell networks in a configuration similar to that of OS/2 Database Manager, with SQL Server, OS/2, and the NetWare OS/2 Requester running on the Database Server.

Language Support   In addition to the software packages previously mentioned, SQL Server supports embedded SQL calls from C, COBOL, and BASIC.[39]

ORACLE Server

Description   Oracle Corporation markets their product as running on more hardware platforms and under more network operating systems than any other database software. Product literature lists more than 80 different platforms that ORACLE supports.[40] In addition to DBMS software, ORACLE offers a full line of development and maintenance tools. These tools can be used to develop both client applications and server databases. The PC

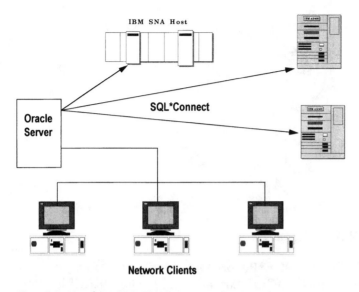

Figure 5.16   ORACLE Multiplatform Environment

LAN ORACLE DBMS can be linked to mainframe DB2 databases via the ORACLE SQL* Connect product, and to ORACLE databases on other platforms via Oracle's SQL*Net.[41] Figure 5.16 shows an example of a multiple platform configuration using ORACLE.

The ability to access data on multiple platforms supports the enterprise data-access concept introduced in Chapter 2 and discussed in detail in Chapter 7. ORACLE Server is ANSI and DB2 compliant and supports many of the common additional SQL commands.[42]

Operating Systems   ORACLE Server is available for a number of platforms. The most popular for client/server databases are OS/2, UNIX, VMS, MVS, and Macintosh.[43]

Network Support   As with operating systems, ORACLE supports a number of network operating systems. These include Novell NetWare, Microsoft LAN Manager, IBM LAN Server, Banyan Vines, and Apple Talk.[44] In an IBM LAN Server environment, ORACLE Server would be configured as shown in Figure 5.17. In a Novell environment, ORACLE Server would be configured as shown in Figure 5.18.

Language Support   ORACLE supports SQL calls from C, FORTRAN, and COBOL.[45] Several of the ORACLE development tools

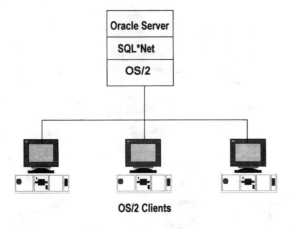

OS/2 Clients

Figure 5.17   ORACLE for OS/2

such as SQL*Forms, SQL*ReportWriter, and SQL*Plus, provide 4GL-type access to ORACLE Server data.[46] The ORACLE Database Add-In for Lotus 1-2-3 and ORACLE for 1-2-3 DataLens allow ORACLE Server data to be accessed from within the Lotus 1-2-3 spreadsheet application.

Gupta SQLBase

Description SQLBase from Gupta is designed primarily as a LAN-based SQL server.[47] In addition to SQLBase, Gupta markets two client application development products, SQL Windows and Quest. SQL Windows is designed for use by programmers and applications developers, while Quest is designed as a graphi-

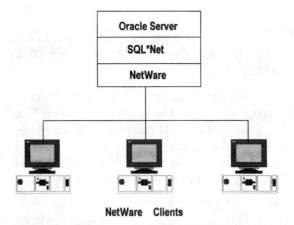

NetWare   Clients

Figure 5.18   ORACLE for NetWare

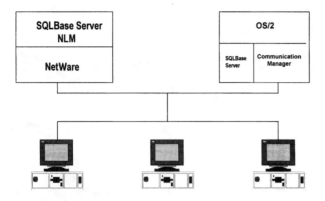

Figure 5.19   Gupta SQLBase for OS/2 and NetWare

cal data access tool for end users. Both of these tools can access DB2, ORACLE, and OS/2 Database Manager databases as well as SQLBase databases.[48] Another Gupta product, SQLNetwork, provides connectivity to other SQL databases on LANs or mini or mainframe platforms. It is similar in function to Oracle's SQL Connect described earlier in the chapter. While not totally conforming to ANSI Level 1, SQLBase does provide a basic functionality similar to the ANSI standards and does support many of the additional common SQL commands.[49]

Operating Systems   SQLBase runs under DOS and OS/2.[50]

Network Support   SQLBase supports Microsoft LAN Manager, IBM LAN Server, Novell NetWare, and other NET BIOS–compatible networks.[51] Figure 5.19 illustrates the configuration of SQLBase on NetWare and OS/2 networks.

Language Support   SQLBase supports SQL calls from C and COBOL. The SQL Windows product previously mentioned can be used to develop applications graphically under Windows or OS/2 Presentation Manager.[52]

Host Database Gateway   In addition to LAN database servers, database servers may also reside on a host mainframe or minicomputer. For a client to access this data, it must use a database gateway. All of the LAN server products described earlier in the chapter support database gateways to host databases. The hardware configuration for database gateways was discussed earlier in the chapter, but now let us consider the software configuration for database gateways.

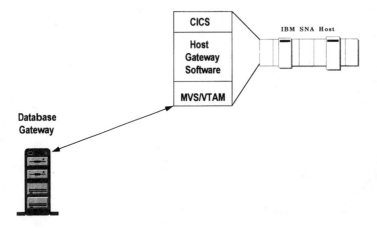

Figure 5.20   LAN Database Gateway

Database gateways generally have software on both the client network and the host server. The software on the client network receives an SQL request from the client applications or from a server on the network and passes the request to the host component. The host component receives the request and executes it against the host database. Figure 5.20 shows a typical software configuration for a database gateway in an IBM environment.

The database gateway software on the LAN communicates with the gateway software on the host via a standard communications protocol. On the host side, the communications software and operating system (MVS/VTAM) pass the request on to the host component of the gateway software. The software then accesses the database, in this case a DB2 database, through a CICS transaction. The completed request then follows the reverse path back to the requesting client. The database gateway may be configured to access a "generic" database such as IBM DB2 or a proprietary database on the host such as ORACLE.

Implementation Considerations

The combination of Windows–OS/2 client applications and SQL Server databases offers a true client/server architecture; however, there are several implementation factors to be considered.

- Location of Data

  The data for an SQL database server must come from one of two sources: a LAN database or a gateway to a host database.

In the case of a LAN database server, the data will in most cases be available to LAN client applications. The data cannot be shared with new or existing host applications. Data residing on a host database is accessible to LAN clients as well as other host applications. In some situations it may be desirable and even cost effective to use an existing host database rather than a LAN database.

- Development Costs

  While many SQL databases and client application development tools are available, initial development cost may be high. This is particularly true if existing staff must be retrained and there is little Windows, OS/2, or SQL expertise available within the organization. Additional technical expertise may be required to set up database servers on the network or install gateways to host databases. LAN administration will become more complex and may require additional staffing and/or training. Database gateways may require the acquisition and installation of additional host software.

- Hardware Requirements

  Additional hardware may be required to support a network database server. In most situations, a dedicated database server is required. For database gateways, additional communications hardware may be required. The additional load placed on the host by the database gateway may impact host performance. Client hardware may need to be upgraded to support GUI applications.

Situations Appropriate for This Approach

In light of the concerns just presented, the combination of Windows–OS/2 client applications and SQL database offers a flexible and cost-effective means to implement a client/server architecture. The following criteria can be used to select those situations suitable for this approach.

- Need for Updated Information

  An SQL database allows client applications real-time access to updated information. On-line systems such as order entry, inventory, and reservation systems are examples of this.

- Multiple Client Applications

  An SQL database provides a means to develop a generic database that can be accessed by a number of different client applications. Client applications can be developed independently. One application can input and update information while another accesses information. SQL databases also support the use of end-user 4GL tools for ad hoc reporting.

- Availability of Existing Host Databases

  An existing host database combined with a database gateway can maximize an organization's investment in existing hardware, software, and data while providing the benefits of client /server computing to LAN clients.

- Availability of Existing LAN Resources

  With the widespread use of local area networks, an existing LAN offers the basic infrastructure required to support an SQL database. While additional hardware and software may be needed, the initial investment in LAN cards, cabling, and software can be maximized.

Implementation Case Study #5

Inventory Management System

Although case studies of client/server applications using SQL databases abound in trade journals and vendors' literature, the following case study is particularly interesting in that it combines a LAN-based SQL database with a host application on a minicomputer.[53]

A manufacturing firm was exploring options to update their existing inventory management system. The growth of the firm combined with an increase in the number of items managed by the inventory system had exceeded the capabilities of their current inventory system on an IBM AS/400. The AS/400 system was shared by a number of divisions in the firm, each of which required access to information about customer orders, inventory, and the status of shipments. As parts were received, they were entered into the inventory system, which tracked all inventory until it was shipped in response to a customer order.

In designing a new system, it was decided that a client/server architecture was required to support the many applications required by the system as well as to provide a central point of con-

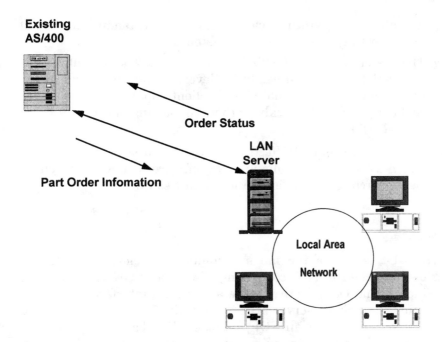

Figure 5.21   Client/Server Implementation Example

trol for system data. Additionally, the new system would need to interact with the AS/400 and its existing applications, and with an automated parts retrieval system.

The new inventory system use Microsoft's SQL Server in conjunction with a communications gateway to meet the requirements of the inventory system and interface with the existing AS/400. The SQL Server provided a reliable and flexible database that managed data for more than 50 client applications. Specialized client applications were developed to support the automated parts retrieval system. A communications server running the OS/2 Communications Manager provided a means to receive parts order information from the AS/400 and pass order status information back to the AS/400. Figure 5.21 illustrates the system configuration.

In this particular situation, this approach was effective because:

- The database was capable of supporting the needs of the LAN client applications in addition to the needs of the host applications. This allowed the existing host applications to be used in addition to the newly developed client applications. The firm was able to acquire new capabilities while extending the life of and investment in the existing systems.

- The system provided flexible client support. The specialized client applications could easily be developed and modified. As requirements change, individual client applications modules could be modified quickly without impacting the operation of the overall system.

- The system was cost effective. As compared to acquiring a second AS/400 and developing new software, a downsized client /server architecture offered a lower-cost solution.

Summary

The GUI is one of the major enabling technologies behind the growth of client/server computing. Two major GUI products are Windows and OS/2. Both provide a graphical interface and multitasking. In a client/server architecture, the GUI is normally used in combination with an SQL database. Databases may exist on either LANs, midrange, or mainframe systems. Client hardware normally consists of a powerful PC capable of supporting a GUI.

LAN database servers are often maximized to handle large volumes of network traffic. To access data on a midrange or mainframe host, a database gateway is used. The software configuration of a client/server architecture involves a client component and a host component. The client software consists of the GUI, the operating system, the network operating system, and the client application. The client application may be an SQL addition to an existing PC application, an application developed with a client/server design tool, or a high-level language application. Server software consists of an operating system, network operating system, and server database management system. Numerous LAN DBMS products are available that use SQL as a data access method. For host database servers, database gateway software would be required on the LAN database gateway and the host database.

When implementing this approach, the following factors should be considered: location of data, development cost, and hardware requirements. Placing data on LAN servers may make it unavailable to other systems such as mainframes. Development costs may be high if there is a lack of in-house expertise and retraining or outside support is required. Additional hardware may be required to support network database servers and client GUIs. This approach would be most appropriate in situations where there is a need for access to updated information, multiple client applications access the database, existing host databases are available, and there are existing LAN resources.

End Notes

1. Shawn Willett, Jayne Wilson, and Cate Corcoran, "Windows NT to Steal Little Thunder Away from Intel," *INFOWORLD*, November 30, 1992, p. 1.

2. Patrick Corrigan and Aisling Guy, *Building Local Area Networks with Novell's NetWare* (Redwood City: M&T Books, 1989), p. 97.

3. Jay Misra and Byron Belitsos, *Business Telecommunications— Concepts, Technologies and Cases in Telematics* (Homewood: Richard D. Irwin, Inc., 1987), p. 138.

4. Ibid.

5. Corrigan and Guy, op. cit., p. 103.

6. "The Database Gateway—MicroDecisionware's Mainframe Data Access Solution for Microsoft SQL Server Environments," in *Mainframe Connectivity Series, Version 1.1* (Boulder: Micro Decisionware, Inc., 1991).

7. *User's Guide for the Microsoft Windows Operating System, Version 3.1* (Redmond: Microsoft Corporation, 1990–1992), p. 55.

8. Ibid., p. 516.

9. Ibid., p. 518.

10. Charles Petsold, "Windows 3.1—Hello to TrueType, OLE, and Easier DDE; Farewell to Real Mode," *Microsoft Systems Journal*, September 1991.

11. Ibid.

12. John Soat and Rob Kelly, "Microsoft Sets Stage for Windows NT," *Information Week*, July 13, 1992, p. 12.

13. Ibid.

14. Gordon Letwin, *Inside OS/2* (Redmond: Microsoft Press, 1988), p. 9.

15. Ibid., p. 4.

16. Charles Bermant, "32-Bit Reality," *INFOWORLD*, August 17, 1992, p. S51.

17. Jennifer Sanders, "Novell's NetWare Still King of the Hill in LAN OS Market," *PC Week*, February 10, 1992, p. S30.

18. Susan Breidenbach and Laura Didio, "NetWare SQL Captures Market; Database Server Quietly Moves In to Win Developers' Hearts," *LAN TIMES*, April 1, 1992, p. 1.

19. *DataLens Driver for Lotus 1-2-3 Product Fact Sheet, Enterprise Data Access/SQL* (New York: Information Builders, Inc., 1991).

20. "Microsoft and MicroDecisionware Announce New Version of the Database Gateway," Microsoft–MicroDecisionware Press Release, March 18, 1991.

21. *Guide to Oracle Products*, Oracle Corporation, 1991, p. 2.

22. *Flashpoint Product Information*, Viewpoint Systems, Inc., 1991, p. 2.

23. Ibid.

24. *EASEL/2 Product Note*, Easel Corporation, Inc., 1990, pp. 2–3.

25. Ibid.

26. Corrigan and Guy, op. cit., p. 128.

27. *Extended Services—Breaking Through*, Product Information, IBM Corporation, 1991.

28. Ibid.

29. *A Comparison of OS/2 SQL Database Servers*, Consulting Study by Performance Computing, Inc., Microsoft Corporation, November 1990, p. 9.

30. *Extended Services—Breaking Through*, op. cit.

31. *A Comparison of OS/2 SQL Database Servers*, op. cit., p. 41.

32. *A Comparison of OS/2 SQL Database Servers*, op. cit., p. 45.

33. *A Comparison of OS/2 SQL Database Servers*, op. cit., p. 44.

34. "Microsoft SQL Server," in *Networking Series, Version 4.2*, Product Information, Microsoft Corporation, 1992.

35. *A Comparison of OS/2 SQL Database Servers*, op. cit., p. 9.

36. "Microsoft SQL Bridge," in *Networking Series*, Product Information, Microsoft Corporation, 1992.

37. *A Comparison of OS/2 SQL Database Servers*, op. cit., p. 41.

38. *A Comparison of OS/2 SQL Database Servers*, op. cit., p. 45.

39. *A Comparison of OS/2 SQL Database Servers*, op. cit., p. 44.

40. *Guide to Oracle Products*, op. cit., p. 2.

41. *Guide to Oracle Products*, op. cit., p. 8.

42. *Guide to Oracle Products*, op. cit., p. 6.

43. *A Comparison of OS/2 SQL Database Servers*, op. cit., p. 41.

44. *A Comparison of OS/2 SQL Database Servers*, op. cit., p. 46.

45. *A Comparison of OS/2 SQL Database Servers*, op. cit., p. 44.

46. *Guide to Oracle Products*, op. cit., p. 28.

47. *SQLBase Server Product Information*, Gupta Technologies, Inc., 1991, p. 31.

48. *SQLWindows 3.0 Technical Summary*, Gupta Technologies, Inc., 1991, p. 31.

49. *A Comparison of OS/2 SQL Database Servers*, op. cit., p. 10.

50. *SQLBase Server*, op. cit.

51. *SQLBase Server*, op. cit.

52. *SQLBase Server*, op. cit.

53. Adapted from "Microsoft Case Study: Automated Inventory Management," *Microsoft Networking Series* (Redmond: Microsoft Corporation, 1991).

6

Peer-to-Peer Communication

The client/server implementation approaches presented so far have all maintained a distinct division and hierarchical relationship between the client and the server. In IBM environments, it is also possible to implement a client/server architecture on a peer-to-peer basis. The client/server relationship still exists; however, the client and server communicate with each other as peers rather than as a subordinate client requesting data from a server. This type of computing architecture relies on IBM's *Advanced Peer-to-Peer Network* (APPN) and *Advanced Program-to-Program Communications* (APPC). APPN is the data communications network system that allows multiple platforms of differing types to communicate as peers.[1] APPC allows applications programs on different hosts to communicate via APPN at an application- to-application level.[2] This peer-to-peer configuration differs considerably from traditional mainframe host configurations as well as from the client/server configurations presented to this point.

Figure 6.1 shows a hierarchical mainframe configuration. In this type of configuration the mainframe or its communications controller manages the communications with all of the attached devices. This includes other computing platforms such as mini-computers and local area networks. Connectivity to the host is established via a 3270-type connection to a dumb terminal or a

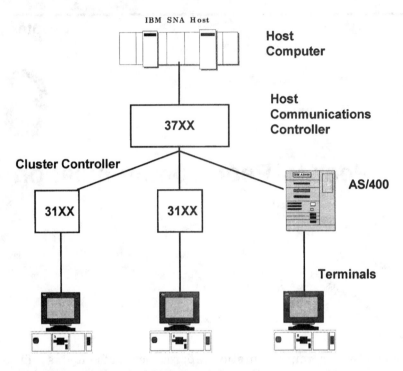

Figure 6.1   Hierarchical SNA Network

PC with 3270 emulation. LANs and minicomputers also utilize 3270 emulation normally through a gateway. With 3270 emulation, the PC or minicomputer was relegated to the same role as a dumb terminal. Acting solely as a display device, the processing power of the PC or minicomputer is not fully utilized. The use of IBM's *High-Level Language Applications Programming Interface* (HLLAPI) can take advantage of the PC's processing power, automate host access, and support GUIs for existing host applications. (See Chapter 4 for more information on HLLAPI and Applications Programming Interfaces.)

APPC makes it possible to exploit the relative advantages of each type of platform. Mainframe host computers excel at data storage and management, while PCs and workstations can accomplish processing tasks and support GUIs with relatively inexpensive MIPS. APPC is in some respects simpler than HLLAPI in that it is not dependent on 3270 screen formats. Because APPC works on an application-to-application level, less "overhead" is required on the host. Rather than generating a complete screen dis-

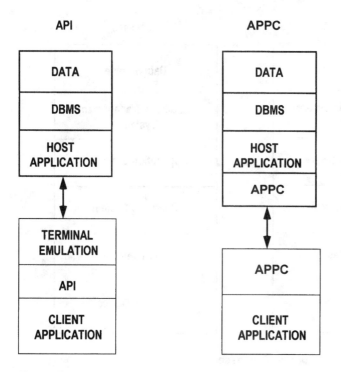

Figure 6.2   API versus APPC

play as with HLLAPI, APPC host applications access the required data and returns it as data to the client. Figure 6.2 illustrates the differences between HLLAPI and APPC.

With APPC, any platform can act as either a client or a server or both. Data may be shared at an application level between programs residing on different platforms. In terms of the computing processes model described in Chapter 2, APPC allows both client and server processes to run on all platforms. Figure 6.3 shows the conceptual computing process model for APPC.

Through APPC, the applications program on a client communicates its request for data to the applications program on a server. The server then uses its applications program to access data stored by its database management system. The data is then returned to the client application where, via its operating system, the user interface and display device present the information to the user. The six computing processes of the conceptual model reside on each APPN/APPC host. Each host may act as a client or a server or both, depending on the applications programs being

Processes   Processes

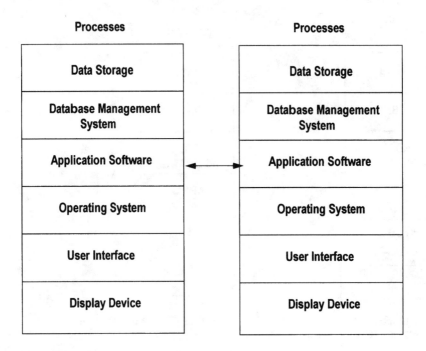

Figure 6.3   APPC Computing Processes

executed. The hosts may be the same type of platform such as an AS/400, or may be a mixture of hosts such as 3090s, AS/400, or OS/2 LAN servers. In either situation, all hosts communicate as peers and as peers can interact at an application level.

In this chapter we will first briefly review IBM's APPN. Next we will discuss APPC and see how applications can be programmed to communicate with each other via Advanced Peer-to-Peer Networking. Finally, an implementation example of APPC will be presented.

Advanced Peer-to-Peer Networking (APPN)

As mentioned earlier in the chapter, IBM mainframe environments configured under the *Systems Network Architecture* (SNA) establish a hierarchical relationship between processing platforms and their attached devices. Normally, the communications processor would control the establishment and management of sessions with various devices. The communications controller is in turn connected to the mainframe host via a high-speed communications channel. Figure 6.4 illustrates this configuration.

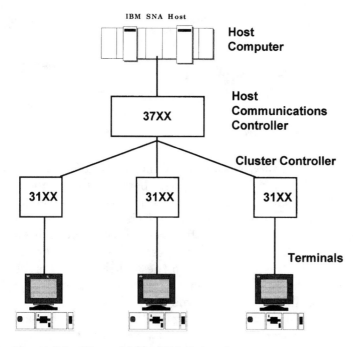

Figure 6.4   Hierarchichal SNA Network

This type of connection is referred to as an LU2- or 3270-type session. LU2 sessions support dumb terminal devices, which act solely as input/display devices with no processing power. Even PCs with terminal emulation capability function only as dumb terminals. In terms of the communications network, all network functions are controlled by the communications controller. It controls routing and establishment of sessions between the devices and one or more host systems. In an APPN network, any system can control the establishment and termination of sessions without a controlling host.[3] Figure 6.5 shows a simple APPN network.

In this example, either host may initiate and terminate a session with the other host. This is in contrast to the configuration in Figure 6.4 where the host(s) and the communications controller are at the top of the hierarchy and all other devices are subordinate to them. In an APPN configuration, each host acts as an equal peer and there is not a higher-level device controlling the interactions between devices. Figure 6.6 shows an example of a more complex APPN network.

In Figure 6.5, each of the platforms or nodes is configured as an end node. An end node allows the origination of sessions or

End Node   **End Node**

Figure 6.5   Simple APPN Network

may be the destination of a session established by another end node.[4] In Figure 6.6, a network node exists between the two end nodes. The network node, in addition to acting as an end node, provides intermediate routing of sessions from other nodes. In this example, System A can establish a session with System C. Additionally, System A may establish a session with System B that is routed through System C. Due to the additional resources required of a network node, it is desirable to configure nodes as end nodes when possible. The other type of APPN node shown in Figure 6.6 is the Low-Entry Networking Node. This type of node may use an APPN network by using a network node. In this example, Node D may establish a session with Node A or B through Node C. Low- Entry Networking Nodes can be used by:[5]

- IBM System /38
- IBM System /36 without APPN
- IBM AS/400 not utilizing APPN
- Personal Computers

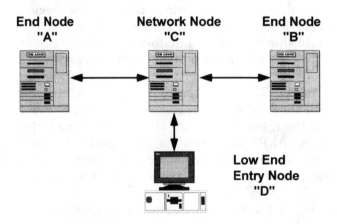

Figure 6.6   APPN Network

Initially, APPN was developed to link AS/400 and System 36 minicomputers together. Recently, IBM has expanded APPN to include the following operating systems:[6]

- AS/400

- OS/2

- AIX (RS6000)

- MVS

- VM

Additionally, APPN is supported on the IBM 6611 router and 3174 cluster controllers.[7] This provides APPN capability to much of the installed base of IBM SNA networks. IBM estimates that 70 percent of the wide area networks in existence today are SNA networks.[8]

APPN and SNA can coexist over the same network, allowing phased conversion to APPN. The expansion of APPN to include LAN servers and LAN workstations will allow the integration of LAN system and mainframe communications networks. In many organizations, parallel mainframe and LAN wide area networks exist because of the inability to route both types of communications protocols over the same network. APPN provides the capability through OS/2 for PCs and LANs to connect with APPN networks. This can require that OS/2 be run on individual workstations. This option is often not attractive due to the high resource requirements of OS/2 and its APPN Communication Manager.[9] Another option is to use a LAN gateway to provide APPN connectivity. This eliminates the high resource demands on individual workstations. (See Chapters 3 and 5 for more information on LAN gateways.)

Advanced Program-to-Program Communications (APPC)

While APPN establishes the peer-to-peer network, *Advanced Program-to-Program Communications* (APPC) allows application programs to communicate with each other over the APPN network. Using an LU6.2 session protocol and APPC verbs, high-level applications programs can communicate with each other on a peer-to-peer basis. The LU6.2-type session is the SNA logical unit that supports peer-to-peer communications between applications. (For more information on SNA and LU types, see Chapter 3.)

APPC applications communicate with each other by establishing a session with a target or server application on another APPN node. This session is established by opening a file and acquiring a program device. A program device is basically a means to direct I/O to a pseudonym that is in actuality an application on another APPN node. Existing high-level languages such as COBOL are not designed to communicate with other applications programs. By using a program device, I/O is directed to what the high-level language believes is an I/O device such as a file. The program device is married to another program device residing on another APPN node. The high-level application on the target APPN node treats the program device on its end just as if it were an I/O device as well. Figure 6.7 illustrates this concept.

In this example, the source node application writes a request, say to store a piece of data, to the program device. The application would in essence treat this as though it were a write request to a local I/O file. The output sent to the program device is then routed via APPC and the APPN network to the target node. There the I/O request is sent to a program device used by the target application. To the target application, the program device acts as if it were a local input file. While this is an extremely simplified explanation of the APPC process, it illustrates the basic concept. In actuality, a great deal more is involved than simply reading or writing to a device married to another application.

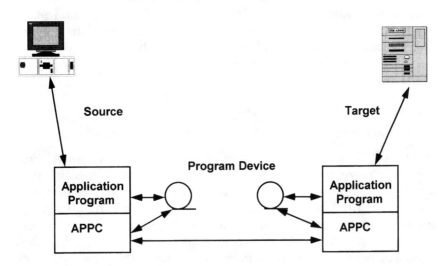

Figure 6.7   APPC Program Device

When a session is established, no single node is in control of all sessions. Control of the sessions is distributed among the nodes in the network. When two systems are connected via APPC, each system may initiate and terminate sessions. Sessions initiated by your local node are called *locally controlled sessions*, and sessions initiated by a remote node are called *remotely controlled sessions*.[10] When an application program requires a connection to a remote application, APPC attempts to establish a session with the remote node. When a session is established between the source and target nodes, the applications program must establish communications with the target application program. The communication between the two applications programs is referred to as a *conversation*.[11] Conversations may be one of two types: mapped or basic.[12] In a mapped conversation, the application program is responsible for only the user data portion of the data stream. In a basic conversation, the application program is responsible for portions of the communications data stream in addition to the user data.

Once a conversation between two applications programs is initiated, the link between them is called a *transaction* (not to be confused with mainframe CICS transaction). Conversations may be either synchronous or asynchronous.[13] A synchronous conversation allows applications to communicate in either direction. Some programming is required to ensure each node is in the proper mode to either send or receive. In an asynchronous conversation, the sending program completes its transmission of data and terminates its conversation before the receiving program receives all the data. This may be necessary due to the speed of the communications links between the two nodes. Figure 6.8 illustrates a synchronous conversation between two applications.

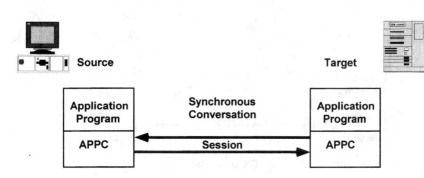

Figure 6.8   Synchronous APPC Conversation

In this example, the source application receives a request from an input device, say a terminal, to make an inquiry on a customer's account balance. The source application initiates a session with the target node and establishes a synchronous conversation. The source program is in a send state and the target program is in a receive state. The source program via its program device sends its request to the target application. The source application switches to a receive state and waits for the reply from the target application. The target application switches to a send state and sends the results of the account balance inquiry back to the target application, which in turn displays the data on a terminal. The conversation could at this point be terminated. Throughout the conversation between the two applications, the send and receive states of each could potentially switch several times.

An example of an asynchronous conversation is shown in Figure 6.9. In this situation, the source application initiates a session with the target application. When the conversation is established, the source application is in a send state and the target application is in a receive state. The target would initiate the transfer of data, say an update of parts received into inventory, and when transmission is complete, terminate the session. The target will continue to receive data from the local system data buffers. This configuration may be required in situations where there are low-speed communications links between the two nodes.

Within an APPC application, specialized commands called verbs are used to initiate and control the APPC session. These verbs are used in the high-level language application programs in

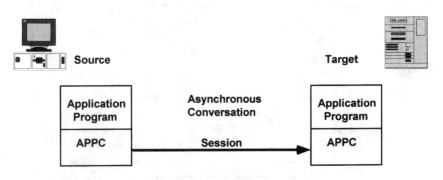

Figure 6.9 Asynchronous APPC Conversation

Verb	Function
OPEN/ACQUIRE	Establishes a session with a remote node.
EVOKE	Starts an application program on a remote host.
FORCE DATA	Sends data in buffer to remote application.
CONFIRM	Confirms acceptance of data.
READ	Reads data from remote host.
READ-FROM-INVITED PROGRAM DEVICES	Obtains data from any one of a number of invited programs.
INVITE	Requests input from remote programs.
RESPOND-TO-CONFIRM	Sends a positive acknowledgment to a confirmation.
REQUEST-TO-WRITE	Requests to stop receiving data and begin transmitting data to remote application.
ALLOW WRITE	Advises remote that send is complete, ready to receive.
TIMER	Time delay.
DETACH	Sending complete, end transaction.
RELEASE	End session.

Figure 6.10   APPC Verbs

conjunction with standard programming commands. Some examples of APPC verbs are shown in Figure 6.10.[14]

Let us now look at how these verbs can be used in an APPC application. In this example, an application accepts a customer account number from a terminal device and requests account balance information from a remote application program. If the customer account number is valid, the account balance is returned. If the account number is invalid, an error message is returned. Figure 6.11 illustrates the configuration of the processing platforms.

Two applications programs are required—one on the source computer system and one on the remote or target computer. Figure 6.12 shows excerpts of the COBOL code for the source program.[15] (*Note:* While a knowledge of COBOL is helpful in understanding this example, the function of the APPC verbs is basically the same regardless of the high-level application program language used.)

In the input-output section, the APPC file and a display file are described. The application will use the APPC file to communicate with the remote application. The display file is used to display input from the user. The file section describes the record format for each of the files. The APPC file contains the APPC record,

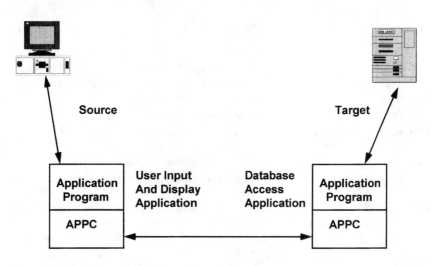

Figure 6.11   Account Balance Inquiry Program

```
000100 IDENTIFICATION DIVISION.
000200
000300 PROGRAM-ID. APPCEX1.
000400
000500************************************************************
000600* SAMPLE APPC SOURCE PROGRAM TO PERFORM A CUSTOMER ACCOUNT*
000700* INQUIRY ON A REMOTE APPC                                *
000800************************************************************
000900
001000 ENVIRONMENT DIVISION.
001100
001200 CONFIGURATION SECTION.
001300
001400 SOURCE-COMPUTER. IBM-S3X.
001500 OBJECT COMPUTER. IBM-S3X.
001600 SPECIAL-NAMES.   I-O-FEEDBACK IS IO-FEEDBACK
001700                  OPEN-FEEDBACK IS OPEN-FBA.
001800
001900 INPUT-OUTPUT SECTION.
002000
002100 FILE-CONTROL.
002200
002300  SELECT APPCFIL ASSIGN TO WORKSTATION-APPCFIL
002400      ORGANIZATION IS TRANSACTION
002500      CONTROL-AREA IS TR-CTL-AREA
002600      FILE STATUS IS STATUS-IND MAJ-MIN.
```

Figure 6.12   COBOL Code Excerpts for the Source Program

```
002700     SELECT DSPFIL ASSIGN TO WORKSTATION-DSPFIL
002800        ORGANIZATION IS TRANSACTION
002900        CONTROL-AREA IS DISPLAY-FEEDBACK
003000        FILE STATUS IS STATUS-DSP.
003100
003200 DATA DIVISION.
003300
003400 FILE SECTION.
003500**************************************************************
003600* FILE DESCRIPTION FOR PROGRAM DEVICE                        *
003700**************************************************************
003800 FD  APPCFIL
003900     LABEL RECORDS ARE STANDARD
004000 01  APPCREC.
004010     COPY DDS-ALL-FORMATS-I-O OF APPCFIL.
004020        05 APPCFIL-RECORD

       [MULTIPLE RECORD FORMATS FOR ICF OR PROGRAM DEVICE FILE.
       EACH TYPE OF REQUEST TO THE REMOTE APPLICATION IS A
       REDEFINITION OF THE APPCFIL-RECORD AND CONTAINS AN INPUT
       AND OUTPUT FORMAT]

004100**************************************************************
004200* FILE DESCRIPTION FOR DISPLAY FILE                          *
004300**************************************************************
004400 FD  DSPFIL
004500     LABEL RECORD ARE STANDARD
004600 01  DSPREC.
004700     05 DSPFIL-RECORD        PIC X(65).
004800     05 PROMPT-I   REDEFINES DSPFIL-RECORD.
004900        06 ACCTN             PIC X(10).
005000     05 PROMPT-O   REDEFINES DSPFIL-RECORD.
005100        06 ACCTB             PIC 99999V99.
005200        06 ERRORL            PIC X(40).
005300
005400 WORKING-STORAGE SECTION.
005500
005600     77 STATUS-IND           PIC XX.
005700     77 STATUS-DSP           PIC XX.
005800     77 MAJ-MIN-SAV          PIC X(4).
005900     77 ERR-SW               PIC X       VALUE "0".
006000     77 INDON                PIC 1       VALUE B"1".
006100     77 INDOFF               PIC 1       VALUE B"0".
006200     77 OPEN-COUNT           PIC 9(1)    VALUE 0.
006300
006400 01  TR-CTL-AREA.
006500     05 FILLER               PIC X(2).
006600     05 PGM-NAME             PIC X(10).
```

Figure 6.12   COBOL Code Excerpts for the Source Program *(continued)*

```
006700     05 FORMAT-NAME          PIC X(10).
006800
006900 01 DSPF-INDC-AREA.
007000     05 CMD3                 PIC 1        INDIC 99.
007100        88 CMD3-ON     VALUE B"1".
007200        88 CMD3-OFF VALUE B"0".
007300
007400 01 IO-FBA.
007500     05 FILLER               PIC X(37).
007600     05 DSP-FMT              PIC X(10).
007700     05 FILLER               PIC X(225).
007800     05 PGM-DEVICE-NAME      PIC X(10).
007900     05 FILLER               PIC X(84).
008000     05 DEV-DEP-AREA.
008100        10 FILLER            PIC X(34).
008200        10 MAJ-MIN-S.
008300           15 MAJ-S          PIC XX.
008400           15 MIN-S          PIC XX.
008500        10 FILLER            PIC X(8).
008600     05 FILLER               PIC XXX.
008700
008800 01 MAJ-MIN.
008900     88 FAIL-RETURNED VALUE "83C9".
009000     05 MAJ                  PIC XX.
009100        88 OK-RETURNED VALUE "00".
009200     05 MIN                  PIC XX.
009300
009400 01 DISPLAY-FEEDBACK.
009500     05 CMD-KEY              PIC XX.
009600     05 FILLER               PIC X(10).
009700     05 RCD-FMT              PIC X(10).
009800
009900 PROCEDURE DIVISION.
009950
010000 DECLARATIVES.
010050
010100 ERR-SECTION SECTION.
010200
010300***********************************************************
010400* INTERSYSTEMS COMMUNICATIONS FUNCTION FILE ERROR HANDLER *
010500***********************************************************
010600
010700     USE AFTER STANDARD ERROR PROCEDURE ON APPCFIL.
010800 APPCFIL-EXCEPTION.
010900     IF MAJ-MIN NOT = "0000" AND MAJ-MIN NOT = "83C9" THEN
011000        STOP RUN.
011100
011200 EXIT-DECLARATIVES.
```

Figure 6.12   COBOL Code Excerpts for the Source Program *(continued)*

```
011300
011400 END DECLARATIVES.
011500
011600 START-PROGRAM SECTION.
011700
011800 START-PROGRAM-PARAGRAPH.
011900
012000    OPEN I-O APPCFIL DISPFIL.
012100    MOVE ZEROS TO DSP-INDIC-AREA.
012150    IF ERR-SW = "1" THEN

       [FILE OPEN ERROR PROCESSING]

012200    ACQUIRE 'ICF00    " FOR APPCFIL.
012300    MOVE "ICF00    " TO PGM-NAME.
012400    PERFORM EVOKE-ROUTINE THRU EVOKE-EXIT.
012500    MOVE SPACES TO DSPREC.
012600    WRITE  DSPREC FORMAT IS "PROMPT"
012700    INDICATORS ARE DSPF-INDIC-AREA.
012800    READ DSPFIL INDICATORS ARE DSP-INDC-AREA.
012900    ACCEPT IO-FBA FROM IO-FEEDBACK FOR DSPFIL.
013000    PERFORM DISPLAY-PROC UNTIL CMD3-ON.
013100    PERFORM END-JOB.
013200
013300**********************************************************
013400* AFTER INPUT IS RECEIVED, SEND TO REMOTE APPLICATION     *
013500* AND PROCESS RESULTS. THEN PERFORM UNTIL F3 KEY PRESSED.*
013600**********************************************************
013700
013800 DISPLAY-PROC.
013900    PERFORM REMOTE-PROC.
014000    WRITE DSPREC FORMAT IS "PROMPT".
014100    READ DSPFIL INDICATORS ARE DSPF-INDC-AREA.
014200    ACCEPT IO-FBA FROM IO-FEEDBACK FOR DSPFIL.
014300
014400 REMOTE-PROC.
014500    MOVE ACCTN OF PROMPT-I TO ACCTN OF ACCTRQ-O.
014600    WRITE APPCREC FORMAT IS "ACCTRQ"
014700       TERMINAL IS PGM-NAME.
014800    IF OK-RETURNED THEN
014900       READ APPCFIL FORMAT IS "ACCTBAL"
015000          TERMINAL IS PGM-NAME
015100       MOVE ACCTBAL OF ACCTBAL-I TO ACCTB
015200       MOVE SPACES TO ERRORL
015300    ELSE
015400    IF FAIL-RETURNED THEN

       [PERFORM ERROR PROCESSING, NO ACCOUNT FOUND]
```

Figure 6.12   COBOL Code Excerpts for the Source Program *(continued)*

```
015500 EVOKE-ROUTINE.
015600     MOVE "APPCEX2" TO PGMID.
015700     MOVE "APPCLIB" TO LIB.
015800     WRITE APPCREC FORMAT IS "PGMSTR"
015900          TERMINAL IS PGM-NAME.
016000
016100 EVOKE-EXIT.
016200     EXIT.
016300
016400 ERROR-RECOVERY.

       [ERROR PROCESSING ROUTINE FOR ERRORS WHEN OPENING FILES]

016500 DETACH-ROUTINE
016600     WRITE APPCREC FORMAT IS "PGMEND"
016700
016800 DETACH-EXIT.
016900     EXIT.
017000
017100 END-JOB.
017200     PERFORM DETACH-ROUTINE THRU DETACH-EXIT.
017300     DROP "ICF00   " FROM APPCFIL.
017400     CLOSE DSPFIL APPCFIL.
017500     STOP RUN.
```

Figure 6.12   COBOL Code Excerpts for the Source Program *(continued)*

which is redefined in a number of formats. These different formats are used for the various APPC commands and read/write requests made by the application. The APPC record may be defined in one format to start a remote application, used again in a different format to request data, then used in a third format to end the remote application. The display record defines how information will be read from and displayed on the user display device. The working-storage section contains various flags and indicators used in the program. The IO-FBA provides information from the APPC file that is used in the program.

The procedure division starts by defining an error-handling routine for the APPC file. If any codes other than the two specified are returned during APPC file operations, the program is ended. The program now begins with the START-PROGRAM-PARAGRAPH, opening the APPC file and the display file. Should there be any errors in opening the files, an error-handling routine is called. A session is started with the remote system by the ACQUIRE command. On the AS/400, an *Intersystems Communication Function* (ICF) file is used to establish a session with a remote device. The ICF contains the routing and communications information required to establish a session. In this example, "ICF00" is the name of the ICF file.

The EVOKE-ROUTINE is called to evoke the target application on the host. The evoke request is built by moving the target program ID and library to an APPC file record and then writing that record to the APPC file. The program then prompts the user for an account number and continues until the F3 key is pressed. When a number is entered, REMOTE-PROC is called. This procedure moves the account number entered to an APPC file record format called ACCTRQ-0. This record is then written to the APPC file, which in turn passes the record to the remote application. If the remote application finds the customer account on file, OK-RETURNED is set to true and it returns the account balance. The APPC file record is read and the balance moved to the display file. If the customer account number is not located, an error procedure is executed. When the F3 key is pressed, the DISPLAY-PROC procedure ends and END-JOB is called. This routine in turn calls DETACH-ROUTINE, which writes an APPC record to the remote application, causing it to end. Next, END-JOB terminates the session by dropping the ICF and then closes the display and APPC files.

The target program that would reside on the remote node is shown in Figure 6.13. The file configuration is the same as that found in the source program in Figure 6.12. The only difference is the replacement of the display file by the database file. The database contains the customer account data. The database records each contain an account number and an account balance. As with the source program, the remote program uses flags and indicators in the working-storage section for program control and information feedback from the ICF.

The procedure division begins by declaring an error-handling routine for the ICF. If any return codes other than "0000" are received from the APPC file, the program terminates. Next the APPC and database files are opened. If any errors occur when opening the files, an error routine is executed. The APPC file is now acquired and the session between the two nodes is established. In the example, ICF00 is the name of the ICF file used. A read against the APPC file to look for an incoming request is made. When a request is received, the READ- REQUEST procedure is executed. This procedure reads the account number from the incoming ACCTRQ-I record and searches the database for a

```
000100 IDENTIFICATION DIVISION.
000200
000300 PROGRAM-ID. APPCEX2.
000400
000500***********************************************************
000600* SAMPLE APPC TARGET PROGRAM TO PERFORM A CUSTOMER        *
000700* ACCOUNT INQUIRY BASED ON INPUT FROM A REMOTE APPLICATION*
000800***********************************************************
000900
001000 ENVIRONMENT DIVISION.
001100
001200 CONFIGURATION SECTION.
001300
001400 SOURCE-COMPUTER. IBM-S3X.
001500 OBJECT COMPUTER. IBM-S3X.
001600 SPECIAL-NAMES.    I-O-FEEDBACK IS IO-FEEDBACK
001700                   OPEN-FEEDBACK IS OPEN-FBA.
001800
001900 INPUT-OUTPUT SECTION.
002000
002100 FILE-CONTROL.
002200
002300    SELECT APPCFIL ASSIGN TO WORKSTATION-APPCFIL
002400       ORGANIZATION IS TRANSACTION
002500       CONTROL-AREA IS TR-CTL-AREA
002600       FILE STATUS IS STATUS-IND MAJ-MIN.
002700    SELECT DBFIL ASSIGN TO DATABASE-DBFIL
002800       ORGANIZATION IS INDEXED
002900       ACCESS IS RANDOM
003000       RECORD KEY IS ACCTN.
003100
003200 DATA DIVISION.
003300
003400 FILE SECTION.
003500***********************************************************
003600* FILE DESCRIPTION FOR PROGRAM DEVICE                     *
003700***********************************************************
003800 FD  APPCFIL
003900     LABEL RECORDS ARE STANDARD
004000 01  APPCREC.
004100     COPY DDS-ALL-FORMATS-I-O OF APPCFIL.
004200        05 APPCFIL-RECORD
```

[MULTIPLE RECORD FORMATS FOR ICF OR PROGRAM DEVICE FILE.
EACH TYPE OF REQUEST TO THE REMOTE APPLICATION IS A
REDEFINITION OF THE APPCFIL-RECORD AND CONTAINS AN INPUT
AND OUTPUT FORMAT]

Figure 6.13   Remote Node Target Program

```
004300*********************************************************
004400* FILE DESCRIPTION FOR DATABASE FILE                    *
004500*********************************************************
004600 FD   DBFIL
004700      LABEL RECORD ARE STANDARD
004800 01 DBREC.
004900      05 ACCTNUM                  PIC X(10).
005000      05 ACCTBAL                  PIC 99999V99.
005100
005200
005300 WORKING-STORAGE SECTION.
005400
005500    77 STATUS-IND       PIC XX.
005600    77 ERR-SW           PIC X     VALUE "0".
005700    77 OPEN-COUNT       PIC 9(1)  VALUE 0.
005800    77 ERROR-FND        PIC X VALUE "0".
005900
006000 01 TR-CTL-AREA.
006100      05 FILLER         PIC X(2).
006200      05 PGM-NAME       PIC X(10).
006300      05 FORMAT-NAME    PIC X(10).
006400
006500 01 APPCFIL-INDC-AREA.
006600      05 DETACH-IND     PIC 1     INDIC 82.
006700         88 DETACH-YES  VALUE B"1".
006800         88 DETACH-NO   VALUE B"0".
006900
007000 01 IO-FBA.
007100      05 FILLER         PIC X(37).
007200      05 DSP-FMT        PIC X(10).
007300      05 FILLER         PIC X(225).
007400      05 PGM-DEVICE-NAME PIC X(10).
007500      05 FILLER         PIC X(84).
007600      05 DEV-DEP-AREA.
007700         10 FILLER      PIC X(34).
007800         10 MAJ-MIN-S.
007900            15 MAJ-S    PIC XX.
008000            15 MIN-S    PIC XX.
008100         10 FILLER      PIC X(8).
008200      05 FILLER         PIC XXX.
008300
008400 01 MAJ-MIN.
008500      05 MAJ            PIC XX.
008600      05 MIN            PIC XX.
008700
008800 01 NOT-FND-MSG         PIC X(40)
008900          VALUE "ACCOUNT NUMBER NOT ON FILE".
```

Figure 6.13   Remote Node Target Program *(continued)*

```
009000
009100
009200
009300 PROCEDURE DIVISION.
009400
009500 DECLARATIVES.
009600
009700 ERR-SECTION SECTION.
009800
009900*****************************************************************
010000* INTERSYSTEMS COMMUNICATIONS FUNCTION FILE ERROR HANDLER *
010100*****************************************************************
010200
010300     USE AFTER STANDARD ERROR PROCEDURE ON APPCFIL.
010400 APPCFIL-EXCEPTION.
010500    IF MAJ-MIN NOT = "0000"
010600       STOP RUN.
010700
010800 EXIT-DECLARATIVES.
010900
011000 END DECLARATIVES.
011100
011200 START-PROGRAM SECTION.
011300
011400 START-PROGRAM-PARAGRAPH.
011500
011600    OPEN I-O APPCFIL DBFIL.
011700    MOVE ZEROS TO APPCFIL-INDIC-AREA.
011800    IF ERR-SW = "1" THEN

       [FILE OPEN ERROR PROCESSING]

011900    ACQUIRE 'ICF01    " FOR APPCFIL.
012000    MOVE "ICF00    " TO PGM-NAME.
012100    READ APPCFIL FORMAT IS "ACCTRQ"
012200         INDICATORS ARE APPCFIL-INDC-AREA.
012300    PERFORM READ-REQUEST THRU READ-EXIT
012400         UNTIL DETACH-YES.
012500    PERFORM END-JOB.
012600
012700*****************************************************************
012800* PROCESS INPUT FROM REMOTE SYSTEM.  SEARCH DATABASE FOR  *
012900* MATCHING ACCOUNT NUMBER AND IF FOUND RETURN ACCOUNT    *
013000* BALANCE. RETURN ERROR MSG IF NOT FOUND.               *
013100*****************************************************************
013200
013300 READ-REQUEST.
```

Figure 6.13   Remote Node Target Program *(continued)*

```
013400     MOVE "0" TO ERROR-FND.
013500     MOVE ACCTN OF ACCTRQ-I TO ACCTNUM.
013600     READ DBFIL FORMAT IS "DBRCD"
013700         INVALID KEY PERFORM RECORD-NOT-FOUND
013800         THRU RECORD-NF-EXIT.
013900     IF ERROR-FND = "0" THEN
014000         PERFORM SEND-RECORD THRU SEND-REC-EXIT.
014100     READ APPCFIL FORMAT IS "ACCTRQ"
014200         INDICATORS ARE APPCFIL-INDC-AREA.
014300
014400 READ-EXIT.
014500     EXIT.
014600
014700
014800*************************************************************
014900* RECORD FOUND, RETURN DATA TO REMOTE PROGRAM             *
015000*************************************************************
015100 SEND-RECORD.
015200     WRITE APPCREC FORMAT IS "ACCTFND"
015300         TERMINAL IS PGM-NAME.
015400     MOVE ACCTBAL TO ACCTBLNC OF ACCTB-O
015500     WRITE APPCREC FORMAT IS "ACCTB"
015600         TERMINAL IS PGM-NAME.
015700
015800 SEND-REC-EXIT.
015900     EXIT.
016000
016100*************************************************************
016200* RECORD NOT FOUND, RETURN MESSAGE TO REMOTE PROGRAM      *
016300*************************************************************
016400
016500 RECORD-NOT-FOUND.
016600     MOVE NOT-FND-MSG TO ERRORM OF ERRORST-O.
016700     PERFORM ERROR-SEND THRU ERROR-EXIT.
016800
016900
017000*************************************************************
017100* SEND MESSAGE TO REMOTE PROGRAM                          *
017200*************************************************************
017300
017400 ERROR-SEND.
017500     MOVE "1" TO ERROR-FND.
017600     WRITE APPCREC FORMAT IS "PGMERR"
017700         TERMINAL IS PGM-NAME.
017800     WRITE APPCREC FORMAT IS "ERRORST"
017900         TERMINAL IS PGM-NAME.
018000
```

Figure 6.13   Remote Node Target Program *(continued)*

```
018100 ERROR-EXIT.
018200      EXIT.
018300
018400**********************************************************
018500* ERROR RECOVERY                                          *
018600**********************************************************
018700
018800 ERROR-RECOVERY
018900      CLOSE APPCFIL DBFIL.
019000      MOVE "0" TO ERR-SW.
019100
019200 ERROR-RECOVERY-EXIT.
019300      EXIT.
019400
019500 END-JOB.
019600      DROP "ICF01   " FROM APPCFIL.
019700      CLOSE DBFIL APPCFIL.
019800      STOP RUN.
```

Figure 6.13   Remote Node Target Program (continued)

match. If no match is found, the RECORD-NOT-FOUND, ER-
ROR-SEND, and ERROR-EXIT procedures are performed. These
procedures first place an error code in the APPC record, send it to
the remote program, and then send a second record to the remote
program with an explanation of the error.

In this example the message "Account number not on file" is
returned to the remote program. If the search is successful, the
SEND- RECORD procedure is executed. As with the RECORD-
NOT-FOUND procedure, first a confirmation that a record was
found was sent, followed by a record containing the account balance. The READ-REQUEST procedure is performed until a detach request is received from the remote program. When a detach
request is received, END-JOB is executed, which drops the session and then closes all open files.

While this is a relatively simple example, it helps to illustrate
the flow of data between the two applications programs. Figure
6.14 graphically illustrates the data flow between the example
programs.

Implementation Considerations

Using APPC and LU6.2 offers many benefits; however, several
implementation concerns are to be considered.

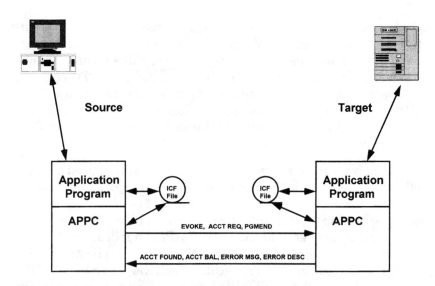

Figure 6.14   Account Balance Program Data Flow

- Cost

    A major consideration of an LU6.2/APPC implementation is cost. It may be necessary to acquire additional communications hardware and software as well as operating system software to support LU6.2. A potentially greater cost is that of rewriting existing programs. Some firms have opted to use HLLAPI (see Chapter 4) rather than rewrite applications for LU6.2/APPC.[16]

- Resource Usage

    LU6.2 and APPC consume a large amount of the resources of the processing platforms they run on. Early APPC software for DOS PCs utilized so much memory there was little memory left for applications. While the OS/2 Communications Manager supports LU6.2 and APPC, it also requires a powerful processor and large amounts of memory. In many cases, an OS/2 Communications Manager gateway on a LAN is used to avoid the expense of running OS/2 Communications Manager on individual PCs. On other platforms such as AS/400s, APPC/APPN also consume system resources.

- Programming Skills

    A major challenge in developing LU6.2/APPC applications is training or retraining programming staff. Estimates are that three months of training would be required for a typical mainframe programmer.[17] This could add significantly to overall implementation costs. In addition to APPC skills on say a mainframe system, a programmer would also need PC APPC training to develop cooperative processing applications. Since APPC applications could conceivably span multiple platforms, it would be necessary to have staff with APPC expertise on all platforms.

- Complexity

APPC applications are more complex than single platform applications. The task of designing and debugging applications becomes more complex as that application is effectively spread out over multiple platforms. Errors can manifest themselves in numerous components of the overall APPC application. The debugging process must not only include the applications programs but also the communication software and the APPN network. CASE Tools for APPC applications development are just beginning to appear on the market. As more development tools become available, some of the design, development, and maintenance tasks may be simplified.

- Compatibility

Although LU6.2 is supported by IBM, there is not yet a large third-party market for LU 6.2 products. Some vendors have developed LU6.2 interfaces, but many non-IBM and even some IBM platforms do not support LU6.2. Multivendor networks may have difficulty implementing APPC until more cross-platform capability is available.

Situations Appropriate for This Approach

In light of the concerns just presented, LU6.2 and APPC do offer a number of advantages when client/server applications are being developed. The relationship between client and server platforms is dynamic with the client and server roles changing as required by the applications program. At any one instant, a particular platform may be a client, a server, or both. The following criteria can be used as a guide to select those situations most appropriate for an LU6.2/APPC approach.

- Availability of Existing Host Database

Existing host databases on multiple platforms combined with APPC can maximize an organization's current investment in hardware, software, and data while providing the benefits of client/server computing. In this type of situation, an APPC implementation would be implemented "on top of" existing applications and databases.

- Need to Access or Integrate Data on Multiple Platforms

  APPC provides this capability through APPN. Via other methods, it may be difficult to access and combine data from multiple platforms simultaneously. Since APPC works at an application level, the complexity of dealing with multiple systems is reduced.

- Need for a Common Interface

  Given data on multiple platforms, it is often difficult for users to master multiple operating systems and log-on procedures. Using APPC, a single interface can be developed for all data access. Users simply learn one interface, and access to other hosts is managed by the APPC application.

- Existing Communications Network LU6.2/APPC Compatible

  An existing communications network that is LU6.2- compatible helps to reduce the cost of an LU6.2/APPC implementation and, again, maximize the firm's current investment in the communications network while increasing its utility.

Implementation Case Study #6

Medical Records System

In this example, APPC is used to link applications running on DOS workstations to a database application on an IBM mainframe.[18] The DOS workstation application is part of a medical record transcription system that requires access to patient data stored on a host DB2 database. The DOS applications communicate with an OS/2 server, which in turn communicates with a CICS application on an IBM host. The DOS application uses an OS/2 interprocess communication service called Named Pipes to establish a program-to-program link to the OS/2 server. Named Pipes are similar to the ICF file described earlier, and allow applications to communicate via file I/O. After receiving a request for data from an application, the OS/2 communications server establishes an APPC link with a host CICS program. The host program then executes and returns the results of the database search to the OS/2 communication server. The server returns the

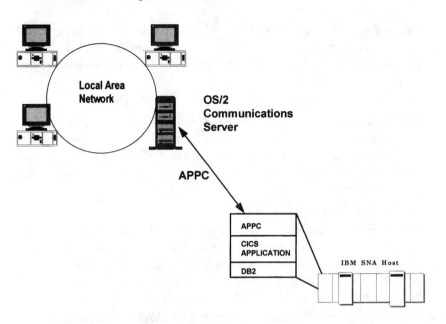

Figure 6.15   APPC Implementation

data to the DOS application. Figure 6.15 illustrates the components of the complete application.

In this example, an APPC approach was effective because:

• The existing host database contained the data required by the workstation application, and it could easily be retrieved. The host database did not require any modification and required only a simple CICS program to give it APPC capability.

• A need existed to integrate data. The workstation application was required to access data from multiple host files and integrate that data with other PC applications.

• The existing communications netware supported APPC/LU6.2. The existing local area network consisted of DOS workstations and an OS/2 LAN server. The server was used as a communications server to eliminate the need to run OS/2 or the DOS APPC software on the individual workstations.

Summary

In IBM environments, client/server computing can be implemented using *Advanced Peer-to-Peer Networking* (APPN) and *Advanced Program-to-Program Communications* (APPC). APPN allows multiple platforms of differing types to communicate with each other as peers. APPC allows applications programs on differing hosts to communicate via APPN at an application-to-application level. This peer-to-peer configuration differs from traditional hierarchical mainframe networks. Any platform may act as a client, a server, or both. In an APPN network, any node or host may initiate or terminate sessions with other nodes. End nodes may be the originators of a session or the destination of a session initiated by another node. Network nodes, in addition to acting as end nodes, provide intermediate routing of sessions from other nodes.

APPC uses the LU6.2 session protocol and specialized APPC verbs to establish application-to-application communications. Applications interface with each other via a program device that redirects I/O between applications. When an application requires connection to a remote node, APPC attempts to establish a session. When the session is established, the two programs communicate with each other in what is referred to as a conversation. Specialized APPC verbs are used to control the APPC session and to exchange data between applications.

Major considerations for using this approach are cost, resource usage, programming skills, and complexity and compatibility. Additional hardware may be required as well as extensive rewrites of existing software.

Situations appropriate for this approach would include those where there is an availability of host data, there is a need to access or integrate data on multiple platforms, there is a need for a common interface, and a communications network exists that can support APPN/APPC.

End Notes

1. *AS/400 Communications: Advanced Program-to-Program Communications and Advanced Peer-to-Peer Networking User's Guide,* IBM, June 1988, p. 2-1.

2. Ibid., p. 6-1.

3. Ibid., p. 2-1.

4. Ibid., p. 2-4.

5. Ibid., p. 2-3.

6. Elinor Pederson, "APPN Makes SAA, but SNA Doesn't," *MIDRANGE Systems*, May 12, 1992, p. 44.

7. Ibid.

8. Ibid.

9. Helen Ridgway, "SNA and LANS Touch Hands." *IBM System User*, June 1991, p. 51.

10. *AS/400 Communications: Advanced Program-to-Program Communications and Advanced Peer-to-Peer Networking User's Guide*, op. cit., p. 6-5.

11. *AS/400 Communications: Advanced Program-to-Program Communications and Advanced Peer-to-Peer Networking User's Guide*, op. cit., p. 6-5.

12. *AS/400 Communications: Advanced Program-to-Program Communications and Advanced Peer-to-Peer Networking User's Guide*, op. cit., p. 6-5.

13. *AS/400 Communications: Advanced Program-to-Program Communications and Advanced Peer-to-Peer Networking User's Guide*, op. cit., p. 6-5.

14. For a complete listing of APPC verbs, see IBM's *AS/400 Communications: Advanced Program-to-Program Communications and Advanced Peer-to-Peer Networking User's Guide*, June 1988.

15. Adapted from *AS/400 Communications: Advanced Program-to-Program Communications and Advanced Peer-to-Peer Networking User's Guide*, op. cit., pp. 6–46.

16. Leila Davis, "Peering at the LU6.2 Choice," *Datamation*, February 1, 1990, p. 50.

17. Ibid., p. 52.

18. Adapted from a case study presented by Bobby Blass, "Implementing a LAN-to-Host Server: Building a Working Model of a Communications Server Using IBM's Named Pipes and APPC," *DBMS*, March 1992.

7

Enterprise Computing

As was noted in Chapter 1, most organizations have multiple and often incompatible computing platforms. At some point the need to access data from multiple platforms prompts the organization to look at its data not in terms of individual systems but rather in terms of the total enterprise. The data generated and maintained by one division of the organization may be vital to another division or to high-level decision makers. Often the processing platforms in an organization have been acquired to fill very specific needs, and functional concerns may have overshadowed the desire for compatibility with other platforms in the organization. Even within a specific vendor's product line many systems are incompatible.

The need to integrate data and applications within an organization has led to the concept of enterprise computing. Enterprise computing has been defined as "seamless integration of applications, data, user interfaces, and other computing resources among heterogeneous systems of all sizes."[1]

This definition supports the user-centered environment described in Chapter 1. In this type of environment, the user interacts with all applications and data in the enterprise through a

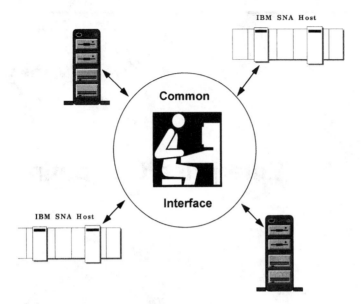

Figure 7.1   User-Centered Environment

single interface. Access to remote applications and data is transparent to the end user. The user is not burdened with mastering each type of operating system used within the organization. Data may be accessed with equal ease from a local LAN file server or a host database located in another city. The desktop cluttered with multiple terminals is replaced by a single workstation that is the user's single point of access to all enterprise data. Figure 7.1 illustrates a user-centered environment such as that supported by enterprise computing.

Let us take a moment to see how enterprise computing relates to client/server computing. Client/server computing in general, and more specifically the implementation approaches presented in this book, represent an applications architecture. In each of the approaches, it was assumed that the client and server platforms were compatible and by some means connected. The major difference in each approach has been the division of the computing processes. Enterprise computing provides the infrastructure to implement client/server computing across an enterprise. With enterprise computing, it would be possible to develop client/server applications that not only ran between compatible platforms, but would be able to access data on any data source in the enterprise.

Server

Client

Figure 7.2   Basic Client/Server Configuration

This greatly expands the scope and potential of client/server computing.

Figure 7.2 illustrates the basic concept of client/server computing. A single client is connected to a compatible server. Given an enterprise computing scenario, the potential servers for the single client shown in Figure 7.2 expand greatly. Figure 7.3 shows the same application under enterprise computing.

The client now has access to data and applications on multiple platforms. Enterprise computing provides interconnectivity and interoperability between platforms. While enterprise computing is not required to implement client/server computing, it does greatly expand the potential of client/server computing.

The Evolution of the Multiplatform Organization

The mix of processing platforms found in most enterprises is a result of the organization's changing needs over time. In the early days of computing, there was usually only one platform, the corporate mainframe. Having a single, centrally controlled platform eliminated in most cases the problem of dealing with distributed data and applications. In addition to limited choices of processing

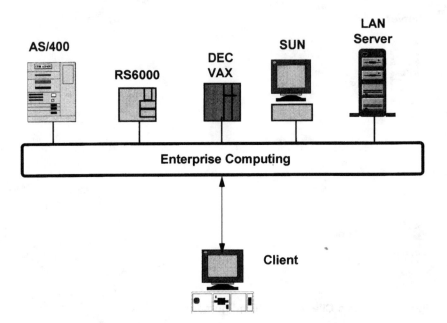

Figure 7.3   Client/Server under Enterprise Computing

platforms, there were also limited options for applications programs, display devices, and user interfaces. Programs were written in high-level languages, dumb terminals were used to access the programs and the users learned whatever interface the system used.

As computing hardware evolved, more choices became available. Rather than adding applications to existing mainframes, it was possible to purchase midrange and minicomputer systems for applications that required less than mainframe processing power. These midrange and minicomputer systems ushered in the concept of departmental computing. Applications and databases resided at the departmental level rather than the corporate level. To overcome application development backlogs and to be able to react more rapidly to changes in the business environment, more and more applications were developed on departmental platforms. So-called "islands of automation" began to spring up in corporations.

The introduction of the personal computer in the early 1980s and the local area network in the mid-1980s served to further expand the type and number of corporate data repositories. The PC and LAN offered some capabilities for accessing multiple data sources. Using terminal emulation such as that described in Chapter 3, it was possible to access mainframe data in addition to PC or LAN data. The terminal emulation software allowed the PC to act as a dumb terminal attached to the mainframe. Utilizing several different terminal emulations, it would be possible to access different hosts such as an IBM 3090, AS/400, or even a DEC VAX.

While terminal emulation provides connectivity, it does little to integrate data. Additionally, end users must master the intricacies of each emulation and host operating system. In effect, multiple terminal emulation simply reduced the number of devices on the desktop. In Chapter 1, the concept of a platform-centered environment was introduced. The growth of the multiplatform organization created this type of environment, in which the user conformed to each individual system accessed. Figure 7.4 illustrates a platform-centered environment.

In some cases, through the use of APIs such as those described in Chapter 4, it was possible to achieve some degree of application and data integration. This had to be accomplished at the workstation level though, and was limited to the ability of the existing host applications to access and present data. Through the use of gateways, multiplatform connectivity could be ex-

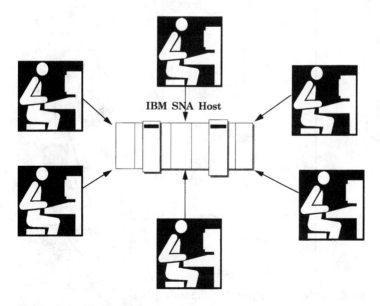

IBM SNA Host

Figure 7.4   Platform-Centered Environment

panded to "dumb" terminals on various platforms. AS/400 terminals could be emulated mainframe 3270 terminals and even non-IBM systems, such as Digital Equipment Corporation's VAX computers, could provide 3270 terminal emulation via gateways to IBM mainframe systems. Figure 7.5 illustrates the evolution of corporate computing systems.

While most hardware connectivity problems can be overcome, there still remains the question of integrating data, applications, and user interfaces across platforms. In some aspects, IBM attempted to solve these problems with their *Systems Applications Architecture*, (SAA). SAA is basically a set of standards for applications development that include user and system interfaces. The purpose of these standards is to integrate applications across platforms, specifically IBM platforms. Within SAA there are three major categories of interfaces. Those are the *Common User Access* (CUA), the *Common Programming Interface* (CPI), and the *Common Communications Support* (CCS).[2] The CUA provides a standardized user interface across platforms by specifying how data is presented and how users interact with the system. Operations such as opening and closing files, selecting menu options,

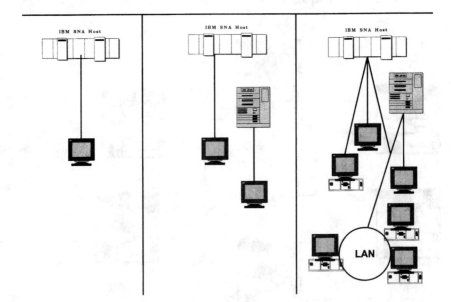

Figure 7.5   The Evolution of Corporate Computing

and other tasks are all accomplished in the same manner from system to system. GUIs developed under CUA provide a standardized graphical interface from platform to platform. This greatly reduces user training, as a person trained to use one CUA-compliant GUI can, with minimal additional training, use a CUA-compliant GUI on another platform. The CPI provides a common interface for programming languages and database management systems. The CCS provides a common communications interface between SAA systems.

While SAA can provide applications integration in an IBM environment, an organization may find itself with a mixture of platforms. The task of implementing enterprise computing becomes more difficult in a multivendor environment. Let us briefly look at two models of enterprise computing.

Enterprise Computing Models

In a recent study, two major conceptual models of enterprise computing—the scalable utopian model and the integration model—are described.[3] In the scalable utopian model, access to enterprise systems is accomplished by running identical software on all platforms in the enterprise. The term "utopian" is used because, while this would be the ideal solution, it is presently and in the near future at least, unlikely to become reality. The more realistic model, and the one on which several enterprise products are based, is the integration model. In this model, the differences between platforms and operating systems are recognized, and an intervening layer of integration hardware and software provides connectivity and interoperability between platforms. Figure 7.6 illustrates the integration model.

To accomplish this integration, it may be necessary to use various methods to achieve the physical connectivity between platforms and the integration of data between platforms. Hardware devices such as bridges and gateways may be necessary to accomplish the physical connectivity between disparate platforms. Since there is no "common ground" for the multiple platforms, it will be necessary to utilize some type of common software interface on all platforms. This interface would allow "generic" requests from other platforms in the enterprise network to be received and processed. The common software interface provides a means to "glue" together the many types of systems that may exist within an or-

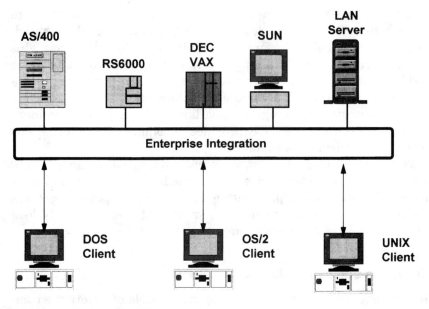

Figure 7.6   Integration Model

ganization. Examples of products that accomplish this are presented later in the chapter.

If the goal is to provide end users with access to all data in the organization, there are options. One option mentioned briefly early in the chapter is to provide the user with access to all platforms in the organization. While this may fulfill the basic requirement, it may prove to be difficult to implement. Given that the technical complexities of providing connectivity to all platforms can be overcome, the task of integrating data, applications, and interfaces still remains. In some limited situations, it may be possible to utilize applications programming interfaces at the workstation level; however, as the number of platforms and applications increase, this approach becomes impractical.

Another option is to move all enterprise data to a common system for all users to access. In some situations, this may be a viable solution. If data is updated infrequently and there is no need for real-time data, this approach could be used. Considerations would include the volume of data to be transmitted, the frequency of updates, and transmission to a central location. Users at all locations must have access to the central system as well as to their own local system. As with the previous option, as the amount of data and number of platforms increases, this option may also prove impractical.

Open Systems

An alternative to proprietary enterprise computing solutions or third-party integration systems is open systems. Open systems have been defined as "hardware and software implementations that conform to the body of standards that permit free and easy access to multiple vendor solutions."[4] An open system is designed to conform to standards that allow it to easily interface with products from other vendors. This alleviates many of the problems and limitations of proprietary systems. Wheeler states that the goal of open systems is to provide application portability, scalability, and interoperability.[5] Portability refers to the ability to move or port applications from one platform to another. This eliminates the need to rewrite programs that may run on multiple platforms in the enterprise. Applications development can be accomplished on one platform, say a PC or workstation, and then ported to a production platform such as a mainframe or midrange system. Scalability refers to the ability to utilize processing power as needed. As processing needs increase, additional processing capability can be added. Interoperability is the ability to interoperate with other systems.

A major initiative in the computer industry to establish open systems is the *Open System Foundation* (OSF).[6] Some earlier efforts were centered around standardizing the UNIX operating system. UNIX offers the ability to run on many different hardware platforms, making it attractive as an open operating system. OSF was founded to establish standards not only for an open operating system, but also for a user interface and distributed computing.

While open systems and enterprise computing seek to provide the same type of functionality, they are at present different paths to the same destination. In its most pragmatic sense, enterprise computing offers a means to overcome a legacy of incompatible systems. Enterprise computing implementations attempt to "glue" together existing systems to provide an enterprisewide view of data and applications through a common interface. Open systems have the same goals but accomplish this task by establishing standards for new systems. It would be difficult if not impossible for organizations to retrofit all of their existing systems to an open architecture. Open systems are more future-oriented, while many present enterprise computing systems are oriented toward existing proprietary systems. In *Enterprise Computing*, Alan R. Simon states that there is currently little overlap between open systems and enterprise computing; but as open standards and enterprise architectures evolve, there will be more overlap between the two.[7]

Enterprise Computing Solutions

In response to the problem of implementing enterprise computing in a multivendor environment, several third-party vendors have developed enterprise computing solutions. These solutions conform to the integration model of enterprise computing. By providing interfaces to existing systems and common applications development tools, these products provide an enterprise computing solution among heterogeneous systems.

FOCUS

Information Builders, Inc. offers a line of products aimed at providing enterprise computing solutions.[8] Primary among these products are the FOCUS 4GL and the FOCNET Connectivity interfaces. FOCUS is a forth generation database access tool designed to run on a variety of platforms and interface with a number of proprietary databases.[9] Applications portability is provided by the use of FOCUS on all platforms. Applications developed on one platform may be ported to other FOCUS platforms. FOCNET provides the communications interface between platforms.[10] Figure 7.7 illustrates how FOCUS and FOCNET could be used to implement a client/server architecture in an enterprise computing scenario. The client application uses FOCUS to create its request for data. This request is passed to the server platform via FOCNET. FOCNET provides the protocol interfaces required between disparate systems. For example, the client could be a PC running OS/2 and the server a DEC VAX under VMS. The FOCNET components on both platforms would provide transparent data access to the client application.

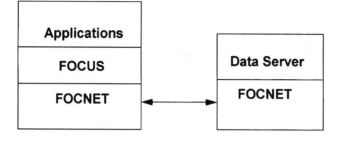

Platform X   Platform Y

Figure 7.7   FOCNET Enterprise Computing

ORACLE

Oracle Corporation offers an enterprise computing solution with its ORACLE Relational DBMS, SQL*NET network software, and SQL*Connect gateways. The ORACLE database system is available for a number of platforms.[11] The SQL*NET product provides protocol interfaces between platforms.[12] This allows physically separated databases to be accessed as if they were a single logical database. Access to non-ORACLE databases is provided by Oracle's SQL*Connect gateway.[13]

In addition to database products, Oracle provides application development tools. Figure 7.8 shows how an ORACLE enterprise computing solution could be configured. In this example, the client application accesses data from multiple servers in the organization via SQL*NET and the SQL*Connect gateway.

The advantages of integration solutions are that they

- provide access to enterprise data. This is predicated on the availability of an interface for each of the platforms in the enterprise and the installation of the interface on each platform.

- build on existing systems and data. In most instances, existing data can be accessed and the need to write applications or replace hardware is eliminated.

- provide a single programming language and interface. This is true providing the enterprise will commit to a third-party standard programming language.

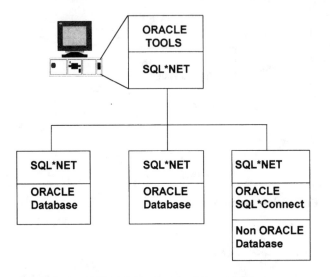

Figure 7.8   ORACLE Enterprise Computing

IBM Information Warehouse

Realizing the growth of enterprise computing, IBM has developed its own framework for an enterprise computing solution. Announced in September of 1991, the Information Warehouse framework describes a set of products and facilities for the access and management of data spread over IBM and non-IBM systems.[14] The concept of the Information Warehouse mirrors that of enterprise computing. Some feel that this indicates a move away from IBM's proprietary architecture of the past and toward a more open model.[15] The Information Warehouse framework is composed of three major elements: Applications and Decision Support, Data Delivery, and Enterprise Data.[16]

Applications and Decision Support   This element provides users with the tools needed to retrieve, analyze, and interpret data. A number of IBM's existing decision support tools, such a Query Management Facility, Application System, Data Interpretation System, Personal Application System, and Lotus 1-2-3/M, are included in the Information Warehouse framework.[17]

Data Delivery   The data delivery element is responsible for the access and transfer of data. IBM's *Distributed Relational Database Architecture* (DRDA) is a key component of this element. DRDA

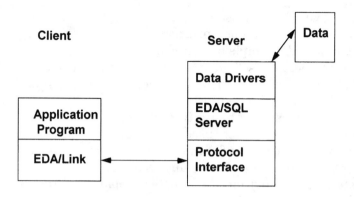

Figure 7.9   EDA/SQL

provides SQL access to remote relational databases such as IBM's DB2, SQL/DS, OS/400, and OS/2 EE Database Manager, and non-IBM databases that implement DRDA.[18]

Enterprise Data   The enterprise data element of the Information Warehouse framework consists of all data and database management systems in the enterprise.[19] To support this element, IBM has recently released a new version of its DB2 Relational DBMS that conforms to the DRDA standard of the Information Warehouse framework.[20]

To provide more products that are compliant with the Information Warehouse framework, IBM has formed partnerships with a number of third-party vendors. One product developed for the Information Warehouse framework is Information Builders *Enterprise Data Access* SQL (EDA/SQL). EDA/SQL provides the capability to access more than 45 types of databases and files on IBM and non-IBM systems.[21] Figure 7.9 shows an example of how EDA/SQL could be used for a client/server configuration.

The Information Warehouse framework is a relatively new entry in the enterprise computing picture and it may be several more years before the number and variety of third-party products is sufficient to provide enterprise computing solutions in a multivendor environment.

Summary

In this chapter the concept of enterprise computing was introduced. Enterprise computing involves the integration of data, applications, and user interfaces across disparate computing platforms. The goal of enterprise computing is to provide an enterprise view of all data in an organization. While enterprise computing is not required to implement a client/server architecture, it does expand the potential of client/server computing. Due to an evolution of needs, most enterprises have acquired multiple and often incompatible computing platforms.

IBM's System Application Architecture attempted to provide a set of standards that could be used to integrate applications across IBM platforms. The standards covered such areas as user interfaces, programming interfaces, and communications. Two models of enterprise computing, the scalable utopian and the integration model, can be used to describe approaches to enterprise computing. The scalable utopian model envisions identical programs running on all platforms. This model is unrealistic in today's environment. The integration model takes a more pragmatic view of the current computing environment and provides for interfaces between disparate systems and the user.

An alternative to proprietary systems is open systems. Open systems conform to a set of standards designed to permit interoperability across platforms. Several industry consortiums have been established to foster the development of open systems standards. Several third-party enterprise computing solutions are available, all of which conform to the integration model and provide a set of software and communications interfaces. IBM's recent entry into enterprise computing, the Information Warehouse, is a framework designed to provide access and management of data across IBM and non-IBM platforms.

End Notes

1. Alan R. Simon, *Enterprise Computing* (New York: Bantam Books), 1992, p. 3.

2. Ibid., p. 138.

3. Ibid., p. 14.

4. Tom Wheeler, *Open Systems Handbook* (New York: Bantam Books), 1992, p. 3.

5. Ibid.

6. Ibid., p. 59.

7. Simon, op. cit., p. 24.

8. *FOCUS in Distributed Systems Environments: The Architecture for the 1990s* (Redwood Shores: Information Builders, Inc., 1990), p. 3.

9. Ibid.

10. Ibid.

11. *Guide to Oracle Products*, Oracle Corporation, 1991, p. 2.

12. Ibid., p. 8.

13. Ibid., p. 10.

14. Al Gillen, "Information Warehouse Open for Business: IBM Releases Revised DB2 Product with DRDA Features" *MIDRANGE Systems*, April 28, 1992, p. 3.

15. Andrew Lawrence and Katy Ring, "Information Warehouse:Triumph of Pragmatism?" *IBM System User*, October 1991, p. 9.

16. "Information Warehouse: IBM Announces Information Warehouse Framework: New Strategy on Managing Data" *EDGE—On and About AT&T*, September 16, 1991, p. 11.

17. Ibid.

18. Ibid.

19. Ibid.

20. Gillen, op. cit., p. 3.

21. *Enterprise Data Access/SQL: EDA/SQL Product Description* (New York: Information Builders, Inc., 1991), p. 5.

8

Implementation Planning

Given that the many benefits of client/server computing justify its use, the next question is how to implement it. Developing a client/server application is more difficult than developing a single-platform application. This is primarily because the application is spread over multiple platforms. In the simplest case, only two platforms, the client and the server, would be involved. Given that most organizations have data on multiple platforms, the situation could rapidly grow to multiple servers serving a variety of client platforms and applications. The client and server platforms could be similar, as with PC clients and LAN data servers, or very different, as with PC clients and mainframe servers. As the number and type of platforms grow, so does the complexity. In some situations, the implementation of client/server computing could drive an organization to enterprise computing.

Client/server applications involve more technologies than single systems applications. Not only must the operating systems and applications for each platform be dealt with, so must data communications and connectivity. As physically separated platforms enter the picture, the data communications portion of the picture becomes more complex. A body of expertise is needed to bring the entire client/server application together. Often it is difficult to find people with the specific mix of skills needed.

As with any new technology there are risks and challenges. Adopting standards early on runs the risk of investing large amounts of time and money in products that may be obsolete as new de facto industry standards evolve. Moving too slowly runs the risk of being left behind technologically and playing catch-up to competitors.

The question still remains: How to proceed in implementing client/server computing. In this chapter we will present a methodology for implementing client/server computing. First we will look at some important factors to consider before initiating a client /server project. Next we will examine some implementation options, and finally we detail steps for planning a client/server implementation.

Evaluation of Current Environment

Before implementing a new system, it is often wise to evaluate the current computing environment. This is particularly true when implementing client/server computing. Because client/server is based on the premise of dividing computing processes among platforms to exploit the relative advantages of each, it is important to fully understand what the capabilities and limitations are within the current environment. Again, since client/server is based on multiple platforms and the ability to communicate between platforms, the current data communications environment will have a large impact on how client/server computing is implemented. In addition to hardware, the applications software and database systems currently in use will affect any move to client /server. Existing databases and database management systems may impact the development of client applications and new server databases. While hardware and software are two tangible pieces of any computing system, a third, potentially more vital but less tangible element is the organization itself. Perhaps more than any other development in the computing industry in the recent past, client/server computing has changed the way in which IS departments and organizations in general view data and information processing. Let us now look at each of these three areas in more detail.

Hardware

Hardware in a client/server architecture covers more than just the primary processing platform. It includes the servers, the clients, and the communications network. In evaluating an organization's current environment it is useful to look at each category separately. Let us start with servers.

Servers   When looking at current platforms and their suitability as servers, there are several factors to consider. First, are there platforms currently being used as database servers or that could potentially be used as database servers? The most likely candidates are those currently running relational databases. Depending on the DBMS used, it may be possible to use an existing platform as a database server. For example, a mainframe running DB2 would have a great deal of potential to act as a server database. A second major consideration is load. A system currently running at or near capacity would not be a good choice. This is particularly true of LAN database servers. In most situations, existing LAN file servers are not suitable as database servers.[1] The additional traffic and load placed on the server may be too much for an existing nondedicated server. A third consideration is storage capacity. If a new database is to be added or an existing database is to be expanded, the impact on storage must be considered.

Figure 8.1 lists the three factors that determine server suitability. Although none of these factors would rule out a client/server implementation, they will help to determine the suitability of existing systems as database servers. Should none of the existing platforms turn out to be suitable, it may be necessary to plan for the acquisition of a database server. At this point, there may not be sufficient information to determine what type of server to acquire. The purpose of looking at existing server platforms at this point is simply to gather data for use during the design of the

- Current Database Servers

- Load

- Storage Capacity

Figure 8.1   Server Suitability

client/server system. This information will also provide a rough idea of how suitable the current environment is for client/server computing.

Workstations   The category of workstation covers all input/display devices in use. This can range from dumb terminals to powerful RISC workstations. The major consideration at this point is the ability of the workstations in use to support a client/server interface and, most probably, their ability to support a graphical user interface. In most organizations, there will be a mixture of devices. As with processing platforms, workstations were added as needs changed. It is important to note the type and distribution of each device. A department with a mixture of dumb terminals, PCs, and MACs is a much less attractive candidate for a client /server implementation than a department equipped only with PCs. When reviewing the workstations, it is useful to note the type of processor, RAM memory and type of display on each. This will aid in determining if current workstations can be used as client platforms or can be upgraded to serve as client platforms. To support graphical user interfaces and multitasking, 386 or higher processors and 4 to 8 megabytes or more of RAM memory may be required.

   Again, as with the server, the specifics of the workstation requirements won't be finalized until further along in the design process. These requirments are outlined in Figure 8.2. This information provides a quick look at the suitability of existing workstations. While GUI-ready workstations are not a prerequisite for a client/server implementation, organizations with an existing base of 386/486 PCs will have a much lower initial investment in client hardware.[2]

- **Type**

- **Distribution**

- **Capabilities**
  -- **Processor**
  -- **Memory**
  -- **Display**

Figure 8.2   Workstations

Communications

Communications may be one of the greatest limitations in implementing client/server computing. In many instances, the appropriate hardware exists on the client side and on the server side; however, the communications link between the two is inadequate. Much of this is due to the shift from a mainframe-centered environment to a multiplatform processing environment. Most mainframe systems perform all the processing and send only a screen image to the display device. This screen image usually consists of a 24×80 screen of characters, a maximum of 1,920 characters. This is a relatively small amount of data, which can easily be transmitted over low-speed data links. In client/server computing, the client application performs much of the processing previously performed by the mainframe and may require large amounts of data from the server. Potentially, the client may pass many megabytes of data between the servers and itself. In most situations, low-speed data lines are inadequate for this task. When reviewing the current communications environment, it is important to note the type of communications links, the speed of the links, protocols supported, and the types of interfaces that exist to other platforms (gateways, bridges). Figure 8.3 outlines these considerations.

With LANs, it is important to note the type of topology as well as any gateways or connectivity to other LANs or systems. Again this information is used solely to judge where the enterprise is currently. Depending on the requirements of the client/server application, it may be necessary to upgrade existing data communications systems. Some client/server approaches, such as simple file transfer or applications programming interfaces, can be implemented using low-speed data communications links.

- **Type**

- **Speed**

- **Protocols**

- **Interfaces**

Figure 8.3   Communications

Given the information collected, it would be possible to get a rough idea of how well the existing hardware is suited for client /server computing. The lack of suitable hardware does not necessarily mandate the purchase of additional hardware to support client/server. If the purchase of new hardware is not possible for whatever reason, the hardware information gathered may help to steer the organization toward a client/server approach achievable with its existing hardware. Chapters 3 through 6 detail specific approaches and their hardware requirements. If the approach chosen requires new hardware, the investment may be significant. Some research indicates that companies initially investing in information systems may pay more for hardware with client /server than with a host-terminal configuration.[3]

Software

The next area to consider is the software existing within the organization. In some instances, existing software may be sufficient to implement client/server computing. In other cases, it may be necessary to acquire new programming and database management software. The major software items to be reviewed are the database management systems and file structures in use, the applications and application programming languages used, and the user interfaces in use.

Database Management Systems and File Structure In reviewing the DBMS and file structures in use, be sure to consider all platforms that could be included in the enterprise system. While a particular database or data file type may not be included in the initial client/server implementation, it may be added later. Knowledge of all the DBMS and file types can be helpful when selecting client/server development tools. The items to note are the type of DBMS or file, such as relational, VSAM, sequential; its compatibility with SQL standards if applicable; and any SQL add-on products that may be available. These considerations are outlined in Figure 8.4. SQL add-on products such as SQL gateways for DB2 provide a means to access the database from other platforms. (See Chapter 5 for more information on SQL gateways.)

Applications and Application Programming Languages A knowledge of the existing applications and programming languages is neces-

- Type

- SQL Compatibility

- SQL Accessibility

Figure 8.4   DBMS—File Structures

sary to determine if existing programs can be modified to support client/server and to determine the suitability of existing programming languages for the development of new client/server applications. In some situations, it may be possible to modify existing applications to client/server. This can save on development time and build on the capabilities of existing applications. Additionally, the programming languages in-house should be reviewed for their suitability for building new client/server applications. The major factors to consider are the language's ability to support SQL, its ability to support GUIs, its portability among platforms, and the availability of design tools. Figure 8.5 lists these factors.

Since SQL has become the access method of choice, a language's ability to use embedded SQL statements is a major factor in determining its suitability for developing client/server applications. While supporting GUIs is not a necessity, it does enhance the utility of an application. This primarily involves the integration of the application with other GUI applications such as spreadsheets and word processors. Another concern is the portability of the programming language and applications developed with it. In multiplatform environments, portability can be a major concern. The last factor to review is the availability of design tools. Design tools can greatly reduce applications development

- SQL Support

- GUI Support

- Portability

- Design Tools

Figure 8.5   Applications and Application Programming Language

- Type
   -- Windows
   -- OS/2
   -- Other

- Distribution

Figure 8.6   Graphical User Interfaces

time as well as provide a means to more easily modify programs developed with them.

User Interfaces   The user interfaces existing in the organization may serve as a base for the development of client applications. Of primary interest are GUIs such as Windows and OS/2. As with the workstation hardware, the type and distribution of GUIs is important to note. Departments or units within the organization that have Windows or OS/2 would be good candidates for a GUI-based client/server implementation, since they could use the existing GUI software and they already have experience with GUIs. Figure 8.6 outlines the factors to note in reviewing user interfaces.

As with hardware, the review of existing software can help to determine what software may be utilized in developing client /server applications. In most situations, additional software will be required, but an understanding of existing software may help in choosing new client/server software products. For example, if the review of the current environment shows that Windows is used widely and has become the de facto standard in the organization, it may not be wise to choose client/server software that runs only under OS/2. An absence of a standardized user interface may offer an opportunity to use the implementation of client /server to set standards for GUIs within the organization.

The Organization

The organization itself and the people in it are as much a part of an automated system as the hardware and software used. End users must use the system, and system designers and developers must understand the user role in the organization. Client/server computing, because of its distributed nature, brings many potentially different units of an enterprise together in a single system.

- Organizational Structure

- Staffing
  -- IS
  -- User Departments

Figure 8.7   The Organization

In *Analysis and Design of Information Systems*, James Senn includes in the feasibility study for a proposed system the test for operational feasibility along with technical and economic feasibility.[4] The purpose of including operational feasibility is to ensure that the proposed system will work within the organization. Senn goes on to suggest that support for the project from management and users be considered along with any other factors that may cause resistance to the new system.[5] While a complete study of organizational behavior is beyond the scope of this book, let us consider two areas within an existing organization that may impact a client/server implementation: the organizational structure and staffing. Figure 8.7 outlines these considerations.

Organizational Structure   In the days of mainframe-only computing, the division of duties between the IS department and the user departments was simple. IS was responsible for the complete system and the user departments simply used the system. With departmental computing, many of the functions that were handled by central IS are now the responsibility of the departmental IS staff. Client/server computing further complicates the situation in that servers from multiple departments as well as central IS could be involved in a single client/server application. The question arises: "Who owns and is responsible for the client applications, the multiple servers, and the communications network?" More than likely, these questions have not as yet been answered for the organization. As part of the project plan, the responsibilities will need to be delineated. At this point, it is important to gather what information is available on the roles and functions of departmental and central IS. This information may be in the form of organizational charts, service agreements, or "corporate knowledge."

Staffing   Staffing covers not only the IS staff that may be involved with the project, but also the end users who will be using the application. It is important to note what type of experience end users have with automated systems, what type of training they have had, and what is the general feeling about changing to a new system. Many of these questions will be answered in more detail during user training for the new system, but a brief look at these factors now can help to select a department or group that will have a successful implementation.

The next area to consider is the IS staff. A major concern is the expertise of the people who will be designing and implementing the client/server applications. A lack of experienced personnel has hampered client/server development in many organizations.[6] An understanding of the skills of the current IS staff may aid in deciding if enough expertise exists or can be developed in-house or if outside help is required. Training to produce qualified staff may be an option. As with the organizational structure, it can be useful to understand who does what within the overall organization. An understanding of the capabilities and skills of departmental and central IS staffs can be useful when planning the division of responsibility for the project.

The information gathered on the organizational structure and staffing can be useful in developing an implementation plan. If the organization lacks the skills and expertise needed to implement a particular client/server strategy, you may choose to bring in outside expertise, plan for training of existing staff, or even select a different approach that is supportable with the existing staff. If the planned implementation crosses departmental boundaries, it may be wise to include members of all affected departments on the project team to ensure buy-in and support. Depending on the level of end-user sophistication, it may be necessary to include end-user training in the implementation plan. If there is resistance to automation and client/server computing specifically, it may be necessary to take some type of management actions to minimize the effects of this resistance. Particularly in mainframe-dominated organizations, there is likely to be resistance to client/server computing. These are just a few examples of the many organizational and human factors that must be considered in implementing a new computing architecture.

The purpose of evaluating the current environment is to get an idea of where the organization is and what obstacles could exist in a client/server implementation. Many obstacles may arise that could change the approach taken in the move to client/server.

Equally likely is that a number of opportunities may be discovered, situations ripe for client/server computing. The two major concerns when looking for applications that are best suited for client/server computing are the need for user interface to enterprise data and the need to integrate data and applications. Client /server via a GUI offers an excellent means for end users to access corporate data for analysis and decision making. Data from multiple sources can be combined and manipulated by end-user tools such as spreadsheets. Capabilities such as these are seldom available in traditional host-terminal configurations.

Implementation Options

A key point to emphasize is that client/server computing spans a broad spectrum of implementation approaches. Client/server computing is not a specific product or combination of products, but rather a means to divide processing tasks between platforms. Chapter 2 presented the computing processes model and Chapters 3 through 6 presented implementation approaches, each based on progressively more complex technologies. An evaluation of the current environment such as that just presented can help determine what approaches may be implemented using existing systems as well as help determine what would be required to implement an approach that requires technology beyond that which the organization currently possesses. In general, client/server implementations fall into one of three categories: new systems, modified systems, or additions to existing systems. These categories are noted in Figure 8.8.

New Systems

This option is often preferable to rewriting an existing system, as new systems are in many cases easier to develop. A recent survey

- New Systems

- Modified Systems

- Additions to Existing Systems

Figure 8.8   Implementation Options

found that 70 percent of those responding had written new client /server applications rather than convert existing systems.[7] New design and development tools allow complete applications to be rapidly produced. In terms of the approaches presented, the Windows–OS/2 and APPC approaches would be best suited for completely new applications. This is predicated on the existence of or the willingness to acquire the required hardware and software. While the file transfer and API approaches could be used to develop a new system, the limitations of these approaches may justify either of the other two approaches. Depending on the technology available in the organization, it may be possible to use existing hardware and software. In this situation, the major investment would be in development time rather than hardware. As was noted earlier, those firms with an installed base of 386/486 PCs are in a good position to realize the benefits of client /server computing with a relatively low initial investment.[8] New systems can range from a large-scale enterprisewide system to a simple, single LAN client/server application. As the scope and complexity of the project increases, so does the risk.

Modified Systems

In many situations, there is a large base of existing applications. To protect its investment in applications and data, firms may wish to convert or rewrite existing systems to take advantage of client/server computing. As was mentioned earlier, a lack of tools for conversion of existing programs has prompted many firms to write new applications rather than rewrite existing ones.[9] A major complication to rewriting existing applications is that new software must run on two platforms rather than just one. In a host-terminal environment, everything was located on and ran on the host. Modifying an existing program to a client/server architecture would potentially involve moving a portion of the application to a client platform such as a PC.

There may be portability and compatibility problems to deal with. Additionally, it may be difficult to incorporate GUIs into existing applications. The likely case for rewriting existing programs would be in situations where the existing application is to remain basically intact, but where client/server will be utilized to acquire data from other sources. The APPC approach presented in Chapter 6 would be appropriate in this type of situation. Rather than transfer updated data between platforms on a periodic basis, APPC could be added to existing applications to access the data at its source, eliminating the need for mass data transfers. The basic functionality of the existing application would not change significantly, but the method by which information is distributed between platforms would be changed.

Additions to Existing Systems

This option offers an easy means of initial entry into client/server computing. An addition to an existing system would take one portion of an existing system and add to it a client/server application. This approach offers a lower degree of risk than that of a completely new system implementation. Additionally, the firm's current investment in systems is retained as well as extending the useful life of the existing systems. Many organizations start by developing "frontware" or GUIs for existing mainframe applications.[10] No modification of the existing application is required and users are given an opportunity to use and buy into the concept of client/server computing. This option allows time for the IS staff to gain experience with some of the client/server technologies that will be needed as the firm moves into more complex approaches.

The simple file transfer and API approaches presented in Chapters 3 and 4 are the most likely approaches to be employed when making client/server additions to existing systems. The more advanced approaches presented in Chapters 5 and 6 may be used to develop add-ons to existing systems, particularly in situations where existing host databases can be used by client applications. Keep in mind, though, that as the application becomes more technically complex, the risk factor increases. As the scope of an add-on project expands, it may move into the category of a new system. While this is not necessarily bad, you may want to choose a low-risk option for a first-time venture into client/server computing. As add-on projects become successful, and the organization gains some knowledge and experience in client/server computing, more advanced approaches can be pursued.

Pilot Projects

When implementing a new system or architecture, it is often useful to pilot the system on a small group in the organization.[11] This allows the complete system to be "field tested" before it is implemented on a larger scale. During the pilot, changes and enhancement can be made to the system. Piloting has been particularly popular with client/server implementations. Eastman Kodak Company is starting its move to client/server computing by piloting projects in several of its divisions.[12] As pilot applications prove successful, they can be expanded to other parts of the organization. In addition to proving the technology, pilot programs help to gain user buy-in and acceptance.

Implementation Planning

After completing an evaluation of the current computing environment and considering the various options available, the next step is to plan for the implementation of client/server. The next section focuses on "tactical" planning as opposed to strategic planning. The overall strategic direction of the organization would be assumed to include moving to client/server computing. The tactical planning framework presented here would be appropriate for a project or series of projects supporting the overall move to client/server computing.

Let us briefly discuss a few general topics on the subject of implementation planning.

Phased Implementation

As mentioned in the previous section, there are three major implementation options: new systems, modified systems, and additions to existing systems. An approach many firms have adopted is to implement client/server in phased fashion, first introducing additions to existing systems, followed by modifications to existing systems if possible, and, finally, the implementation of totally new systems. This type of phased migration allows organizations to move to client/server through a series of small manageable steps.[13] Figure 8.9 shows how a phased migration could be planned.

Initially existing applications would provide a beginning step into client/server computing. This would most likely include GUI front ends to applications that have a high degree of user interaction, require access to corporate data, or require integration of data. Appropriate approaches would most likely be simple file transfer or an API strategy.

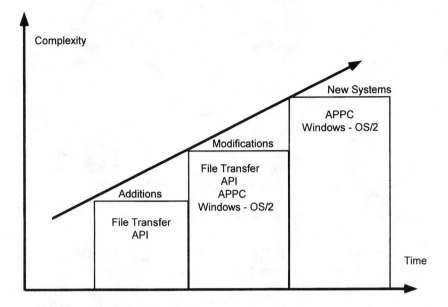

Figure 8.9   Phased Implementation

The next phase would involve the modification of existing applications if possible to take advantage of client/server. In the previous phase, client/server applications were glued on, so to speak, in front of existing applications, and modification of existing applications was not required. Due to the factors mentioned earlier in the chapter, there may be some benefit in creating new applications rather than rewriting existing ones.

The last phase would involve the complete development of new client/server applications. By the time the organization reached this point, client/server would hopefully be well established and there would be sufficient knowledge and expertise in the organization to tackle major projects. Let us now look at an example of how this phased approach has been used.

A moderate-sized local government maintained its financial management system on an IBM mainframe computer. The system consisted of a number of COBOL programs that processed input from several sources to maintain a general ledger. Much of the data fed into the system was entered via a host-based data entry system. Information from the system was available through on-line access or hard copy reports that were produced daily. Ac-

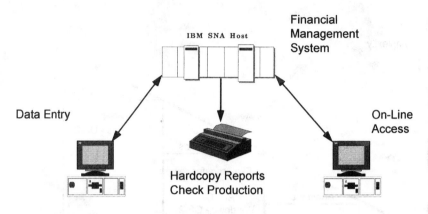

Figure 8.10   Phased Implementation Initial System

cess to the system was accomplished via dumb terminals or PCs with 3270 emulation. Figure 8.10 illustrates the original system.

While a complete replacement of the financial management system was planned for a future date, rising costs, new requirements, and declining budgets necessitated a search to find ways to

1. lower processing costs.

2. improve productivity.

3. provide additional capabilities until a new system was acquired.

4. extend the useful life of the existing system.

A phased approach was taken to achieve the above goals. First, functions such as data entry and check production were moved off the host platform and onto a local area network. This was accomplished via a combination of simple file transfer and APIs. PC clients on the LAN accomplished data validation and editing and produced files that were uploaded to the host. Check production previously accomplished on the host was offloaded to the PC clients. A new budgeting package was installed on an IBM RS6000 rather than on the host 3090. Using file transfer, data was moved between the host and the RS6000 as needed. Minimal programming was required on the host to support data extraction and transfer. By moving these functions off the host and onto other client platforms, the host now functions as a server for the client data entry, check production, and budgeting applications. Figure 8.11 illustrates this relationship.

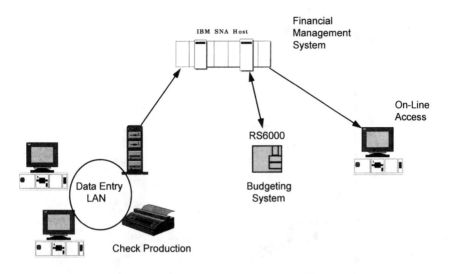

Figure 8.11   Phased Implementation with Client Additions

The next step in the progression of a client/server strategy would be the implementation of SQL database servers and the development of GUI-based client applications. Due to the file structure of the existing host application and the planned acquisition of a new accounting system, this last step will be incorporated into the design of the new system.

In all, the stated goals were achieved. By offloading data entry and check production to client applications, operating costs were reduced. Productivity was increased due to more user-friendly client applications that handled data entry tasks faster than the host system. New capabilities were provided by the addition of a client system to accomplish budgeting tasks. In general, the life of the system was extended, maximizing the investment in current hardware, software, and data, while providing time to develop expertise in client/server computing.

Scalable Implementation

Another option is to implement an application that is scalable. In this context, scalable refers to the ability to expand the application. This expansion may be either horizontal or vertical. For example, a small personnel application could be piloted in the Human Resources Department that utilized data stored on the Human Resources database server. When the application is

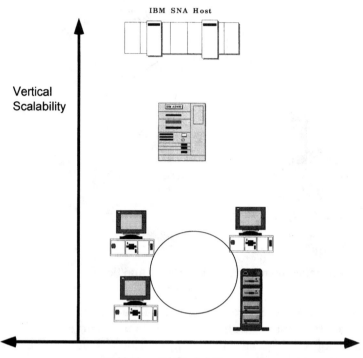

Figure 8.12   Application Scalability

deemed ready for widespread use, it would be expanded horizontally across the organization to other departments. If the application were then modified to access payroll information stored on a corporate mainframe, the application would have expanded vertically. Horizontal scalability refers to expansion across equivalent systems, while vertical scalability refers to expansion to other platforms of greater or lesser processing capability. Figure 8.12 is a graphic presentation of scalability.

Now let us continue with some important factors to consider in implementation planning.

Identify an Application

While the direction of the organization may be to move to client /server, the big question becomes where to start. A course followed by many is to start small and work up to larger systems.

This is the basic concept behind pilots, phased implementations, and scalable applications. A wise move would be to choose a visible but not mission-critical application as the first to be implemented under client/server. Visibility can help to build acceptance of the client/server concept. Unless you are a great risk-taker, choose a non-mission-critical application. If something goes wrong, as it inevitably does on a new implementation, a mission-critical application could give you and the client/server project more visibility than you'd like. Pick something that will provide a needed new capability, and that won't be seriously impacted by delays or problems. After achieving a few successes and obtaining some experience, then tackle the high-visibility, mission-critical applications. The section on conducting an evaluation of the current environment in this chapter contains some tips on identifying those applications that would be likely candidates. Generally, those applications that require a high degree of user interaction, access to corporate data, or integration of data and applications fall into this category.

Form a Project Team

As was mentioned earlier in the text, client/server applications are more complicated than single system applications in that they involve multiple platforms, data communications, and, potentially, multiple applications programs. Usually it is difficult to find one person who has the necessary skills and expertise for such an undertaking. Most likely, it will require forming a project team consisting of people with the necessary skills from various areas of the organization. In addition to applications programmers, you may need data communications, LAN, and PC expertise. If the application involves a host database, you may require the involvement of the database administrator. In organizations that have gone to departmental computing, the project team may also involve the IS staff of multiple departments. This may be desirable not only from a technical standpoint, but also from an organizational standpoint. The project team can be useful in building consensus and acceptance of the project as well as resolving technical issues.

The project team will play a major role in determining the "ownership" of the project. Because client/server computing can potentially span multiple systems and cross many organizational boundaries, the issue of ownership is an important one to resolve. Specific responsibilities for the maintenance of applications, data, and communications should be spelled out early in the project. Not only will this be important during development and implementation, it will also be important for later support and maintenance of the system. Procedures for coordination of changes, modifications, and downtime of individual components that could affect the overall system should be formalized early in the project.

In addition to the technical team it is important to ensure the project has management support and, ideally, a management member who will champion the project and work to resolve issues outside the scope of the project team. Again, if the project crosses organizational boundaries, it is important to obtain support from all involved departments. Appendix A contains further information on forming project teams.

Select Hardware and Software

A task of the project team will be to select the hardware and software for the project if any are required. The evaluation of the current environment will provide the team with useful information. The selection of hardware and software will be greatly influenced by existing systems and any requirement to interface with those systems. The strategic direction of the firm, such as toward open systems, will also influence the selection of hardware and software. This particular activity may be a part of the development methodology used for the project. Many of the major system development methodologies include steps for the evaluation and selection of hardware and software. For relatively small projects, say an application on a single LAN, the evaluation and selection of hardware and software would most likely consist of a comparison of LAN SQL databases and a client development tool.

Develop a Project Plan Using a Systems Development Methodology Appropriate for the Project

In some cases, difficulties in implementing client/server computing have stemmed not only from a lack of expertise, but also from failure to follow project management practices.[14] Many organizations have formalized system development methodologies they use for implementing new systems. Often these methodologies break the development process into phases with defined deliverables for each phase. Senn lists the following activities in the development of a system:[15]

- Preliminary Investigation
- Determination of Requirements
- Development of Prototype Systems
- Design of System
- Development of Software
- Systems Testing
- Implementation

In the absence of an existing methodology, these activities and the subordinate steps included under them provide a good basic design methodology.

It is important to select a design methodology that is appropriate for the project. A small project may be best served by a simplified version of the methodology listed above. A more formalized methodology with extensive documentation and set deliverables would be more appropriate for a large project. It may be necessary to tailor existing methodologies to fit the scope of a particular project.

Summary

The implementation of a client/server architecture is more complicated than that of a single host architecture. This is because client/server computing can potentially involve multiple applications running on multiple platforms. The addition of remote platforms further complicates the situation and introduces new data communications complexities. Client/server computing is a relatively new phenomenon, and it is often difficult to find people with the required combination of skills. Before embarking on a client/server project, it is useful to evaluate the current computing environment. This evaluation should include hardware, software, and the organization itself. The evaluation of hardware should include servers, workstations, and data communications. Software should include database management systems, applications, and graphical user interfaces. The review of the organization should include the organizational structure and the skills and training requirements of the staff.

When implementing client/server there are three major options: new systems, modification of existing systems, or additions to existing systems. Developing a new system is sometimes preferable to modifying an existing system. Modification of existing systems is often difficult due to a lack of tools to rewrite existing applications into the client/server mold. Additions to existing systems can prolong the useful life of systems by providing them with some client/server capabilities.

Pilot projects are a useful means to introduce a client/server application. Client/server applications may also be phased, and can utilize the approaches presented in Chapters 3 through 6. Scalable applications are those that can be expanded across the organization or expanded to include additional database servers. Applications that require a high degree of user interaction, require access to corporate data, or require integration of data or applications are prime candidates for client/server computing. Initial applications should be useful and visible but not mission critical.

The project team for a client/server implementation may require people from a number of specialized areas and, depending on the organizational structure, people from a number of departments. The selection of hardware and software for the project will be controlled by existing systems, new system requirements, and the strategic direction of the organization. A systems development methodology appropriate for the size and complexity of the project should be chosen.

End Notes

1. "Guru Sheds Light on Client/Server," *Network World*, November 16, 1992, p. 71.

2. Mary Martin, "Reaping the Rewards," *Network World*, November 16, 1992, p. 63.

3. Ibid.

4. James A. Senn, *Design and Analysis of Information Systems* (New York: McGraw-Hill, 1984), p. 53.

5. Ibid.

6. Dwight B. Davis, "Where Client/Server Fits," *Datamation*, July 15, 1991.

7. Ibid.

8. Martin, op. cit., p. 63.

9. Davis, op. cit.

10. W. James Fischer, "Client/Server Reshapes Corporate Computing," *Chief Information Officer*, Summer 1992, p. 31.

11. Senn, op. cit., p. 534.

12. Bob Violino, "Kodak's Next Step," *Information Week*, February 3, 1992, p. 10.

13. Fischer, op. cit., p. 31.

14. Wayne Eckerson, "The Sobering Slide of Client/Server Move," *Network World*, September 28, 1992, p. 93.

15. Senn, op. cit., p. 18.

9

Future Trends

As rapid as change is in today's computing industry, it is important to look to the future as well as deal with the present. Considering that client/server computing is in its infancy, it is particularly important to be cognizant of trends in the industry that may impact its future direction. In this chapter, we will briefly review some recent developments in hardware, software, and in the industry in general that relate to the future of client/server computing.

Hardware

The major areas in which to expect innovations in hardware are workstations, servers, and LANs.

Workstations

If the advances in hardware made since the introduction of the PC 10 years ago are any indication of what to expect in the future, it can be expected that the trend of more powerful, less expensive desktop computers will continue. As more power moves to the desktop, so does more processing. A big question in the workstation market of the future is which processor will emerge as the dominant client workstation—PCs based on the next generation of Intel microprocessors or the RISC-based workstation. At present, the Intel chip and the PC dominate the business market while RISC workstations are primarily found in calculation-intensive applications such as engineering and drafting. The RISC platform is starting to move into more and more business applications and is gaining ground in the traditional PC market. Major players in the RISC workstation arena include Sun and IBM's line of RS/6000 workstations. As more software becomes available for RISC platforms, it can be expected that they will gain an even larger share of the market.

Servers

Initially, servers were simply PCs with additional memory and disk storage. As networking grew, the server developed into a more specialized piece of hardware, but still retained much of the same basic architecture as a workstation. Several hardware manufacturers have recognized that as firms move more to client /server computing and to downsizing, they become as dependent on LAN file servers as they were on mainframe hosts. Many CIOs feel uncomfortable about leaving the security of a mainframe environment, regardless of the benefits and potential cost savings. To fill the need for a reliable, high-performance LAN server, a new generation of file servers is appearing on the market. IBM has recently announced its new line of PS/2 servers.[1] These servers are designed to provide a LAN server with the reliability of a mainframe system. Features of this new line of servers include multiple processors, a high-speed data bus, and multiple disk drives utilizing RAID (Redundant Array of Inexpensive Disks) technology.[2] RAID technology provides a fault-tolerant data storage system that uses relatively inexpensive PC-type disk drives.

A new entry into the server market is the UNIX Server. In some situations, RISC workstation performance has exceeded the ability of the server to provide data.[3] To overcome the server bottleneck, vendors such as Auspex are marketing specialized UNIX Superservers capable of high-speed, high-volume I/O.[4] As the UNIX workstation market grows, the UNIX Server market can also be expected to grow.

As with workstations, server buyers will be faced with the RISC–Intel platform decision. Again, RISC platforms are gaining ground in what were traditional PC and PC-server markets. More and more business applications are being developed under the UNIX operating system for RISC processors. Networks combining multiple types of servers are becoming more prevalent as firms attempt to build enterprise networks from existing servers. New network operating systems, described later in the chapter, support these types of heterogeneous networks.

Local Area Networks

The term local area network may soon be outdated as corporate networks evolve into MANs, WANs, and GANs (metropolitan area networks, wide area networks, and global area networks). Today it is not uncommon to have corporate networks that have tens of thousands of users, and hundreds of servers spread across several countries.[5] Hardware for wide area networking is becoming less expensive and may soon become as common as plug-in cards are for PCs today. Deregulation of the telecommunications industry has led to competition in the "long haul" data communications market and lower data communications costs.

To support emerging high-bandwidth applications, such as imaging, video, and multimedia, network speeds can be expected to increase. The common 10 and 16 megabit per second speeds of today can be expected to be replaced with 100 megabit per second LANs in a few short years. As with other hardware, networking hardware prices are dropping as capabilities are increasing. The concept of a corporate "backbone" is becoming the centerpiece of telecommunications strategies. Again the need for high-speed, higher-capacity communications links is driven by the applications that will be running on the network. Client/server computing requires the ability to move data (potentially very large amounts of data) from the server to the client. Moving client /server computing into an enterprise computing scenario further expands the need for high-speed corporate data communications. Even though current and perhaps even planned systems don't require 100-megabit speeds today, they may in the future.

An area of networking that can be expected to grow in the future is peer-to-peer networking. In this type of configuration, there is no central server, but rather the ability to share data and files between workstations. Figure 9.1 illustrates the differences between a peer-to-peer LAN and a client/server LAN.

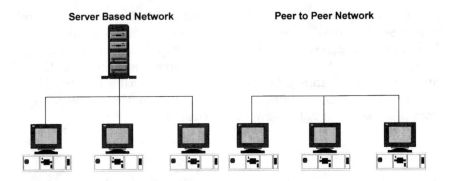

Figure 9.1   Peer-to-Peer Networking

Peer-to-peer networks are growing in popularity due to their low cost, ease of installation, and simple administration.[6] Peer-to-peer networking has in the past been relegated to small, simple LANs. One indicator of the future of peer-to-peer networking is the recent decision of a major airline reservation system to switch up to 50,000 network nodes to a peer-to-peer system.[7] This decision was based on the low cost and support requirements of peer-to-peer as compared to server-based networks.

Another emerging LAN technology is that of wireless networks. These networks utilize a radio or infrared connection between the workstation and server. This eliminates the need for costly, relatively fixed network cabling. Workstations or even complete networks may be physically relocated within the limits of the wireless system. This gives rise to the possibility of a "portable" client that could be moved or, in the case of a laptop, carried to where work needs to be performed within the physical plant of a firm. One vendor supports a "roaming" feature, which allows a portable client to operate much like a cellular phone in that it communicates with the closest server in the wireless network, but continues its session with a specified server.[8]

Software

As with hardware, the future direction of client/server software products remains to be determined. It is safe to assume that GUI-based client applications and SQL databases will be the dominant client/server applications software products. Further growth can be expected in graphical design and development tools. Some areas of client/server software are more unsettled and as of yet have not produced a de facto industry standard. Two major software products in this category are client operating systems and network operating systems. Client/server computing has also spawned the growth of a new family of software products—that of client/server management tools. Let us now consider each of those areas in more detail.

Client Operating Systems

A major decision in implementing client/server is which GUI to select. Many in the industry are waiting for a clear winner in the Windows–OS/2 battle to emerge. The recent announcements of Windows NT and Windows for Workgroups have positioned the Microsoft line of software products for a large share of the client /server market. Of primary interest is Windows NT, the recently released 32-bit operating system.[9] This product is aimed at overcoming the limitations of the current version of Windows, which is forced to run on top of an existing DOS operating system and is constrained by architecture. Windows for Workgroups combines the features of Windows 3.1 with basic networking capabilities such as file and printer sharing.[10] Networking is on a peer-to-peer basis rather than on a server-based configuration. Some feel that this product could jeopardize the server-based LAN operating systems that currently dominate the market.[11] The big question is Windows NT. If it proves as successful as its predecessor, Windows 3.1, it could become the dominant client operating system in the future.

The other major contender in the client operating systems arena is OS/2. In addition to offering a 32-bit operating system and multitasking, a major advantage of OS/2 is its availability. OS/2 has been on the market for quite some time, and some firms opted to go with OS/2 rather than wait for Windows NT. OS/2 has an installed base approaching 1.5 million users; given its earlier release than Windows NT, it may capture a significant portion of the client market.[12]

The client operating system decision remains unresolved. There may not be one best solution for all situations. Most likely, there will be a mixture of client operating systems in use. Some organizations may find themselves with a mixture of client operating systems based on the specific needs of each business unit. In looking to the future, a survey published in *Information Week* indicated that 63 percent of respondents felt that by 1994 Windows would be their dominant client operating system, followed by Windows NT at 17 percent and OS/2 at 14 percent.[13]

Network Operating Systems

Along with client operating systems, server operating systems are a major question for the future. Given that the LAN will be the corporate information distribution system of the future, network operating systems will become critical to client/server implementations. While there are many products on the market, the dominance of Novell can be expected to continue in the immediate future. The *Information Week* study previously cited reported that 44 percent of respondents felt NetWare would be the dominant server operating system, followed by UNIX at 22 percent, Windows NT at 18 percent and OS/2 at 16 percent.[14]

Two recent announcements by Novell seem to indicate their strategy for maintaining their current market position in the future. First is the introduction of NetWare 4.0. Designed as a follow-on to version 3.11, NetWare 4.0 has added features such as Directory Services, designed to support large wide area networks.[15] This product provides organizations with existing Novell LANs the means to move individual networks into a single enterprisewide LAN. A major limitation of previous versions of NetWare was its inability to manage resources across a group of connected LANs. The second major product announcement by Novell, UNIXWare, a UNIX server operating system, positions them to move into the expanding UNIX server market. UNIXWare is designed to share printers and files with DOS, Macintosh, OS/2, and Windows clients.[16]

It appears that Novell will be a major player in the server operating system market for some time to come. This most likely will give rise to a number of Novell-compatible third-party software products for servers.

As networks become larger and multiple networks become interconnected, network management becomes much more complex. Client/server computing further complicates the management problem by adding multiple databases on multiple server platforms. Enrolling and maintaining users on a systemwide basis can become a monumental task. Some firms have found that while client/server computing has provided more productive, lower-cost applications, LAN management issues have caused them to slow down their move to client/server.[17] As enterprise networks and client/server computing grow, so will the demand for more advanced network management tools.

The management of a client/server configuration includes three major areas: network management, system management, and database management. Network management deals with the LAN and WAN links used to connect multiple servers. System management deals with the administration of individual systems or platforms within the enterprise network. Database management involves the administration and maintenance of server databases. While tools exist to deal separately with each of these, there are few tools currently available that integrate all three areas into one tool. IBM is currently developing an OS/2-based platform for managing enterprisewide, multivendor networks.[18] In addition to IBM, third-party vendors are beginning to provide integrated management tools. One such third-party vendor is ECO Systems, which provides integrated management tools for UNIX Servers.[19]

As client/server computing matures, more products will likely be developed to meet the increasing needs for multiplatform network, system, and database management. Management tools will become an increasingly more important part of client/server implementations, particularly in large enterprisewide scenarios.

The Industry

In the immediate future, the move to client/server computing can be expected to continue. In a 1992 survey of top IS executives, 85 percent indicated that they planned to increase spending on client/server technologies in 1993.[20] This is particularly significant in light of the sluggish economy of the early 1990s. The overall market for client/server hardware, software, and services is expected to be one of the faster growing markets in the computing industry. One report projects that the client/server market will grow to $44 billion by 1995.[21]

Another sure sign of the viability of client/server computing is the move by many traditional mainframe applications vendors away from centralized mainframes to client/server. Vendors of mainframe human resources and financial management software are offering PC client software that uses mainframe databases as servers, as well as new client/server packages for midrange and LAN systems.[22] Even financial management software long held as the one application to remain on centralized mainframe systems is moving to client/server. Major vendors such as Integral and Dun & Bradstreet are fielding client/server financial software.[23] These moves are all prompted by a growing demand for client/server applications. Rather than reinvent the technological wheel and develop their own client/server applications, many firms are looking to major software vendors to provide packaged client/server solutions.

Many vendors have realized that the demand is for client/server products rather than traditional host-based systems. Dun & Bradstreet recently reorganized to focus development efforts on client/server and rightsizing.[24] One of the most prominent signs of the continued growth of client/server is IBM's formation of a business unit to specifically promote client/server computing.[25] When the leader in mainframe hardware acknowledges the need to support client/server computing at the risk of losing a portion of its mainframe market, it is an important sign indeed. This move was in all likelihood prompted by declining sales of mainframe hardware and demands by customers for client/server solutions.[26]

In general the future looks bright for client/server computing. The basic architecture will most likely remain the same; the major issues will revolve around the selection of specific hardware and software. Some have billed 1993 as "The Year of the Client" with the pending introduction of Windows NT and other client /server products.[27] Regardless, it appears that client/server computing will remain a major force in the computing industry for some time to come.

Summary

Given the rapid change that is prevalent in the computing industry, it is important to be cognizant of trends that may impact the direction of client/server computing in the future. Primary areas of concern include hardware, software, and the industry in general. Client platforms can be expected to become more powerful as advances in microprocessor technology continue. The major players in the client workstation market will be the next generation of Intel processors and RISC-based workstations. Servers that were initially powerful workstations have evolved into specialized platforms designed for high-volume, high-speed I/O.

As with work stations, more RISC-based servers can be expected in the future. Local area networks can be expected to grow in size, complexity, and speed. Growth is likely in the areas of peer-to-peer networking and wireless networking. In the area of client software, the major client operating systems will most likely be Windows or Windows NT and OS/2. Given its present market share and announced products aimed at enterprise computing, Novell NetWare can be expected to be the dominant server operating system in the future.

As networks become more complex, there will be a growing demand for network management products. The client/server market is expected to continue to grow through 1994. Vendors of traditional mainframe software applications are moving to develop client/server solutions. A major indication of the viability of client/server computing is IBM's formation of a client/server business unit. Client/server computing can be expected to be a major force in the computing industry for some time to come.

End Notes

1. *IBM Personal System/2—Servers*, IBM Corporation, 1992.
2. Ibid., p. 10.
3. David Stamps, "UNIX Server Clout," *Datamation*, March 1, 1991, p. 22.
4. Ibid.
5. Tom McCusker, "Novell Casts a Wider Net," *Datamation*, December 1, 1992, p. 34.
6. Kevin Strehlo, "Windows for Workgroups is Painless Peer-to-Peer," *INFOWORLD*, September 28, 1992, p. 109.
7. John McMullen, "Covia Takes Alternate Route," *Information Week*, December 7, 1992, p. 98.
8. Paul Strauss, "Roaming the LAN Scape," *Datamation*, December 1, 1992, p. 98.
9. Anthony Vecchione with Bob Violino, "Microsoft's Overture." *Information Week*, November 2, 1992, p. 12.
10. *Focus on Microsoft Windows*, Microsoft Corporation, 1992, p. 4.
11. Vecchione with Violino, op. cit., p. 12.

12. Rob Kelly, "OS/2 Lands a Starring Role," *Information Week*, November 2, 1992, p. 13.

13. "Client/Server Stats," *Information Week*, November 23, 1992, p. 16.

14. Ibid.

15. McCusker, op. cit., p. 28.

16. William Brandel, "UNIX Is Front Runner in 32-Bit Race," *LAN TIMES*, September 14, 1992, p. 1.

17. Stephanie Stahl, "LANs: Much Agony, Little Ecstasy," *Information Week*, May 25, 1992, p. 82.

18. Bob Violino with Chuck Appleby, "IBM Completing Puzzle, or Just Adding Pieces?" *Information Week*, May 4, 1992, p. 12.

19. Jeff Moad, "Client/Server Management Arrives," *Datamation*, November 15, 1992, p. 28

20. Chuck Appleby, "Spending for a Rainy Day," *Information Week*, December 7, 1992, p. 40.

21. Paula Musich, "Client/Server Wave to Continue Unabated, Study Says," *PC Week*, April 20, 1992, p. 52.

22. Mike Ricciuti, "Here Come the HR Client/Server Systems!" *Datamation*, July 1992, p. 38.

23. Ned Snell, "Mainframe Accounting Moves Down," *Datamation*, November 1, 1992, p. 113.

24. "Layoffs at Dun & Bradstreet," *Information Week*, December 7, 1992, p. 102.

25. Bob Violino with Robert Moran, "IBM Serves Up New Unit," *Information Week*, November 30, 1992, p. 14.

26. Ed Scannell and Shawn Willett, "Losses Force IBM to Refocus," *INFOWORLD*, December 21, 1992, p. 1.

27. William Brandel, "1993 Will Be the Year of the Client," *LAN TIMES*, December 21, 1992, p. 9.

Organizing a
Client/Server Project

Forming a Client/Server Project Team

As was mention earlier in the text, client/server applications are often more complicated than single system applications. This is due to the fact that they frequently involve multiple platforms, multiple databases, and multiple applications programs. It is usually difficult, if not impossible, to find one person with all the necessary skills and expertise for such a project. Because client/server is a relatively new phenomenon, there is a lack of experience in client/server applications development. As more firms move to client/server, the availability of skilled programmers should increase. Some suggestions on how to bridge the "expertise gap" are included in Appendix B.

Assuming that staff are available with the prerequisite skills, most client/server applications will require the formation of a project team. A team is usually necessary due to the following:

- Need for diverse skills

  While it may be possible to find programming expertise, the project may require skills from other areas such as data communications, local area networking, database design and management, and PC hardware. It may be necessary and even desirable to include someone on the project team with functional expertise. For example, on a financial application an accountant would bring functional expertise to the project team.

- Scope of the project

  A client/server application may span many platforms and involve multiple applications. The size and scope of the project may warrant the use of a team to allow it to be completed in a reasonable amount of time.

- To build consensus

  A project that spans multiple functional areas or divisions within a firm often faces organizational as well as technical challenges. A project team comprised of representatives from all involved business units can help to build consensus and acceptance of the project. Additionally, the project team can play a major role in determining "ownership" of the project. A client/server project can cross many organizational boundaries, and the issue of ownership in this situation is an important one to resolve. Operational issues such as who owns the data, the communications system, the applications, and who is responsible for the maintenance of each can be resolved by the project team before the application is implemented. Answering these questions in the initial stages of the project can help to reduce the "finger pointing" after the application is in place.

Given the above rationale for forming a project team, let us now look at who should be on it. The recommendations listed below should be viewed as descriptions of functions and not necessarily as job descriptions for individual members of the project team. Depending on the size of the project, one person may accomplish several of the functions or, on large projects, several people may be assigned to a single function. Let us now examine each function in detail.

Project Manager

The project manager is responsible for the overall direction and management of the project. While it is desirable to have a project manager who is technically skilled in client/server computing, it is not absolutely essential. A basic understanding of the technology would be acceptable, providing sufficient technical expertise is available from the other members of the project team. The project manager should be skilled in project management techniques and the use of project management tools. Additionally, he or she should have good "people" skills to allow him or her to effectively deal with the team members, end users, and upper management.

Programmer/Programmer-Analyst

The programmer or programmer-analyst is responsible for the design and development of the application. This may involve the following tasks:

- Development of systems requirements and specifications
- Development of prototypes
- Development and testing of the application
- Implementation of the application
- Documentation
- Maintenance of the application after installation

The development of the application includes both the client and the server component. Generally, the programmer will be involved in the development of the client application and, depending on the size and complexity of the overall application, he or she may also be responsible for the server application. In larger, more complex, applications, the server application may be handled by a database analyst. The programmer should have experience in the development of Graphical User Interfaces (GUIs), as well as knowledge of the design tools to be used. Knowledge of SQL and database management systems would also be required. The programmer should have a basic understanding of Local Area Networks (LANs), gateways, and data communications. While an in-depth knowledge of these areas is not required, a general knowledge of these areas is useful and can be beneficial in diagnosing system problems.

Database Analyst

A database analyst or database administrator may be required on complex applications or on applications that access existing databases on host platforms. The database analyst responsibilities could include:

- Design and implementation of new databases
- Development of new server database applications
- Testing

- Documentation
- Database maintenance and administration

Most host database systems require an administrator to support and maintain them. LAN and midrange database administration is often accomplished by the LAN administrator or system manager. On smaller, less complex, projects, these functions are often accomplished by the programmer. The skills required by the database analyst would include knowledge of the particular database system, knowledge of database design, and an understanding of SQL. For follow-on support, the database analyst should be able to maintain the database to include security and recovery. Often the skills of the database analyst are particular to one vendor's product such as IBM's DB2.

LAN Specialist

The LAN specialist is required on projects that involve the use of an existing LAN or the installation of a new LAN. The responsibilities of the LAN specialist would include:

- Design of new LAN systems
- Review of existing LAN systems
- Capacity planning/analysis
- Installation of LAN hardware
- Installation of LAN software
- Configuration of file servers/workstation
- Documentation
- Training
- On-going support and maintenance

These functions may be accomplished by technical staff from the central IS function or by appropriately qualified departmental IS staff. Several vendor certifications such as Novell's Certified NetWare Engineer or CNE program are generally recognized professional credentials. The skills required by the LAN specialist would include knowledge of LAN design and installation, knowledge of networking topologies and protocols, and knowledge of PC and LAN hardware. The LAN specialist should be capable of installing network operating systems as well as network applications software. Knowledge of network communications equipment such as bridges, routers, and gateways may be required on larger networks or on Wide Area Networks (WANs). Depending on the size and complexity of the data communications system, some of these functions may fall under the responsibility of the data communications specialist. As with the database analyst, most training and certification programs are vendor specific.

Data Communications Specialist

The data communications specialist is responsible for designing and implementing any required communications links between physically separated client/server platforms. The responsibilities of the data communications specialist would include:

- Design of new communications systems
- Review of existing communications systems
- Capacity planning/analysis
- Installation of communications hardware
- Installation of communications software
- Configuration of host gateways
- Documentation
- On-going support and maintenance

The functions of the data communications specialist are generally performed by the central IS staff, since they usually encompass enterprisewide communications. In smaller organizations, these functions may be performed by the LAN specialist. The data communications specialist should have knowledge of data communications principles, knowledge of data communications hardware, and familiarity with the specific hardware and protocols used by the organization. An understanding of Local Area Networks is useful, particularly in situations where LANs are interconnected or connected to corporate platforms. While the skills of the data communications specialist are generally more generic than those of the LAN specialist, they still may be somewhat vendor specific.

User Representative

Often overlooked, the user representative is a key member of the project team. His or her responsibilities include:

- Development of systems requirements and specifications
- Development of user procedures

- Testing of the application
- Implementation of the application
- Training

The user representative acts as the liaison between the project team and the end users. He or she protects the interests of the user department and ensures that the system meets its needs. With applications that span several functional areas in the organization, there may be one or more user representatives from each functional area. As was mentioned earlier, the user representatives are crucial to achieving consensus on system requirements. The end-user representatives can be very useful in gaining acceptance for a client/server project and can help to overcome organizational resistance to change. They play a major role in the definition of system requirements. The user representatives should be skilled in their particular area of expertise. This is important to ensure the required functionality is identified during system design. Knowledge of automated systems is not required but would be useful. Experience in systems design and analysis is desirable. The user representative is often well suited to conduct end-user training. He or she has knowledge of the functional area as well as knowledge of the design and function of the new system. Additionally, the user representative may have a closer rapport with the end users in his or her department.

These are examples of some of the members of a project team and their functions. Again, depending on the scope and size of the project, it may be necessary to have additional members on the team. If the project is large and encompasses many areas of the organization, the use of focus groups may be beneficial. Focus groups are often used to develop systems requirements. The focus groups are given the task of defining requirements for a specific functional area. For example, in a project to implement a financial system, separate focus groups could be used to define the requirements for accounts payable, accounts receivable, and general ledger. The members of the group would be selected for their expertise in each functional area. The focus groups would be primarily involved in the requirements definition and would not be part of the overall project team. This reduces the time commitment for the members of the focus groups but still provides for input from a broad group during requirements definition. Additionally, the core project team is kept to a manageable size. If required, the focus groups can be recalled later in the project.

Sponsorship

A key factor in the success of any project, particularly a client/server implementation, is the degree of support the project has from upper management. This support is necessary to obtain the resources required for the project. These resources include such things as funding, equipment, and staff time. The problem is somewhat simplified if the project is limited to just one department or functional area. As the scope of a project expands and it crosses organizational boundaries, the need for management support increases. In highly centralized organizations, sponsorship is somewhat easier to obtain and often comes in the form of a directive from higher management. In today's business environment, however, most organizations are highly decentralized and individual business units function autonomously. The goals of decentralization and enterprise computing are often at odds with each other. In this type of situation, the need for broad management support is crucial. Obtaining this support is dependent on how the overall organization manages IS projects. Two common approaches are the steering committee and the executive committee.

The Steering Committee

The Steering Committee approach utilizes a standing committee of top managers who review and approve all IS projects. Requests for major IS projects are generated by the user departments or by the IS department. The committee then reviews and approves the requests. Depending on the degree of decentralization in the organization, the role of the Steering Committee can range from full authority to review, approve, and fund, to simply reviewing projects for compatibility with corporate IS standards and strategic direction. In highly centralized organizations, the Steering Committee would have the authority to approve or deny a project. Approval by the Steering Committee would serve as approval to utilize needed resources in the organization. In a decentralized organization, the Steering Committee would not have the same degree of control as in the centralized organization. The role of the Steering Committee in this situation would be to approve the project under a set of very broad guidelines such as a statement of strategic direction for the organization. This allows for the flexibility desired in decentralized organizations, while providing some common direction and standardization for information systems. Often the requesting department is responsible for providing funding and other required resources. Since approval in a decentralized organization does not carry the force of law that it does in a centralized organization, it is often necessary to coordinate needed support with other departments within the organization. For instance, if division X were implementing a system that required data from divisions Y and Z, it would need to request that support directly from those divisions. Approval from the Steering Committee would simply validate that the project was in line with the overall strategic direction of the organization.

The Executive Committee

Another approach is that of the Executive Committee. The Executive Committee is similar to the Steering Committee; however, it is not a standing committee and is formed as required by each project. This approach is somewhat more flexible in that the committee can be formed with only those top mangers who would be directly involved in the particular project. For example, the Executive Committee for a personnel/payroll system may only involve the Chief Financial Officer, the Chief of Human Resources, and the Chief Information Officer. There are some disadvantages to this approach in that unless the overall strategic direction of the organization is well known, the Executive Committee may act in its own interest and not in keeping with the desired strategic direction of the firm. The Executive Committee provides management approval in that the top management of all involved business units are on the committee.

Given that approval for the project has been obtained in some fashion from the appropriate body, it is important that this approval be communicated to those who will be working on the project. This can be accomplished via a letter or memo to the heads of the affected divisions explaining the charter and scope of the project along with a request for a commitment of resources. Often this is a request for staff resources for a project team or focus group. An estimate of the time commitment and project duration should be included. The letter should come from the Steering Committee or the Executive Committee that approved the project. In addition to the letter to the department head, a letter directly to the affected individuals is often useful. Sample letters are included at the end of this appendix. Plan to send the letters well in advance to allow for schedules to be changed if necessary. Often the success or failure of a project is determined before it even starts by how well it is planned and how well it is staffed.

User Groups

Another type of group that may be useful in the implementation of a client/server application is a user group. User groups are usually formed after a system has been implemented; however, it can be helpful to plan for the establishment of a user group as part of the implementation project. The function of user groups varies widely from informal information sharing to formal systems review and recommendation of system changes. Many software vendors have user groups that vote on system enhancements and help set product direction. Depending on the scope of the client/server project, a user group could be a very effective means to increase end user knowledge, obtain feedback on the operation of the system, and increase the rapport between users and developers.

Sample Letter to Department Head

```
                    XYZ Corporation
                Corporate Headquarters
                  10 West Main Street
                Los Angeles, CA 90212


December 10, 1992


Mr. John Smith, Director
XYZ Corporation, Widget Division
1212 East 5th Street
Palo Alto, CA 94065


Dear John:

As you may be aware, the Information Systems Steering
Committee has recently approved a project to design a
corporate-wide inventory management system. We believe that
this system will result in overall cost savings for the entire
organization as well as provide each division with a means to
quickly locate parts in other divisions rather than buying
them on the open market.

Since this project involves every manufacturing division, we
are asking for your support in this effort. The project team
has identified two people in your division, Jim Clark in
Inventory Control and Sue Jones in Data Systems, as key
members of the project team. We estimate the time commitment
for Jim and Sue to be four hours per week for the next four
months. After that time, the project will be reviewed, and we
will contact you regarding the implementation of the system.
We appreciate your support.



John Williams, Chairman
Information Systems Steering Committee
```

Sample Letter to Project Team Member

```
                        XYZ Corporation
                     Corporate Headquarters
                       10 West Main Street
                     Los Angeles, CA 90212

December 10, 1992


Ms. Sue Jones, Systems Analyst
XYZ Corporation, Widget Division
1212 East 5th Street
Palo Alto, CA 94065


Dear Sue:


The Information Systems Steering Committee has recently
approved a project to design a corporate-wide inventory
management system. We believe that this system will result in
overall cost savings for the entire organization as well as
provide each division with a means to quickly locate parts in
other divisions rather than buying them on the open market.

You have been identified as a key member of the project team.
A letter has been set to the director of your division
requesting your support. We estimate the time commitment to be
four hours per week for the next four months. You will be
contacted regarding your role in the project and to schedule
the first meeting of the project team.



William Carpenter, Project Manager
```

B

Training for Client/Server

Given that there is currently a shortage of trained and experienced client/server applications developers, most firms are faced with two alternatives: hire new staff or retrain existing staff. If your organization is growing and in a position to hire experienced programmers and pay them what the market demands, your problems may be solved. In most situations, however, this is not the case. Many IS departments are heavily staffed with "legacy" programmers and are faced with user departments demanding the latest technology. Training and retraining will be a major task of IS departments in the coming years. Should you just send everyone off to the first class that comes up and hope for the best? A bit of prior planning can help to ensure that your investment in training is maximized. Before sending your programmers off to school, there are a few basic questions to be considered.

What Skills Are Needed?

To answer this question, the firm must first make some decisions regarding its choice of client/server products. Many client/server products require vendor-specific training. Decisions about what types of operating systems, applications development tools, and databases will be used must be made before the training issue is addressed. If you plan to utilize OS/2 on client workstations, it makes little sense to spend time and money on Windows training. While some of the knowledge may be transferable, the best use of both financial and human resources would be to train the staff in the specific products they will be using. Additionally, various levels of training are often available. Listed below are specific training needs for each of the project team functions identified in Appendix A.

Project Manager

As stated in Appendix A, an in-depth knowledge of client/server technology is not required by the project manager; however, generalized training in the following areas is desirable:

- The architecture of client/server computing
- Graphical User Interfaces (Windows, OS/2)
- Use of client applications development tools (vendor specific)
- Server databases (vendor specific)
- Local Area Networks
- Project management

Programmer/Programmer-Analyst

The programmer/programmer-analyst will most likely require the most technical training or retraining of any member of the project team. The skills and training required by other members of the group have not been impacted as greatly by the introduction of client/server computing as those of the programmer. Specific training needs for the programmer include:

- The architecture of client/server computing
- Client operating systems (vendor specific, i.e., DOS, OS/2, UNIX, Windows NT)
- Graphical User Interfaces (vendor specific, i.e., Windows, OS/2)
- Client applications development tools or languages (vendor specific, i.e., EASEL, Mozart, Presentation Manager, C, Visual BASIC)

- Structured Query Language (as required by the specific applications development tools or languages used)
- Server databases (vendor specific, i.e., Gupta, ORACLE, DB2, Sybase, OS/2 Database Manager)
- Local Area Networks (basic principles)
- Data communications (basic principles)

Database Analyst

Depending on the database management systems already used by the organization, the database analyst may only require minimal additional training. If the functions of the database analyst are to be performed by the programmer, these training requirements should be added to those previously listed for the programmer. Specific training needs for the database analyst include:

- The architecture of client/server computing
- Server operating systems (vendor specific, i.e., OS/2, Novell, UNIX, Windows NT, MVS)
- Server databases (vendor specific, i.e., Gupta, ORACLE, DB2, Sybase, OS/2 Database Manager)
- Database design tools (vendor specific, i.e., Gupta, ORACLE, DB2, Sybase, OS/2 Database Manager)
- Structured Query Language (as required by the specific applications development tools or languages used)
- Database administration and security (vendor specific, i.e., Gupta, ORACLE, DB2, Sybase, OS/2 Database Manager)

LAN Specialist

The LAN specialist will in most situations not require any additional specialized skills for a client/server project above and beyond those normally required for this position. As was previously mentioned, there are several industry recognized training and certification programs for LAN specialists. Basic training needs for the LAN specialist include:

- Client operating systems (vendor specific, i.e., DOS, OS/2, UNIX, Windows NT)

- Network operating systems (vendor specific, i.e., Novell, Banyan, IBM, Microsoft)
- Client hardware installation and support (vendor specific)
- Server hardware installation and support (vendor specific)
- Local Area Networks (design and installation)
- Data communications (to include LAN-to-LAN connectivity)

Data Communications Specialist

As with the LAN specialist, the data communications specialist will in most situations not require any additional specialized skills for a client/server project above and beyond those normally required for this position. If the functions of the data communications specialist are to be performed by the LAN specialist, these training requirements should be added to those previously listed for the LAN specialist. Basic training needs for the data communications specialist include:

- Data communications (to include LAN-to-LAN and LAN-to-host connectivity)
- Network operating systems (vendor specific, i.e., Novell, Banyan, IBM, Microsoft)
- Communications hardware installation and support (vendor specific)

User Representative/End Users

While the user representative and the end users in general may not require any technical training at the initiation of the project, they will in all likelihood require some degree of training when the new system is implemented. Issues of how much training, how it is to be provided, and by whom should be resolved early in the project. Areas of training for end users should include:

- Introduction and basic operation of PCs/workstations (vendor specific based on hardware platform)
- Graphical User Interfaces and how to use them (vendor specific, i.e., Windows, OS/2)
- How to use a Local Area Network (basic user instruction, vendor specific, i.e., Novell, Banyan, IBM, Microsoft)
- Client applications software (application specific)

- Reporting tools (if required will be specific to the reporting tools used with the server database)

How to Obtain Training

The second major question is, how to accomplish the training. Should training be provided by the software vendor, by self-study, or by a third party? What other options are available and how will training impact the overall move to client/server? Let us look at each of these questions in more detail.

Training can be accomplished by a number of methods. Several potential sources include:

Vendor Training

The vendors of specific software products often offer training programs to their customers. These training programs can range from simple, end-user training to in-depth application development training. Depending on the vendor, these programs may be included with the purchase of a product, say a database management system, or may be available for an additional charge. Vendor training tends to be very comprehensive; however, travel costs and class scheduling may be considerations.

Third-Party Training Courses

As the demand for training has increased, there has been growth in the third-party training market. These firms provide training on general topics, such as client/server computing, as well as specific technical training on particular database products or application development tools. Often, third-party training is more readily available than vendor training but may be more expensive. Given that the training is provided by someone other than the vendor, it may be wise to ask for references and check with firms that have used a particular program in order to verify the quality of the program. If you have a large number of employees to be trained, it may be cost effective to arrange for on-site training. Shop around for a program that meets your needs and budget.

Courses Offered by Public/Private Educational Institutions

Many educational institutions are now offering courses that include client/server topics. Some even offer courses on vendor-specific products such as database management systems and programming languages. These courses can be part of a degree program or, as in the case of many institutions, part of extension services that offer continuing education programs. Generally, these courses are less expensive than other training methods; however, it may be difficult to find courses on specific products. Additionally, it may be difficult to find a mix of courses that meet your overall training needs. One advantage to this type of training is that it may help individual employees obtain a formal degree or certification.

In-House/Self-Study

While in-house training can be tailored to meet the specific needs of the organization, it can be very expensive. Trainers must be trained and courses prepared. This approach is often reserved for only larger organizations that may have on-going training needs. Self-study is another option; however, it may yield mixed results. Many video training programs are now available that provide flexible, low-cost training while still maintaining the structure and completeness of vendor courses.

Training Options

There are a number of ways to accomplish the training of staff. One approach is to train everyone at once. While this completes the task in a relatively short period of time, it may be expensive and may adversely affect on-going operations. Another approach is to schedule training for selected groups of employees until all are trained. One caution for both approaches is that once an employee is trained, he or she should be allowed an opportunity to practice his or her skills. The longer the break between training and the time the skills are used, the less effective the training. If a project is planned, try to have training completed immediately before the project begins.

Projects completed by outside consultants also offer training opportunities for your existing staff. Combined with the training sources listed above, experience on a project that utilizes outside consultants can be a low-risk means to gain expertise in client/server. Other options include training a "core" group of programmers who can later be used to spread their expertise to other programmers in the organization.

Training should be viewed as an important element of any client/server project. Until the mix of required skills becomes more common in the work force, training and retraining of existing staff will be an important factor in any organization's move to client/server computing.

Client/Server Product Summary

Note: The following pages contain brief summaries of various client/server products. Several of these products and vendors were mentioned in the text. This information is provided for the convenience of the reader and is not an endorsement or recommendation of any specific vendors or products. Product information was provided by individual vendors and was adapted from the *Microsoft Client/Server Applications Catalog.* The accuracy of this information cannot be guaranteed; please contact individual vendors for specific information. All trademarks and tradenames are the property of their respective owners.

Database Servers

ASK Computer Systems
Ingres Products Division
1080 Marine Village Parkway
Alameda, CA 94501

INGRES Tools for DOS, along with INGRES Server for OS/2, is a modular system that works together to form a powerful, integrated SQL database development environment for LAN Manager networks. Users benefit from enhanced productivity and flexibility through the use of full-function, nonprocedural fourth generation language (4GL), visual programming, application portability, and network transparency.

The INGRES Server takes full advantage of OS/2's multitasking capabilities for lower overhead and greater performance. In benchmark tests, the INGRES Server delivers the best price/performance of any major server on the market.

Gupta Technologies, Inc.
1040 Marsh Road
Menlo Park, CA 94025

SQLBase Server, a NetBIOS LAN-compatible SQL database server for DOS and OS/2 is optimized for graphical applications, OLTP, and decision support. Its standard automatic crash recovery, password protection, on-line backup, remote monitoring, and diagnostic tools duplicate features found on minicomputers and mainframes at a fraction of the cost. Multiple users can simultaneously perform data entry, browse between PC front-end applications and multiple sets of data records, and do background reporting at any time while data is being updated. Front ends for SQLBase Server include SQL Windows, SQR, Access SQL, C, COBOL, Clipper, DBXL/SQL, Forest & Trees, JAM, Objectview, PC Nomad, Quicksilver/SQL, R&R Reportwriter, SQLVision (for Lotus 1-2-3 and MS Excel), Superbase, VP-Expert, and many others.

IBM
Old Orchard Road
Armonk, NY 10504

Database Manager provides a full-function relational database manager based on the same relational data model found in IBM host computer database products: IBM Database 2 (DB2) and IBM Structured Query Language/Data System (SQL/DS). Database Manager is also consistent with the SAA specification in its support of the SQL Database Interface and the Query Common Programming Interface.

Database Manager makes extensive use of IBM database technology to provide database consistency, integrity, and optimized performance. It uses the IBM SQL to define and update tables, perform data entry and edit tasks, and retrieve information from the database. Database Manager includes facilities to create, maintain, and back up databases, update information, review existing data, print reports, reorganize tables, and generate statistics. Database Manager also provides extensive application programming support. Database Manager consists of three parts: Database Services, Query Manager, and Remote Data Services.

Informix Software, Inc.
4100 Bohannon Drive
Menlo Park, CA 94025

Informix-SQL is a relational database management system that provides the tools required for sophisticated applications building. Based upon SQL, the Structured Query Language, Informix-SQL offers users a powerful and flexible data management environment. It includes a complete SQL-based query language, a menu creation facility, a relational report writer, and an easy-to-use forms module.

Microsoft Corporation
One Microsoft Way
Redmond, WA 98052-6399

Microsoft SQL Server is the Sybase high-performance, multi-user relational database management system for PC-based LANs. It is designed to support high-volume transaction processing as well as decision-support applications.

SQL Server employs advanced software technology that gives it reliability, performance, and data processing capabilities equal to or better than those found in production-oriented minicomputer or mainframe database management systems.

Microsoft SQL Server runs on OS/2, using a client/server architecture to support DOS, Windows, and OS/2 client applications. SQL Server is also part of an extended product family, which includes compatible versions from Sybase for UNIX and VMS platforms.

Many popular third-party software products support SQL Server today. SQL Server is supported by Microsoft LAN Manager, IBM LAN Server, Novell NetWare and other LANs that support the named pipes protocol.

Novell Inc.
6034 W. Courtyard Drive, Suite 220
Austin, TX 78760

Btrieve is a key indexed file management system for use with most programming languages. It allows file structure with record lengths up to 64KB, 24 different keys/files, maximum key size of 255 bytes and maximum file size of over 4 billion bytes. There is no limit to the number of files open at one time and segmented, duplicate, null, and modifiable keys are allowed.

Ontologic Inc.
Three Burlington Woods
Burlington, MA 01803

Ontos DB is a complete object-oriented database system. It includes a transparent interface to C++, which activates objects into memory as needed.

Oracle
500 Oracle Parkway
Redwood Shores, CA 94065

ORACLE relational database management software includes development tools and decision-support tools for the PC. It includes ORACLE RDMBS, SQL*Plus, SQL*Forms, SQL*Report, SQL*-Calc, & Pro*C. It allows developers to create large PC applications that can be ported to other environments or seamlessly connected to ORACLE running on other PCs connected over a LAN.

XDB Systems, Inc.
14700 Sweitzer Lane
Laurel, MD 20707

XDB-Server for OS/2 is an SQL database server that brings IBM's mainframe DB2 power and integrity to your LAN. XDB-Server is 100 percent DB2 compatible.

Document/Image Management Applications

Cirrus Technologies
8965 Gilford Road, Suite 210
Columbia, MD 21046

The Unite application combines the latest technology for image and data storage, manipulation, and retrieval with a state-of-the-art graphics interface. Functionality allows users to scan, view, index, store, retrieve, fax, and print document images. Designed to run on Microsoft LAN Manager and other local area networks, Unite immediately benefits an end-user organization by providing increased speed for file retrieval, simultaneous access to files by multiple users, reduced storage space, and overall improvement of document management.

Fulcrum Technologies Inc.
785 Carling Avenue
Ottawa KIS 5H4 Canada

Ful/Text Software Developer's Kit (SDK) allows C program developers to access over 250 C library routines for building proprietary text information retrieval applications.

Ful/ft is a complete full-text retrieval package for corporate users. Both products feature full client/server architecture, excellent performance, and complete portability across all major computer platforms.

GeneSys Data Technologies, Inc.
11350 McCormick Road
Executive Plaza 111, Suite 1300
Hunt Valley, MD 21031

ImageFind Network System is a cost-effective way to replace traditional paper documents with electronically scanned images. It provides customers a more efficient and affordable means of storing and retrieving information over a PC LAN-based network.

C02 Network System is a cost-effective way to replace computer hard copy, printer backup tape, or COM systems. It provides a means for storing and retrieving page-formatted computer output. Scanned paper capability can easily be added to provide both COM and replacement and scanned images on one system.

The C02 system can be enhanced with a workflow option that provides intelligent document routing and management.

Imara Research Corp.
111 Peter Street, Suite 804
Toronto, Ontario M 5V 2H1, Canada

IMARA provides businesses with a computerized alternative to paper-based document management. Primarily a workgroup product, IMARA enables network users to store, share, and retrieve information using familiar filing cabinet structure.

With IMARA, businesses can dramatically increase their productivity by streamlining their paper flow, eliminating misfiled documents, and improving communication. IMARA is intuitive and easy to use, yet flexible and adaptable to the needs of all corporate offices. The power and efficiency of IMARA results in significant cost savings. IMARA is the first image and information processing system for personal computer workgroups to blend the most powerful elements of OS/2, Presentation Manager, LAN Manager, and SQL databases with today's most widely accepted image processing standards. IMARA is designed for paper-intensive industries such as financial, insurance, commercial, and government.

Kofax Image Products
3 Jenner Street
Irvine, CA 92718

The Kofax Image Processing Platform (KIPP) is a comprehensive set of hardware and software that serves as a platform for the development of PC-based document image processing systems. KIPP provides high-level imaging libraries, development tools, demo programs, and sample applications that, when used in conjunction with a DBMS, allow the developer to design imaging systems or add imaging into existing hardware systems or software applications. SQL Server can be used with KIPP to provide the DBMS functions in a target document storage and retrieval system. KIPP consists of KF-9200 Document Processor, KF-9100 Document Retrieval Engine, and Software Developer's Toolkit.

Saros Corporation
10900 N.E. 8th Street
Suite 700
Bellevue, WA 98004

FileShare 2.0 is a Microsoft Windows or DOS "front end" for the Mezzanine system. It is a file-management application that uses the services and facilities of the Mezzanine platform.

Mezzanine 2.0 is a network server "back-end" software system. It resides on servers in the network and is a set of integrated services and facilities that provide secure network-transparent file cataloging, management, and access control for both stand-alone and group applications on single and multiserver LANs. It runs on OS/2 servers on LAN Manager or Novell NetWare LANs. The SQL Server database engine is embedded in the Saros engine.

Valinor
239 Littleton Road
Westford, MA 01886

Imaginetworking integrates image and data on a LAN using SQL Server as the database engine. Valinor's integration techniques allow for multiple inputs, networkwide access, and multiple outputs. Using industry standards, the Imaginetworking system accepts scanned and faxed images. Text images are optionally converted to document format while graphical images are stored on network optical media. The heart of the system is a Microsoft SQL Server engine that maintains information about images on the network. Access to any image on the network is driven through this central database. Once identified, the image can be easily directed to a variety of output devices, including network facsimiles, printers, and both high- and low-resolution monitors.

ViewStar Corporation
5820 Shellmound Street
Emeryville, CA 94608

ViewStar Release 2.3 is a network-based software system for document management/workflow processing which facilitates the automation of paper-intensive business functions within large corporations. It processes/manipulates image, text, and other format documents over local and wide area networks, including functions for document capture, storage, management, display, annotation, editing, routing, distribution, and output. It also provides an advanced application development toolkit with an object-oriented programming language for customization/extension of the system to address customer-specific application needs.

Gateway and Communications Products

Attachmate Corporation
13231 S.E. 36th Street
Bellevue, WA 98006

EXTRA! for Windows is high-function, 3270 connectivity software written as a Microsoft Windows application. It is compatible with all major IBM interfaces, for PC/AT and PS/2. EXTRA! supports coax, LAN, and token-ring connections. It offers the fastest file transfer speeds available and includes support for PS/CICS Import/Export and Send/Receive (IND$FILE) file transfer protocols. It also provides complete printer emulation (LU3 and LU1) and will support up to 26 mainframe sessions.

EXTRA! Extended for DOS is high-function, memory-efficient, 3270 connectivity software compatible with all major IBM interfaces, for PC/AT and PS/2. It supports coax, LAN, and token-ring connections. It can support expanded memory specification (LIM 4.0 EMS) and provides many powerful features including simultaneous foreground and background file transfers, concurrent use of up to four mainframe sessions and a DOS session, windowing, keyboard record-playback macros, and an IBM-compatible Applications Program Interface.

EXTRA! Entry-Level provides essential 3270 functions plus IBM-compatible interfaces for coax or LAN connections. It provides a single session link to the mainframe through coax or LAN connections. It also supports IBM standard Send/Receive (IND$FILE) file transfer and provides IBM-compatible 3270 PC API and HLLAPI.

3270 Gateway Option is a high-function, flexible LAN-mainframe link that supports LAN workstations running Attachmate or IBM PC/3270 connectivity software. It lets you take your choice of connections, including SDLC modem links, coax-DFT, and even IBM's high-speed Token Ring Interface Coupler (TIC). Plus, it supports up to 128 SNA logical units and allows you to pool sessions or assign users to dedicated sessions.

Capella Systems, Inc.
8601 Dunwoody Place, #632
Atlanta, GA 30350

Capella's new family of products, SmartScreen and SmartScreen Open, features color icons and an improved functional layout, simultaneous access to multiple PROFS and OV/VM functions, automatic processing, and file transfer capabilities (including PC-to-PC file transfer). The SmartScreen product family was designed to increase user productivity and decrease training and support costs. SmartScreen Open's HostView function lengthens the life of DOS emulation investments by providing a Windows interface to existing emulation independent of your communication environment.

Cross Communications Co.
1881 9th Street, Suite 212
Boulder, CO 80302-5151

LAN+MODEM is the leading modem sharing software available. It is a software-only solution allowing users to share as many as 20 modems located anywhere on Novell or NetBIOS LAN, across LAN bridges, or via multiport PC hardware cards. LAN+MODEM saves memory and dollars—memory requirements are less than 10KB and price is 10 percent of a comparable hardware solution. LAN+MODEM has its own easy-to-use built-in communications package and is compatible with many popular communications packages such as FutureSoft Dynacomm, DataStorm-Procomm, DCA CrossTalk, cc:Mail, and all other systems that support an interrupt 14 interface. Future versions of LAN+MODEM will be enhanced to provide for automatic modem queuing, more file transfer capabilities, higher modem speed support, a Windows interface, and support for a wide range of multiport hardware cards.

DCA
1000 Alderman Drive
Alpharetta, GA 30202

DCA/Microsoft Select Communications Workstation (Select CW) is OS/2 Workstation software for host-connected applications including LU6.2 and 3270 terminal emulation. It supports Token Ring, DFT Coax, SDLC, and X.25 connections.

DCA/Microsoft Select Communications Server (Select CS) is client/server software for distributed host-connected applications of LAN manager with 3270 emulation and APPC, LU6.2 support. Hardware connections supported are Token Ring, DFT Coax, SDLC, and X.25. It is an OS/2-based server supporting OS/2 and DOS clients with Windows compatibility.

Eicon Technology
2196 32nd Avenue
Montreal, Quebec H8T 3H7
Canada

Eicon Technology provides advanced communications solutions for micro-to-mainframe, micro-to-mini, and LAN-to-LAN connectivity. All software is NetBIOS compatible and operates with the EiconCard, an intelligent communication card for the IBM PC and PS/2. 3270 Access for Windows is a 3270 emulation package for Windows. Third Party Emulation Support (ITI) for Windows allows users to access ASCII hosts over X.25 networks transparently under Windows.

IBM
Old Orchard Road
Armonk, NY 10504

Communications Manager is a component of IBM OS/2 Extended Edition, and it manages the information exchange between workstations and between workstations and host computers and includes interfaces for network communications. Connections between workstations and a wide range of systems, from IBM and non-IBM mainframes to personal computers, are supported.

Communications Manager supports multiple, concurrent communications options in various combinations. These options eliminate the need to start and stop programs when communicating with different systems.

Communications Manager offers extensive support to both the users of network communications and programmers who want to write or customize applications.

Communications Manager includes systems management functions for the network management of workstations, as well as tools to gather traces, dumps, errors, and messages locally.

Features of Communications Manager are:

- Terminal emulation:
  - 3270 terminal emulation (including file transfer support) 3270 host-directed print
  - 5250 Work Station Feature
  - ASCII (IBM 3101 and DEC**VT100**) terminal emulation (including file transfer support)
- Asynchronous communication support
- SNA gateway
- System/370 Graphical Data Display Manager (GDDM)
- Support for the following network configurations:
  - IBM Token-Ring Network
  - IBM PC Network* (broadband and baseband)
  - Synchronous Data Link Control (SDLC) connection
  - SNA and non-SNA communication over an X.25 connection
  - Utilization of an ETHERAND* Network

Micro Decisionware
2995 Wilderness Place
Boulder, CO 80301

Database Gateway allows PC applications using Microsoft SQL Server APIs to access DB2 databases through the same interface those applications use to access SQL Server databases. Both corporate-developed clients and vendor-developed clients such as Microsoft Excel, DataEase, and others gain transparent access to DB2 under MVS/CICS using APPC/LU 6.2, the SAA peer-to-peer communications method. Database Gateway can be used in a variety of configurations: as an OS/2 stand-alone client without a LAN; as a gateway for multiple clients on the LAN, to provide concurrent and independent access to SQL Server and DB2; or to enable direct data transfer between SQL Server and DB2. It includes both DOS and OS/2 versions.

PC/SQL-link is a data access and transfer tool that provides expert assistance to PC users for accessing data stored in a variety of relational databases including Microsoft SQL Server, IBM

DB2, SQL/DS, and others. By providing nontechnical end users with a common interface to centralized data, PC/SQL-link enhances the use of databases as decision-support tools. Character based DOS or Windows users can use PC/SQL-link to easily locate relational data and prepare SQL statements, without having to know SQL, to extract or update information. Data extracted from these databases is automatically reformatted for use with popular PC applications. PC files can also be uploaded to the host database.

MicroTempus, Inc.
800 South Street, 2nd Floor
Waltham, MA 02154

Enterprise Router: a NetBIOS NCB/SMB router that connects multiple LANs via an IBM mainframe in a completely transparent manner. The first general-purpose, mainframe-based internetwork router that creates a virtual LAN using your existing SNA network. The Enterprise Router eliminates the need to install expensive, redundant network equipment bridges and routers in order to interconnect LANs as well as coax-connected PCs.

Tempus-Share: NetBIOS and SMB-compatible file server implemented under MVS/VTAM. It uses DOS-compatible disk technology on the host. It provides an extremely powerful facility that allows end users to easily and simply access virtual disks on the mainframe as well as archive data to the mainframe using standard PC commands. At the same time, MIS can manage the creation of virtual disks, often on a production basis, while also retaining appropriate security and administrative control.

Tempus-Link: Mainframe-based virtual disk software issues commands directly from DOS without ever being aware of the mainframe as anything more than aPC disk drive.

Tempus-Transfer: supports the transfer of files from VSAM, TEMPUS-LINK, and TEMPUS-SHARE virtual disks to the PC. It has extensive field manipulation facilities, which allow only specific fields to be selected, edited, and converted.

Tempus-Talk: Scripting facility that runs on PCs and offers dialog management, reads commands from a user-driven script, then uses those commands to drive a 3270 or asynchronous terminal session. In most cases the user is required to press only one key to begin the conversation.

Peer Engine: provides a consistent meta-API (Peer API) over the 40 communications protocols that MicroTempus supports. It is the underlying technology in most MicroTempus products. Comprised of a set of software modules on both the PC and mainframe, Peer Engine enables one or more PC applications to initiate and control communications with one or more host sub-routines.

XcelleNet, Inc.
1800 Century Blvd.
Suite 700
Atlanta, GA 30345

XcelleNet Wide-Area Network Management System is a comprehensive, graphics-based wide-area network and management system. Using one 386-based PC and our network controller software, the system allows normal users to configure, administer, and manage networks of thousands of PCs. It features automatic communications execution, bidirectional transmissions, advanced data compression, multiple telco carrier support, error detection and correction, checkpoint interruption transmissions, and SQL database support.

Workgroup Applications

AT&T
One Speedwell Ave., North Tower
Marstown, NJ 07962-1921

RHAPSODY is a business solution that enhances the way people work together. Work inputs and outputs easily flow from person to person, group to group, company to company—enabling you to orchestrate all aspects of your business. Fully integrated desktop capabilities support work, communications, and information access on both an individual and group basis.

Its client/server operating environment includes a full range of the industry's leading MS-DOS applications. It also features full local area network functionality via AT&T's StarGROUP Software LAN Manager Server.

Coordination Technology, Inc.
35 Corporate Drive
Trumbull, CT 06611

TOGETHER creates a graphical workplace on networked PCs where people, organize their work to become more productive, interact with others to foster innovation, and manage their work so goals are achieved sooner without anything falling through the cracks. With a strong object orientation, TOGETHER encapsulates applications (e.g., Microsoft Word and Excel, WordPerfect, and user-defined applications), enabling users to leverage their existing skills and training. A graphic office metaphor enables users to manipulate objects easily across time and places. Users actually execute work within this robust environment, aided by work status notification, task management, and more.

Lotus Development Corporation
55 Cambridge Parkway
Cambridge, MA 02142

Lotus Notes is a group communication product for people who need to create and access shared information on networked personal computers.

NCR Corp.
1700 S. Patterson Boulevard
Stakeholder Relations Division W1405
Dayton, OH 43479

Cooperation is an enterprisewide, integrated environment that integrates users, applications, information, and networks to dramatically improve the productivity and effectiveness of users and applications developers. It is designed to provide new levels of integration for the entire enterprise by connecting islands of information and allowing information systems users to efficiently utilize information and application resources.

Three concepts underlie the design of Cooperation: object-oriented technology, client/server architecture, and open systems.

Vertical Applications

Desktop Data Inc.
1601 Trapelo Road
Waltham, MA 02154

NewsEDGE/LAN delivers real-time news information from as many as eight different news providers to network clients in Windows or DOS character-based user interfaces. Users set up their own interest profiles based upon keywords and phrases. As stories are received, users are alerted to the ones that match their specific interests. A full database of all the news stories is maintained on the news server for later searching. NewsEDGE/LAN requires a dedicated 386- or 486-class PC with 16MB RAM and 150MB hard disk running OS/2 version 1.1 or 1.2. NewsEDGE/LAN clients require a 286- or 386-class PC running DOS 3.1 or higher with 1MB RAM and 3MB free hard disk space.

Dynix Marquis, Inc.
151 E. 1700 South
Provo, UT 84608

Marquis Dynix is a complete "library automation package." It includes modules for cataloging circulation and an on-line public-access catalog. The system is designed using library standards and procedures. Dynix is designed around client/server architecture and a GUI. The database engine is SQL Server running under OS/2 on an 80386 computer. The workstations use OS/2 Presentation Manager for their user interface. LAN Manager completes the client/server architecture by interconnecting the workstations and the server.

International Financial Tech.
1933 Landings Drive
Mountain View, CA 94043

The INFINITY SQL System is comprised of client/server applications for front-to-back office transaction processing of fixed-income securities, including derivative products for interest rate, commodity, and equity-based instruments. These modular applications come with broad analytical and reporting capabilities for

Dealer Support, Risk Management, and Operations. Central to the system is Montage, INFINITY'S SQL relational model, which houses bonds, options, swaps, futures, and other derivative instruments. Lotus 1-2-3 and Microsoft Excel spreadsheets, as well as in-house C or COBOL software programs, directly access the database as client applications.

INFINITY client applications are available in a variety of GUIs: Microsoft Windows, OS/2 PM, and X11/Motif. The System can be networked over any TCP/IP- or NetBIOS-compatible LAN. Source code is C, C++, and SQL, ensuring portability across hardware environments, as well as several relational database engines: Sybase, Microsoft SQL Server, Ingres, ORACLE, SQLBase, Informix, Teredata, and DB2.

MIDAK International, Inc.
6303 E. Tangue Verde
Suite 100
Tucson, AZ 85715

IMACS: MIDAK has combined automated carousels, bar code technology, knitting matrices, and the SQL Server-based Inventory Management and Control System software (INMCS) to automate the stock rooms of Fortune 500 companies. IMACS incorporates real-time communication with a host computer and monitors each part as it moves through the system. Parts are inducted into IMACS and put away onto automated carousel or manual shelving devices. Work orders are generated for the parts and issue requests are sent to individual work locations for the parts to be picked. Issued parts are sent to the kitting station for collection and final distribution.

PC Quote
401 South La Salle, Suite 1600
Chicago, IL 60605

QuoteLan provides real-time financial market quotations and related information on North American stocks, options, and commodities, maintained by a network quote server and accessible on sophisticated workstation displays. Transmission speeds to quote server are: 19,200 bps (via satellite or land line) and 56,000 bps HyperFeed(sm). Market news is available from Dow Jones News/Retrieval, Capital Markets Report, Scrolling and Interactive News, and Comtex OmniNews. It is compatible with Basket

Maker, Theoretical Value Option Page, and other PC Quote decision-support tools. It supports third party portfolio management.

PeopleSoft
1600 S. Main Street
Walnut Creek, CA 94596

The following PeopleSoft applications will soon fully exploit the client/server architecture using SQL Server. PeopleSoft also supports IBM's DB2 using available gateway software and will support other databases as gateways become available. The applications comply with IBM's Systems Application Architecture (SAA). CUA is provided by PC workstations running Microsoft Windows and/or OS/2. The applications were developed in People-Tools, PeopleSoft's fifth-generation application development environment.

PeopleSoft HRMS is an integrated human resources, payroll, and benefits application software package. It supports employee benefits administration, compensation, career development, EEO/AAP, employee and union relations, payroll and tax processing, position control, recruitment, and training administration.

PeopleSoft Payroll is a business application software package that supports all facets of payroll processing and management. It supports both U.S. and Canadian payroll processing, including time reporting; table-driven earnings, deductions, benefits, and tax definitions; payroll calculations; check printing; payroll and tax reporting; unlimited history; direct deposits; and general ledger interface.

PeopleSoft Benefits is a complete benefits application software package. It supports administration for such benefit plans as health and welfare, life and disability insurance, savings and investment, retirement, flexible benefits, COBRA, and sick and vacation leave plans.

Terminal Applications Group
495 Central Park Avenue
Scarsdale, NY 10583

TAG Star Alpha System is a complete distribution and financial system that handles all aspects of wholesale distribution aspects. It runs under SQL Server. It includes sales order and quotation entry, invoicing, pricing, inventory management and purchasing, and all general accounting. Features include: SAA-style pull-down menus and screens; context sensitive, active Help; multicompany/division/branch/warehouse; pop-up windows; add-on selling and promotional product prompts in sales order entry; credit and collection tracking system; "codeless" access; bar code capability; commission system; "Gordon Graham" inventory management; bin/lot number control, serial number tracking; purchasing library; systemwide context-sensitive notes; unlimited expandability (branches, warehouses, keywords, etc.); and it is migratible/scalable for OS/2, UNIX, and DEC VAX. It is user friendly yet comprehensive.

Accounting Applications

Advanced Business Microsystems, Inc.
15615 Alton Parkway, Suite 300
Irvine, CA 92718

The Platinum Series, manufactured by Advanced Business Micro-systems, Inc., is the most powerful accounting and management information software ever developed for microcomputers. Whether your business is large or small, highly specialized, or diversified across a broad range of activities, the Platinum accounting series offers you a wholly integrated solution for now and for the future. Platinum is a complete management information system (MIS), which handles all your bookkeeping, managerial accounting, and information resource management needs.

Macola Inc.
333 E. Center Street
Marion, OH 43302

Macola software consists of a modular, yet fully integrated ac-counting/distribution system with vertical links to manufacturing, retail, sales management, shipping, and professional services. PC-based, Macola can be run as a single user system or on a multi-user LAN. Macola's feature-rich and easy-to-use system will provide a financial management and reporting system for virtu-ally any size business.

Timberline Software Corp.
9405 S.W. Gemini
Beaverton, OR 97005

Timberline markets a wide line of OS/2- and LAN-compatible modules for Accounts Payable, General Ledger, and report writ-ing.

4th Generation Languages/Databases

Ashton-Tate Corporation
20101 Hamilton Avenue
Torrance, CA 90502

dBASE IV Server Edition brings the power of dBASE IV to the client/server environment. It includes all the capabilities of dBASE IV, as well as allowing dBASE IV to operate as a client to remote database servers.

dBASE IV Server Edition, in combination with the Microsoft SQL Server, provides an attractive solution for database workgroup computing—a solution that combines the power and flexibility of dBASE IV with the advanced relational power of database server technology.

dBASE IV is an ideal client for a variety of reasons, including its comprehensive SQL implementation, a high level of application portability, and its highly productive development environment.

Borland International
1800 Green Hills Road
Scotts Valley, CA 95067

Paradox is the complete database for all your information management needs. As the leader in database technology, Paradox now extends its ease and sophistication to access SQL data. Paradox with Paradox SQL Link makes the perfect front end to SQL data. Paradox provides an unmatched combination of interactive user support, powerful programming capabilities through the Paradox Application Language (PAL), and support for a variety of SQL servers. For querying, Paradox's industry standard QBE is the perfect complement to SQL data. Users get the high performance of optimized queries on database servers, with the intuitive, familiar access that Paradox QBE provides. In addition, all the functionality of Paradox is available to manipulate, query, report, or graph SQL data. Use Paradox's menu-driven, table-level operations (create, data, entry, copy, delete, empty, rename) on remote SQL data. PAL is a complete application development language. It provides a powerful development environment to build applications based on local and remote data. With Paradox, PAL and SQL have been integrated so that any SQL statement may be embedded within a PAL program. In addition, PAL variables can be included within SQL statements to be evaluated before the SQL is passed to the server. Programmers can also use PAL to open cursors on the SQL table for record-oriented operations.

DataEase International, Inc.
7 Cambridge Drive
Trumbull, CT 06611

DataEase SQL is the front-end application development system for SQL database engines in the client/server environment. DataEase SQL provides rapid application development capabilities, distributed database support, transparent access to data, easy migration from file server environments, and application scalability across platforms, combined with the performance, integrity, and connectivity of SQL Server. DataEase SQL automatically translates all DataEase functions, including sophisticated 4GL procedures, into SQL that is optimized for SQL Server. DataEase functions requiring no programming include single form updating of multiple tables, single key viewing of records in related tables, and QBE reporting. DataEase SQL uses the following LAN Manager APIs: print destination, print job, print queue, user, and workstation. It includes both DOS and OS/2 versions.

DataWiz International
1291 E. Hillsdale Boulevard
Suite 210
Foster City, CA 94404

dBSQL is a dBASE/SQL Server software interface that allows any program written in dBASE (dBASE III PLUS, Foxbase, Fox Pro, DBXL, and QUICKSILVER) to send SQL statements to SQL Server, get the results from SQL Server, and insert them into predefined memory variables (one row at a time). dBSQL uses the DB-Library provided with each copy of SQL Server.

dBSQL-IV is a dBASE IV/SQL Server software interface that allows any program written in dBASE IV to embed SQL statements that can be executed on SQL Server, get the results from SQL Server, and insert them into predefined memory variables (one row at a time). dBSQL-IV uses the DB-Library provided with each copy of SQL Server.

dBSQL-C is a Clipper/SQL Server software interface that allows any program written in Clipper (Summer '87 and Version 5.0) to send statements to SQL Server, get the results from SQL Server, and insert them into predefined memory variables (one row at a time). dBSQL-C uses the DB-Library provided with each copy of SQL Server.

Information Builders
1250 Broadway
New York, NY 10001

PC/FOCUS for OS/2 is a 4GL and DBMS that fully supports SQL Server. It includes a full set of application development tools, including a report writer, window builder, financial reporting, graphics statistics, and forms builder. Applications written in PC/FOCUS are directly portable to other Focus platforms. The product supports DOS and OS/2 and will use LAN Manager Net-BIOS and named pipes APIs. The PC/FOCUS database server runs and executes on the LAN Manager server, which acts as a traffic cop for database transaction.

PC/FOCUS PLUS for DOS provides features similar to PC/FO-CUS for OS/2, but it is a DOS extender product running on 286 and 386 machines.

mdbs-KG Software Division
Two Executive Drive
P.O. Box 5268
Lafayette, IN 47093

Guru is a high-productivity 4GL programming environment that offers a wide variety of information processing tools, all integrated in one program. Features such as an RDBMS, inference engine, business graphics, text processing, report generation, communications, a natural-language interface, and more can be accessed at any time within Guru. It is fully compatible with SQL and supports direct interface to SQL Server. Guru is available for single user, multiuser, and LANs on DOS, OS/2, VAX VMS, and Sun OS4 systems.

KnowledgeMan/2 is a high-productivity 4GL programming environment that offers a wide variety of information processing tools, all integrated into one program. Features such as an RDBMS, spreadsheet, business graphics, text processing, report generation, communications, a natural-language interface, and more can be accessed at any time within KnowledgeMan/2. It is fully compatible with SQL, can be used with Guru, and supports a direct interface to SQL Server in both the DOS and OS/2 environments. KnowledgeMan/2 is available for single user, multiuser, and LANs on DOS, OS/2, VAXVMS, and Sun OS4 systems.

MUST Software International
101 Merritt 7
4th Floor
Norwalk, CT 06856

NOMAD version 3.0 for PC-DOS and OS/2 is an application development product for applications accessing SQL Server in a multiuser LAN environment. In a single environment, NOMAD provides a robust report writer, full nonprocedural and procedural language facilities, a window user interface, and a suite of CUA-compliant tools for applications developers. NOMAD 3.0 incorporates several SQL capabilities including CREATE-VIEW and SQL SELECT for joining and accessing multiple SQL Server tables as well as GRANT, REVOKE, and SET transactions for the multiuser environment. A run-time version of NOMAD is available for cost-effective distribution of multiuser NOMAD applications, and support is provided for English, French, German, Italian, Spanish, and Dutch languages.

Nantucket
12555 W. Jefferson Boulevard
Los Angeles, CA 90066

Clipper 5.0 is an application development system for PCs. It includes user-extensible command and function sets, a preprocessor, replaceable database driver, compiler, linker, and utilities. Client/server requirements are met through Nantucket's Database Driver Series for Clipper, used to supplement or replace Clipper's stock DBF file driver. The series will include a driver for SQL Server, and the technology will permit concurrent use of multiple database drivers within a single Clipper application.

The Database Driver Series for Clipper: SQL Server offers Clipper programmers a method for accessing SQL Server databases from Clipper applications. Only minor changes of syntax are required to execute SQL-stored procedures. For higher performance,

SQL statements can be embedded directly into Clipper code, or SQL statements can contain Clipper variables, functions, and user-defined functions. Clipper developers will be able to include SQL data access in their applications without having to learn a new technology.

Revelation Technologies, Inc.
2 Park Avenue
Suite 2300
New York, NY 10016

Advanced Revelation delivers to developers a complete application development environment for DOS and OS/2 workstations, one which enables the rapid development of mission-critical applications, especially those that operate cooperatively with existing mainframe, minicomputer, or PC-based information system investments.

Advanced Revelation facilitates the prototyping, design, implementation, and maintenance of applications by providing essential tools such as an application generator, an ANSI SQL-compatible programmer's toolkit, and an active data dictionary, used for centralizing an application's intelligence and business rules. Environmental Bonding, exclusive to Advanced Revelation, enables the development of applications independent of data format or location, without the need for cumbersome links, bridges, or interfaces, permitting the same application to operate single user, multiuser, or cooperatively with intelligent database servers. Combined with the MS-SQL Server Bond, Advanced Revelation becomes an ideal environment for developing applications that work cooperatively with Microsoft SQL Server.

Wordtech Systems, Inc.
P.O. Box 1747
Orinda, CA 94563

Arago dBXL is a dBASE IV-compatible database manager with full support for SQL Server. Arago dBXL is fully compatible with dBASE IV commands and programs, data, report, label, and other files. It can use data either from dBASE DBF files or from SQL Server. SQL Server transactions can be controlled using either the dBASE language (in Invisible SQL mode) or Embedded SQL in dBASE. It features a CUA-compliant user interface with full mouse support and many language extensions, including commands for creating applications using panels, dialog boxes, and pushbuttons. An easy-to-use menu system allows beginners to add, delete, and modify data and define and run reports and labels without having to learn dBASE or SQL commands.

Arago Quicksilver is a compiler for dBASE IV and Arago dBXL applications. It supports the dBASE IV programming language with the Arago dBXL extensions (including Invisible SQL and Embedded SQL extensions for interacting with SQL Server). Arago Quicksilver compiles dBASE source code into independently executable files that may be distributed without run-time fees. A dynamic memory management system creates overlays automatically, and compiled C and assembly routines can be linked into the final executable file.

Case and Development Tools

American Digital Technologies, Inc.
23041 Avenida De La Carlota
Suite 210
Laguna Hills, CA 92653-1503

ADT's Forms Data Dictionary (FDD) for Sybase APT and SQL Server uses Microsoft SQL Server or Sybase SQL Server to build a database of Sybase APT Workbench forms and report procedures. Programs are written in C and Transact-SQL. Source code is available.

Automated Design Systems, Inc.
375 Northridge Road, Suite 270
Atlanta, GA 30350

The Windows Workstation SQL Server Library for SQL Windows provides a transparent interface between Gupta's SQL Windows and Microsoft SQL Server so that applications written in SQL Windows, or that use Gupta's Dynamic Link Libraries, will run on SQL Server with little or no modification. It also allows complete SQL Server security to be available to all SQL Windows applications.

Bigtec
P.0. Box 13242
Reading, PA 19612-3242

DE DE is the database front end that makes it easy to create or change definitions of SQL Server objects (entities). Carefully designed features allow your staff to build the database entities efficiently. With DE DE's development environment, the process of retrieving, editing, adding, and testing entity definitions is simplified. DE DE integrates your editor, SQL Server Utilities, and specially developed features.

DataWiz International
1291 E. Hillsdale Boulevard
Suite 210
Foster City, CA 94404

SQL Server Toolkit for Windows facilitates the development of SQL applications with a GUI. The Toolkit is a library of C source code modules for use in a Windows and SQL Server environment. SQL Server Toolkit for Presentation Manager facilitates the development of SQL applications with a GUI. The Toolkit is a library of C source code modules for use in a Presentation Manager and SQL Server environment.

CAPTURE provides immediate and direct access from PCs to remote data for strategic planning, decision support, and information management. The CAPTURE software system captures existing data out of transaction-processing files and directly loads the data into SQL Server. It enables transparent and efficient data communication between mainframe systems, public-access systems, or other microcomputers, minicomputers, and PCs. Any files that have been transferred by any of the popular communications products or protocols can be used by CAPTURE.

Gupta Technologies, Inc.
1040 Marsh Road
Menlo Park, CA 94025

SQL System Programmer's Toolkit provides a quick and reliable method for C and COBOL programmers to design, prototype, code, and test complete DB2 SQL database applications on the PC, completely independent from the mainframe. Accelerate DB2 application delivery by 30 to 50 percent by freeing up mainframe scheduling and response time dilemmas. Features include Load/Unload, full backup and recovery for existing development databases, and full dynamic link library compatibility. A single user engine for SQLBase and SQL Talk are part of the SQL System Programmer's Toolkit.

JYACC Inc.
116 John Street
New York, NY 10038

JAM is the core of an advanced 4GL application development toolset. JAM includes a screen painter; integrated data dictionary; a user-extensible 4GL; hooks for attaching 3GL function calls; a run-time executive; and utilities for storing forms and procedures in source code control systems, completely documenting the flow and logic of an application. Applications written in JAM are portable without changes or recompilation to hundreds of hardware platforms and ten operating systems. There are no run times or royalties with applications written with JAM.

JAM/DBi is an add-on layered product for JAM applications, which provides seamless portable integration with the most popular relational databases (e.g., ORACLE, Ingres, Sybase, RDB, Progress, Ultrix SQL, OS/2 SQL Server, and many others). JAM/DBi permits JAM applications to interactively access and store data in local and distributed databases by attaching standard SQL to event points in an application. JAM/DBi provides complete support for the native features of databases including those with a client /server architecture. There are no run times with JAM/DBi.

JAM/Presentation interface is an add-on layered product for JAM developers whose applications are GUI-based. JAM applications contain forms that are independent of the presentation type. By using JAM/Presentation interface, developers can instantaneously and/or simultaneously show JAM forms in character or GUI-mode. Support is planned for OSF/Motif, Open Look, Microsoft Windows, and DEC Windows. Support for graphical bit-mapped applications using Regis, GKS, or other graphical toolkits is available now. Support for character and block-mode devices is bundled into the standard JAM product.

JAM/ReportWriter gives JAM developers the ability to link in production-level reports in their applications. These reports can entail highly complex calculations, invoke line item and row level detail, have multiple break levels, and be device independent. Developers "paint" sections of a report using JAM's screen painter. Sections are reusable modules. JAM/ReportWriter currently requires JAM and JAM/DBi.

Jterm is a full-featured terminal emulator that is "JAM smart," allowing PC users to take full advantage of the colors and graphics of a PC while connected to a JAM application running on a host device. It also supports other terminal emulation modes.

Logic Works
601 Ewing Street, Suite B7
Princeton, NJ 08540

ERwin/SQL is a powerful Entity/Relationship (ER) database design tool for SQL database professionals. With ERwin/SQL, you define entities (tables), attributes (columns), and relationships (referential integrity constraints). Then you add physical information to manage indexes and tables for improved database efficiency. ERwin/SQL generates SQL CREATE TABLE and CREATE INDEX statements for your target DBMS.

ERwin/ERX adds import and export capabilities to ERwin/SQL. In addition to all of the ERwin/SQL features, with ERwin/ERX you can import data from external data dictionaries, repositories, and DBMS catalogs using Logic Works' ERX file format.

Microsoft Corporation
One Microsoft Way
Redmond, WA 98052-6399

Now everything you need for serious BASIC programming comes in one package: new language additions for developing business applications; extensive support for creating large-scale programs and smaller, faster executables; plus a complete set of powerful tools that allow you to create front-end applications to SQL server. Microsoft BASIC Professional Development System: It's the complete solution for professional programmers.

Now it's easy to create fast, powerful database applications. Microsoft Professional ISAM supports advanced features such as transaction processing, a data dictionary, and combined indexes. You can handle data retrieval and manipulation directly from BASIC source code. And several utilities are included to perform tasks such as converting other database files (including dBASE, Btrieve, and earlier Microsoft ISAM files) to the correct format.

And, of course, Microsoft BASIC is still the only BASIC product that supports DOS (MS-DOS or PC-DOS operating system) and OS/2 systems, letting you create both protected-mode and real-mode BASIC programs.

It's never been easier to integrate personal computers into your corporate computing environment than now with the Microsoft COBOL Professional Development System. A complete, integrated environment, Microsoft COBOL provides all the tools you need to code, edit, compile, debug, cross-reference, and execute powerful COBOL applications on a PC. You can write Presentation Manager and client/server SQL applications using the extensions we've added to the COBOL language. Access SQL through embedded SQL statements or call-level support for SQL APIs.

An important new addition to Microsoft COBOL is the Microsoft Programmer's WorkBench. Ideal for mixed-language programming, it contains an editor, a compiler, source browsing facilities, a project management utility, and Online Help, all in one place. A new, improved run-time system to reduce EXE size is included, as well as a utility for easy screen painting. Naturally, Microsoft COBOL is ANSI 85 certified and compatible with all major COBOL dialects.

Netwise, Inc.
2477 55th Street
Boulder, CO 80301

NETWISE: System for OS/2 and LAN Manager, a Client/Server Application Integration System. It enables development of client/server applications, providing Remote Procedure Call (RPC) technology for developers to use in creating client/server applications on OS/2, MS Windows, and approximately 30 other platforms including DOS, UNIX, VMS, and IBM mainframes. By using these tools in conjunction with versions for SNA and TCP/IP networks, applications developers can create information gateways to integrate mainframes, UNIX servers, and desktop systems into a single information network.

Nevis Technologies
300 Corporate Pointe
Culver City, CA 90230

Nevisys is a networked PC application platform and authoring environment that uses the functions of SQL Server. It is designed around a client/server architecture and supports OS/2 version 1.2, LAN Manager version 2.0, and Windows. The basic application platform is horizontal in design with full office automation functionality. Microsoft Excel and Word for Windows, Samna's Ami Professional Aldus PageMaker, Micrografx Designer, and other applications can be authored into the application-launch facility environment with data flow being facilitated by the DDE interprocess communications facility. The authoring toolkit is a single Presentation Manager application for access to numerous editors. This set of tools allows for development, modification, or deletion of applications without the requirement for programming. Available with the basic platform is a "proof-of-concept" application layer that addresses the functional requirements of retail banking.

Popkin Software & Systems, Inc.
11 Park Place, 19th Floor
New York, NY 10007

System Architect is a CASE tool supporting Yourdon/DeMarco, Gane/Sarson, and Ward-Mellor (real-time) methodologies. It also allows users to do structure charts and entity relationship modeling.

SA-SQL-VIEW converts the System Architect Data Dictionary/Encyclopedia to SQL Server format and permits SQL to view a design interactively.

Solutions by Design, Inc.
7 Partridgeberry
Hamilton, MA 01982

Designers Visual SQL is an object-oriented program that enables SQL relational database users to create visual representations of standard SQL queries. SQL queries are performed visually through a representation schema that consists of icons, pull-down menus, and point-and-click boxes. Designers Visual SQL acts as a front-end query tool supplying a baseline set of object-oriented classes for the X-Window System, Microsoft Windows, and OS/2 Presentation Manager. The product supports the Windows environment and OS/2 version 1.1 and is compatible with Microsoft Networks. The product's database administrative facility and SQL interfaces reside and execute on the LAN Manager server; it acts as an SQL front-end user interface for SQL Server.

Strategic Technologies Group
P.O. Box 32464
Richmond, VA 23294

SQL Commander for Windows is a front-end utility to SQL Server for querying and administering SQL Server databases. It implements SQL Server's interactive Transact-SQL command set, allowing users to interactively create, query, edit, secure, and import/export SQL Server databases without using SQL command syntax. End-user, database-administrator, and developer functions are grouped accordingly in pull-down menus so that each user's workstation can be customized for any subset of SQL functions.

Vinzant, Inc.
4 Skyline Drive
Portlage, IN 46368

SQL BASIC Library allows users to write programs that can access data stored in SQL Server using the Microsoft BASIC Compiler. It includes library files and sample programs.

SQLFILE System is an application development system that lets users easily create application screens and reports that can access SQL Server. It includes a sample application and easy-to-follow instructions; it also has an easy-to-use utility for editing data. Both DOS and OS/2 versions are available.

Windows and Presentation Manager Development Systems

Blyth Software
1065 Hillsdale Boulevard
Suite 300
Foster City, CA 94404

OMNIS 5 is an application development tool that enables developers to create a GUI front end for a SQL database that is completely portable between Macintosh and IBM PC compatible computers. It seamlessly connects to one or more databases running on Microsoft SQL Server by creating SQL scripts that are transmitted via an OMNIS 5 driver. OMNIS 5 gives corporate developers their choice of development platforms on which to create an application (Macintosh, Microsoft Windows, or OS/2).

EASEL Corporation
25 Corporate Drive
Burlington, MA 01803

EASEL/2 (EASEL for OS/2) and EASEL/WIN (EASEL) provide developers with powerful features for creating graphically oriented cooperative processing applications. These features include support for SQL Server, the APPC protocol, and DDE.

EASEL provides direct support for creating OS/2 Presentation Manager client applications that take advantage of SQL Server. Developers can manipulate a SQL Server database by issuing dynamic SQL statements from within their EASEL/2 applications. EASEL/2 creates the query statements, formats the data returned by the server, and also manages error handling.

ENFIN Software Corporation
6920 Miramar Road, Suite 307
San Diego, CA 92121

ENFIN/2 introduces a new generation of development tools for OS/2 and other platforms. ENFIN/2 extends the proven concept of 4GL development systems through its integrated object-oriented

4GL development environment. The following main functions are supported by ENFIN/2:

An intuitive Graphical User Interface Management System: supports CUA objects and Workplace Model with pick, drag, and drop functionality and is available for the rapid development of SAA graphical user interfaces.

4GL Tools: an interactive SQL Editor, a Database Create and Data Entry Facility, a graphical Report Generator, and an Object-Oriented Information Pool.

A Modeling Facility: with an Interactive model editor—allows the creation of financial or general-purpose mathematical models.

LU 6.2 APPC Support: Applications can be developed to communicate with other programs.

Object-Oriented Development Environment: includes a rich set of reusable classes, class browser, inspector, profiler, interactive debugger, and more. Dynamic Link Libraries (DLL) and Dynamic Data Exchange (DDE) are fully supported. ENFIN/2 will interface to AD/Cycle in the near future.

GUIdance Technologies, Inc.
800 Vinial Street
Pittsburgh, PA 15212

Choreographer is an object-oriented application development environment that makes the creation of highly graphical user interfaces easy in OS/2 Presentation Manager. A SQL class library included with the product provides full connectivity from within the Choreographer application to a SQL Server database across a network. Other connectivity options include an API that enables other applications to call Choreographer, the ability to call any application in a DLL, local communications via DDE, and mainframe communications via 3270 or 5250 terminal protocols.

Gupta Technologies, Inc.
1040 Marsh Road
Menlo Park, CA 94025

SQL Windows, for professional developers and entry-level programmers, is used to develop graphical SQL database applications that run under Microsoft Windows and OS/2 Presentation Manager without using C or the Microsoft Windows Toolkit (SDK). Its point and click, object-oriented programming and SAL (SQL Windows Application Language—a fourth generation language) help accelerate product development, while industry-standard SQL provides access to SQL database servers running on PCs, PC LANs, minicomputers, and mainframes, including Gupta's SQLBase Server, Microsoft's SQL Server, DB2, ORACLE and OS2/EE. SQL Windows comes with Express Windows, a powerful application generator; Report Windows; a graphical report writer, and a single user version of SQLBase engine.

Intelligent Environments
2 Highwood Drive
Tewksbury, MA 01876

AM (Applications Manager) is a high-level, full life-cycle application development tool designed for OS/2 applications. AM is targeted at business applications in the OS/2 Presentation Manager environment with extensive support for database and mainframe connectivity. AM supports APPC through LU 6.2 and includes IBM EHLLAPI 3270 terminal emulation, DDE, and C APIs. Programmers' tools include a dynamic data dictionary, an outliner for structured program listings, and a graphical flow chart of the program logic. AM's SQL Server facility supports the complete SQL language as well as features such as stored procedures, command batches, and the ability to handle multiple concurrent users. AM is a well-designed OS/2 Presentation Manager application development environment with rich connectivity tools.

Matesys
900 Larkspur Landing Circle
Suite 175
Larkspur, CA 94939

ObjectView helps design Windows applications for Microsoft SQL Server. With ObjectView, users can design attractive screens, forms, and reports without writing a line of code. ObjectView's outstanding benefit is that it allows straightforward development of Windows-based SQL applications by providing high-level tools for interactive interface design such as icons, pull-down menus, and tables.

mdbs-Client/Server Division
Two Executive Drive
P.O. Box 248
Lafayette, IN 47902

Object/1 is an object-oriented environment for graphical applications. Available for OS/2 Presentation Manager and MS-DOS with Windows, Object/1I allows immediate creation of GUIs through its Forms Painter. Additional tools include browsers, a debugger, an inspector, and a multiuser relational DBMS.

Professional Pack for SQL Server is a series of class libraries written in Object/1 that abstract DB-Library calls. This companion product to Object/1I and SQL Server provides an object-oriented approach to data manipulation and reduces by more than 40 percent the amount of code necessary to interact with SQL Server. It is especially effective in accessing and manipulating bit-mapped images and large text items in SQL Server. Source code is provided.

Multi Soft, Inc.
123 Franklin Corner Road, Suite 207
Lawrenceville, NJ 08648-2526

Infront from Multi Soft supports the development of PC-based front ends that run in front of host applications. These front ends, developed without making any changes to host code, allow an application user to work with state-of-the-art, PC-based interface instead of awkward, difficult-to-use interface commonly implemented in mainframe programs.

For the developer, Infront offers an easily learned development environment that is tightly integrated. The developer employs a point and click interface to capture host screen images; convert those images into modern, PC forms; define editing logic for each field; and link forms together to build a front-end processing application.

Neuron Data
444 High Street
Palo Alto, CA 94301

NEXPERT OBJECT, a standard expert system shell for commercial and industrial integration, offers a software bridge between

NEXPERT and Microsoft SQL Server. With this bridge, applications developers can dynamically map SQL Server records into NEXPERT's object structure. NEXPERT provides applications developers with the ability to build expert systems that can access, manipulate, and update live database information. NEXPERT features a GUI; a flexible and powerful reasoning model; an AI library of callable routines; an API that allows for easy integration with other programming languages and programs; and support for all major computing platforms, including OS/2, DOS, Macintosh, UNIX workstations, Digital VAX computers, and mainframes.

Powersoft Corporation
70 Blanchard Road
Burlington, MA 01803

PowerBuilder provides a graphical development environment for creating the next generation of applications. Designed and built initially for the Microsoft Windows or OS/2 Presentation Manager (PM) environments, PowerBuilder is the toolset of choice for organizations that are building industrial-strength, business-oriented applications employing a client/server architecture with a graphic user interface (GUI) client environment coupled with a server-based relational (SQL) database manager.

PowerBuilder has been designed to support several relational database management systems. Version 1.0 of PowerBuilder supports Microsoft SQL Server, Sybase from Sybase Corporation, and SQLBase from Gupta Technologies, Inc. Additional database support is planned for subsequent releases.

Precision Software, Inc.
8404 Sterling Street
Irving, TX 75063

Superbase 4 provides a rich Windows development environment for client applications using SQL Server. Superbase 4 users can incorporate embedded SQL statements in Superbase programs and forms using specialized connectivity software to interact with SQL Server databases. SQL statements can be constructed using any method available in Superbase. Pushbuttons, menus, and other controls can be used to trigger actions and determine user choices. Superbase also provides the ability to select items such as tables and columns from list dialogs. Experienced SQL users can enter SQL statements as text. Once constructed, SQL statements are executed via DDE or DLL.

Superbase 4 SQL applications can easily be set up to select rows of data from a SQL Server database for display or other local processing. The full SQL command set is supported, making SQL insert, delete, and update commands as easy to implement as select statements. Superbase 4 supports embedded SQL syntax, including bind variables, allowing Superbase programmers maximum flexibility when designing applications.

Software Publishing Corp.
1901 Landings Drive Road
Mountain View, CA 94043-7210

InfoAlliance is a forms-based front end to SQL and dBASE data that transparently integrates multiple data sources (SQL Server, OS/2 DBM, and DB2) to generate client/server LAN applications and reports. Capabilities include scanner-assisted forms creation, full field and record validation, data import/export, transaction commit control and rollback, point and click applications generation, WYSIWYG, and security.

Viewpoint Systems
1900 S. Norfolk, Suite 310
San Mateo, CA 94403

Viewpoint is a visual design tool for creating graphical user interfaces for host-based applications and LAN-based and local SQL servers. Using a "point and click" development approach, interfaces can be created in a fraction of the time and cost of traditional programming. Viewpoint's powerful features allow the developer to easily integrate data from multiple host applications, multiple databases including SQL Server, and from PC-based applications through DDE. Viewpoint supports the development of client applications for SQL Server under Windows and Presentation Manager. Developers can execute any SQL statement from within their Viewpoint application and access the results of that statement.

XcelleNet, Inc.
5 Concourse Parkway
Suite 200
Atlanta, GA 30328

The X/Forms option extends the OS/2-based Xcellenet Network Manager. This graphical communications manager lets a central MIS site configure and monitor automated data collection from hundreds of PCs linked through dial-up lines. Users who gather prepared files from branch office, warehouse, or point-of-sale PCs will be able to design forms for on-screen reporting by inexperienced personnel at the remote sites. The Xcellenet system distributes these forms to remote Windows PCs and posts inbound data to the central database, automating traditional paper report procedures.

Xcellenet users will be able to reach out and collect more than files. The editor running under OS/2 Presentation Manager provides a toolbox for building forms with text, graphics, and bit-mapped images. It also defines database field types for standard input, custom masks, text with editing capability, nested windows, and file lookups.

The forms server runs under OS/2 with Xcellenet Network Manager and ships data from remote nodes to Microsoft SQL Server or flat file databases created with the forms editor. Databases may run on the same OS/2 system or LAN-connected servers.

XDB Systems, Inc.
14700 Sweitzer Lane
Laurel, MD 20707

With XDB-Windows, C developers can write Windows applications utilizing XDB's powerful Windows-based SQL database engine. The SQL database engine runs as a Windows task. The engine supports DDE. Access to the engine can be made directly from an application DLL. Also included is a Windows-based redirector that allows Windows front-end applications to utilize XDB's powerful LAN-based SQL database servers. Along with a C API, a C precompiler is also included so that programmers may take advantage of embedded SQL.

Spreadsheets and Decision-Support Systems

Channel Computing
53 Main Street
New Market, NH 03857

Forest & Trees utilizes graphical user interface (GUI), local area network (LAN), and client/server technologies to provide revolutionary end-user capabilities for data access. It is currently available for MS-DOS, MS-Windows, and HP New Wave–based workstations. Forest & Trees runs on most major network operating systems including Novell NetWare, Microsoft LAN Manager, IBM LAN Server, IBM PC Net, and Banyan Vines networks. Also, it can access data in Lotus 1-2-3 and Excel spreadsheets; dBASE, Paradox, R:Base, DataEase, ASCII, and Btrieve files (including the Great Plains and Platinum accounting system); and Microsoft/Sybase SQL Server, Gupta SQLBase, ORACLE, and IBM AS/400 SQL database servers.

Forest & Trees is an ideal component of employee or executive information systems, valuable for financial applications, and strategic in operations management. Forest & Trees capitalizes on existing investments in information technology and data resources, providing a cost-effective and timely solution to users who need more timely and accurate electronic information.

Digital Composition Systems
1715 W. Northern Avenue, #201
Phoenix, AZ 85201

dbPUBLISHER/SQL is a WYSIWYG report writer and desktop publisher for personal computer workstations. It is used to design and publish high-quality typeset documents directly from information stored in SQL databases. Report-generation technology coupled with the Microsoft Windows environment make designing complicated documents a simple task. Users are not required to know SQL to make use of the advanced features and functions that dbPUBLISHER/SQL provides. However, users with a knowledge of SQL can incorporate SQL statements directly into the design of a document for unlimited flexibility and control.

Lotus Development Corporation
55 Cambridge Parkway
Cambridge, MA 02142

The Lotus DataLens Driver for SQL Server is designed to connect 1-2-3 Release 3.0 and 1-2-3/G to SQL Server databases. An add-in product called Lotus @SQL is designed to connect 1-2-3 Releases 2.01 and 2.2. Using familiar 1-2-3 commands, these products enable 1-2-3 users to perform a wide variety of database management and reporting tasks directly from within the spreadsheet, such as querying a database, inserting, deleting or updating database records, and creating or deleting database tables.

Microsoft Corporation
One Microsoft Way
Redmond, WA 98052-6399

Microsoft Excel offers the ability to extract data from dBASE, SQL Server, and text files through a fully graphical database tool. Microsoft Excel includes a version of Pioneer Software's Q+E, which allows users to browse, select, sort, search, perform calculations, change values, add or delete records, and more to external databases. A macro installs Q+E commands on the Microsoft Excel data menu, and this macro can be used to drive Q+E's functionality from within Microsoft Excel. The programs use DDE to pass data and commands back and forth.

Q+E provides three ways to retrieve data into Microsoft Excel worksheets: You can use the macro provided to query external databases, using the familiar Microsoft Excel database commands; you can enter SQL statements as formulas; or you can interactively query a database with Q+E itself and hot link the results into your spreadsheet.

Pansophic Systems, Inc.
2400 Cabot Drive
Lisle, IL 60532

EASYTRIEVE PLUS PC is an information retrieval and data management system for both the experienced and inexperienced user. Its English-like command language provides a user with the tools needed to produce comprehensive reports, while enhanced facilities provide the experienced data processor with capabilities to perform complex programming tasks. Users of SQL Server can use EASYTRIEVE PLUS PC for a wide range of reporting, decision support, ad hoc queries, and application development, with no conversion of data necessary.

EASYTRIEVE PLUS PC consists of the same programming language utilized in over 6,000 mainframe shops. It incorporates well-structured syntax, complete Boolean logic, screen development facilities, and customized and ad hoc reporting capabilities. It supports both DOS and OS/2. The Natural Language interface allows transparent access to SQL Server data without any coding. With the SQL Server interface, users of SQL Server can become immediately productive.

Pioneer Software
5540 Centerview Drive
Suite 324
Raleigh, NC 27606

Q+E is a fully graphical database tool that combines the ease and elegance of Microsoft Windows and OS/2 Presentation Manager with the power of relational databases. Q+E's intuitive point and click interface lets you edit your databases as easily as a text editor lets you edit text. You can easily browse, select, sort, search, perform calculations, change values, add or delete records, and more. Q+E also integrates your data with any Windows or Presentation Manager application by supporting industry standards like SQL and DDE, as well as Microsoft Word and Excel. Q+E accesses data stored in dBASE, ASCII text files, and SQL Server.

Software Products International
10240 Sorrento Valley Road
San Diego, CA 92121

Access SQL is a full-featured front end designed to help managers and other decision makers gain access to information quickly and easily, from all authorized sectors of an organization. Features include forms creation, ad hoc query facility, and Report Writer. Data may be entered and retrieved through customized forms or by using a table format. No knowledge of SQL is needed; queries are built using dialog boxes and pushbuttons.

The Microsoft Windows GUI provides intuitive ease of use. With automatic-default forms creation, even new users can access or modify data. Forms creation provides tools for complex applications. Access SQL provides functionality beyond SQL by pulling information from different tables into the same form and allowing changes, additions, or deletions to be committed back into different tables at the same time. The Report Writer and on-screen forms can include fonts and bit-mapped graphics.

SQLSoft
10635 N.E. 38th Place
Building 24, Suite B
Kirkland, WA 98033

SQL SoftLink is a utility for the Windows environment that allows software developers with Windows DDE applications to connect to SQL Server. SQL SoftLink works with most Windows applications that support DDE, including Microsoft Word for Windows, Microsoft Excel for Windows, and Gensoft Software dbFast/Windows, a language compiler with DDE capability.

SQL Solutions
8 New England Executive Park
Burlington, MA 01803

SQR, or Structured Query Report Writer, is an advanced report writing and procedural language tool for SQL databases currently available for Microsoft SQL Server, ORACLE, Ingres, DEC RDB, Sybase, SQLBase, and XDB. SQR combines SQL query definition with print control, formatting, and procedural logic in a single structured paragraph. Features include complete SQL support (select, insert, update, delete, create, drop), interactive query modification, multidimensioned arrays and in-memory table lookup. SQR can also read and write external files, supporting data load/unload and other requirements. Both DOS and OS/2 versions are available.

Easy SQR is a user's report writer with menus, pop-up windows, a full-screen layout editor, and on-line help. Easy SQR creates finished reports as well as SQR programs that can be further enhanced. Easy SQR requires no programming or SQL knowledge to create and run reports. Easy SQR is available for Microsoft SQL Server, Sybase SQL Server, and ORACLE.

TELEBIT Software
Corporate Headquarters
1315 Chesapeake Terrace
Sunnyvale, CA 94089

InquirePlus is a new kind of application that allows business professionals to browse and manipulate data from corporate databases to get at the "why" behind current business performance and then formulate the "how" of tomorrow's successes.

An intuitive graphical interface makes asking questions easy. InquirePlus users can specify the general information they want, apply constraints to further refine it, create new information by manipulating existing data, and transfer the results to other Windows applications for presentations, analysis, and executive document generation.

InquirePlus makes accessing and viewing related groups of data easy by working with logical sets of information called "collections." Designed in conjunction with the database administrator, collections provide views of only the pieces of information relevant to a decision-maker's responsibilities.

Network Utilities

Automated Design Systems, Inc.
375 Northridge Road, Suite 270
Atlanta, GA 30350

Windows Workstation is a collection of software utilities for networking with Microsoft Windows and is compatible with LAN Manager. Several features of Windows Workstation include: Print Manager, which manages network or local printers and print queues from within a Windows application; Workstation Meter, which measures total concurrent Windows applications usage; MultiSet, a network scripting language, which provides centralized administration of Windows and applications with any Windows menuing system; and Menu, which allows LAN administrator control in creating/updating group menus and allows users to create personal menus. Windows Workstation is available in ELS or Server Licenses, individual features available separately.

Brightwork Development
766 Shrewbury Avenue
Tinton Falls, NJ 07724

The Automated Help Desk, LAN Support Center is an integrated database system, which tracks your LAN support activity, creates user profiles, and maintains complete inventories of the equipment you support. It automates your help desk(s). It generates trouble tickets for problems as they are reported. With trouble ticket summary reports at your fingertips, you'll always know how your staff is spending time, plus you will have complete profiles of user strengths and weaknesses and equipment inventories. It even tracks your warranties. LAN Support Center provides the information you need to stay aware of user problems and maximize your staff efficiency in solving them.

NETremote+ provides instant access to LAN PCs: You see the screen, control the keyboard, and solve the problem from across the building, the street, or the country. NETremote+ provides dial-in and on-LAN PC control, as well as real-time PC and LAN diagnostics. It also can be used to share modems, fax boards, high performance machines, and CD-ROMS. NETremote+ allows you to support any user, no matter how the user is connected, through a WAN, LAN, or modem, and uses less than 19K of RAM for even complicated graphics. The current version (4.1) now has advanced diagnostics, including the ability to analyze network traffic, determine server connections, view LAN adapters and IPX statistics, and access PC configurations such as programs in memory, type of PC available, version of DOS, and network set-ups—all from a remote PC.

Certus International
13110 Shaker Square
Cleveland, OH 44120

Certus LAN safeguards your LAN environment by providing virus protection, detection, identification, and removal.

Chronos Software, Inc.
555 De Haro Street, Suite 240
San Francisco, CA 94107

Enterprise-Who-What-When is a total management system. It turns your network into an integrated productivity tool. It links personal and office calendars, project schedules, milestones and Gantt charts, card files, phone lists, memos, and messages all with complete security.

Emerald Systems Corp.
12230 World Trade Drive
San Diego, CA 92128

EM SAVE for LAN Manager provides LAN administrators with reliable, centralized backup for OS/2 servers. Network administrators can conveniently manage backup from their own workstations. It provides centralized access to server data so the network environment remains secure and controlled, multiple server backup, and restores and simplifies multiserver network environments. Library Management (EMLIB) combined with ENSAVE delivers the most advanced storage management solution available in the LAN marketplace today.

Fifth Generation
10049 N. Reiger Road
Baton Rouge, LA 70809

DirectAccess Network is a network management menu system that organizes all of your programs and lets you access them instantly with a single keystroke. You can create your own menus or let DirectAccess Network create them for you. It recognizes over 800 popular applications and automatically sets up menus. Supervisors can easily set up custom menus and distribute the menus to one or more users. DirectAccess Network automatically tracks computer and program usage for every user and includes Software Metering to control multiple access to programs. Direct-Access Network is not memory resident.

Fresh Technology Group, Inc.
1478 N. Technology Boulevard
Gilbert, AZ 85234

MODEM Assist is a complete network modem sharing software package, providing access for up to 20 modems for local area network users. With MODEM Assist, users can access any installed modem from any workstation on a LAN. With MODEM Assist, a dedicated communications server and the cost of rerouting all modem phone lines are completely eliminated. MODEM Assist works with multiport serial cards, from a variety of manufacturers, which support up to 16 modems on a single workstation. MODEM Assist requires less than 10KB of memory and runs entirely in the background on the workstation with the modem.

FTP Software, Inc.
26 Princess Street
Wakefield, MA 01880-3004

LANWatch is a sophisticated network analyzer for Ethernet, Token Ring, and StarLAN. It captures and parses packets in real time, showing information about the packet including protocol type and source and destination addresses. Zoom mode shows header fields and packet contents.

PC/TCP provides the link between your PCs and other computers, from minis to supercomputers. You can log-in to a mainframe across a network, transfer files to or from a workstation, back up a hard disk to a tape drive, send files to a remote printer, and exchange mail, all using the industry standard protocol (TCP/IP) for communicating between disparate computer types.

LAN Manager and PC/TCP can run concurrently in your DOS or OS/2 PCs, allowing you to switch seamlessly between network activities. PC/TCP is effectively hardware independent, running on Ethernet, StarLAN, Token Ring, X.25, and SLIP and supports over 40 different network interface cards.

LAN Systems
300 Park Avenue South
New York, NY 10010

LANSpool allows users to attach multiple printers to DOS-based workstations and have them available as shared resources. LANSpool has been implemented using client/server architecture and thus uses only 2.5KB of memory at print server.

Maynard Electronics, Inc.
36 Skyline Drive
Lake Mary, FL 32746

MaynStream provides OS/2 users with the ability to fully back up and recover data in an OS/2 LAN Manager environment. Both menu-driven and command-line OS/2 interfaces are provided to allow use by both the novice as well as the seasoned user. Full backup and recovery of the OS/2 system files and LAN Manager system and ACL information are supported, as well as full unattended capabilities through the MaynStream scheduler, Autoback. MaynStream systems provide capacities of 20MB to 2.2G of storage on a single tape and support multiple drive installations with our SCSI-based MaynStream 525Q, MaynStream 1300DAT, and MaynStream 2200HS systems, providing up to 30.8G of total storage.

MemSoft Corp.
621 N.W. 53rd Street, Suite 240
Boca Raton, FL 33487

POLYMOD2 turns OS/2 into a multiuser system, providing the multitasking power and flexibility of OS/2 to every user through local or remote connections. It allows DOS users to keep and use their existing equipment, as well as their favorite applications, while migrating over to an OS/2 environment. POLYMOD2 supports terminals or terminal emulators attached through serial ports, over a local area network, or any combination of these. Terminals can be ASCII, Macintosh, stand-alone DOS PCs, or DOS LAN workstations.

Network General Corporation
4200 Bohannon Drive
Menlo Park, CA 94025

THE SNIFFER is a LAN Protocol analyzer. It attaches to the network and fully decodes all seven layers of the OSI Reference Model, providing insight to LAN communication protocols, as well asdetermining which one of 11 protocols is presently being used.

Norton Lambert
P.O. Box 4085, 5290 Overpass Road, Bldg. C
Santa Barbara, CA 93140

Named "Editor's Choice" and "Best of 1989" by *PC Magazine*, Close-Up-LAN connects PCs on a LAN or WAN, allowing you to instantly share screens/keyboards with one or more people on your network. It can connect computer offices at any location and share printers, modems, faxes, and computers. It is ideal for teaching, training, and conferencing and lets people work together in real time using any popular application.

Ocean Isle Software
730 14th Street
Vero Beach, FL 32960

Reach-Out is a remote control software for Windows on LAN manager networks. Reach-Out allows a LAN workstation to control, support, or monitor any other Windows workstation on the network in real time. Additionally, file transfer and remote printing capabilities are provided without the need of a file server.

Peer Logic, Inc.
555 Delfaro Street, Suite 300
San Francisco, CA 94107

PIPES Platform is a Communications Management System that adds distributed operating system functionality to existing operating systems. It provides the reliable, symmetrical connections between processes which are the foundation for message-passing architectures. The PIPES Platform kernel handles all of the resource and session management functions required, providing a consistent error-handling mechanism, automatically retrying on errors, and rerouting communications after network failures. The application programmer is presented a consistent logical view of the network, independent of network operating systems, protocols, and media used, with an API of 12 function calls that can be made either synchronously or asynchronously.

PowerCore, Inc.
One Diversatech Drive, P.O. Box 756
Manteno, IL 60950

PowerCore, Inc., publishes the LAN shared calendaring software, Network Scheduler II. It is the de facto standard in Group Scheduling, with over 600,000 current users, and supports both DOS and Windows users. Network Scheduler II is available in single server and Internet versions with support for all major e-mail systems.

ProTools, Inc.
14976 N.W. Greenbrier Parkway
Beaverton, OR 97006

The Protolyzer is a LAN analysis and management tool that is combined with a powerful, graphical user interface that makes it easy to learn and use. Its capabilities go beyond traditional protocol analysis and system monitoring to include simulation, benchmarking, and troubleshooting.

Saber Software Corp.
5944 Luther Lane, Suite 1007
Dallas, TX 75225

Saber Menu Systems for DOS lets you create custom menus for users or groups and uses absolutely no RAM overhead when running applications. Also, it provides its own formatted log-on panel for controlling the log-on process. It includes a variety of application control and menu maintenance utilities. Saber Menu Systems for DOS is fully compatible with Saber Menu Systems for Windows and Saber File Manager.

Saber Menu Systems for Windows is a complete set of tools, which work together with Microsoft Windows and LAN Manager for a successful combination. In addition to the applications menu processor, it also simplifies the Windows installation process for each network node. Running DOS applications from Windows is as easy as running Windows applications from Windows.

Saber File Manager lets you update all user configuration files from one place. It is truly network oriented in that it does not log existing files and uses absolutely no RAM overhead when running applications.

Saber Meter monitors LAN access and usage by user and by application. With each access, the application name, status, server, log-on ID, station, date in/out, and time in/out are automatically recorded.

Saber Secure provides workstation security without application exit or log-off. It combines a screen blanker, a pop-up screen cover with password, forced log-off, and local disk drive disable in one package.

Share Communications, Inc.
1809 7th Avenue, Suite 1000
Seattle, WA 98101

FAXSHARE is a user-friendly integrated fax package designed for LANs. Fax commands are accessed via pull-down menus/pop-up screens. FAXSHARE provides LAN/MAN users complete desktop fax capabilities, including automatic routing of incoming faxes. Offices with heavy fax traffic can choose eight phone lines per fax server. FAXSHARE supports a wide range of fax boards and can run single or multichannel configurations.

Sitback Technologies
9290 Bond #104
Overland Park, KS 66214

SitBack is a memory resident (16KB) software backup utility which makes total and incremental backups in the background. It completely automates backup function for stand-alone PCs, workstations, and file servers. Backups can be activated to take place during computer idle and/or preset times of the day or week. SitBack guarantees file backups are complete and up to date without user involvement. It writes to any DOS storage device, is compatible with LAN Manager, and is also available for Windows.

Sytron Corp.
117 Flanders Road
Westboro, MA 01581

Sytos Plus File Backup Manager is a powerful Presentation Manager file backup and restore utility designed for the LAN Manager environment. Used either as a client- or server-based backup solution, this utility offers easy file selection; flexible retry options for busy files; support for OS/2's High Performance File System (HPFS), including extended attributes and long path names; inclusion of all network security and system files; and the highest data throughput rate on a variety of storage devices, including floppy disk, quarter-inch tape, DAT, and 8mm helical scan.

Sytos uses procedures to store all selections and options about a particular backup or restore operation. Procedures can then be edited, shared, previewed, loaded, or scheduled for unattended automated backups.

Ultinet Development, Inc.
9724 Washington Boulevard
Suite 200
Culver City, CA 90232

PRINT+ configures a DOS network workstation as a true print server. Print jobs are sent directly to the "PRINT+ Server" and are processed and spooled at that local workstation. The file server is completely bypassed with PRINT+.

SPOOL+ runs as a task on your LAN Manager file server and redirects print jobs from the file server to a local DOS or OS/2 network workstation hosting local printers. All print processing, spooling, and queues are maintained on the file server and are administered with LAN Manager print administration. SPOOL+ requires Presentation Manager running on the file server or on the OS/2 workstation.

FILE+ allows users to access hard drives, CD-ROMS, or optical drives attached to local network workstations. The connection is transparent and takes up no memory on the requesting workstations. FILE+ configures your DOS workstations as true peer-to-peer file servers.

DISK+ allows administrators to back up all of their local hard drives from anywhere on the network.

REMOTE ACCESS lets administrators physically take control of a Remote DOS or OS/2 workstation. This product is ideal for user support or tutorials.

Vortex Systems, Inc.
800 Vinial Street
Pittsburgh, PA 15212

The TC376 RetroChron Intelligent Storage Management System provides continuous, fault-tolerant, on-line backup for LANs and multiuser computer environments. "Lost" data is quickly and easily recreated, eliminating the need for daily file-by-file backup to tape.

Mail Systems

cc:Mail, Inc.
2141 Landings Drive
Mountain View, CA 94043

The cc:Mail Post Office Pack is a powerful and easy-to-use electronic mail package for local area networks. It can support a few or hundreds of users using DOS, Macintosh, Windows, and OS/2 workstations. It adds wide area networking connectivity capabilities to LANs by supporting any combination of server-to-server, LAN-to-LAN, and remote PC-to-LAN messaging. cc:Mail also provides connectivity to public e-mail services and facsimile transmission directly with Group 3 fax machines worldwide. This package provides complete support for the Windows environment and is the first cc:Mail offering to be based on the company's third generation messaging architecture.

Consumers Software, Inc.
73 Water Street
7th Floor
Vancouver, B.C. V6B 1A1, Canada

Network Courier is a PC LAN–based electronic mail package that supports mixed LAN environments to provide LAN-to-LAN messaging, remote capabilities, and gateways to anyone, anywhere, on any system.

DaVinci Systems Corp.
P.O. Box 5427
Raleigh, NC 27650

DaVinci eMAIL is an electronic mail program that features pull-down menus and pop-up windows, full mouse support, and a completely context-sensitive help system. Security is top-notch, any number of files can be paperclipped to your eMAIL message, and receivers are notified of incoming messages by a pop-up and a tone.

Retax
2644 30th Street
Santa Monica, CA 90405

Retax Open Server 400 brings standardized enterprisewide communications to PC LAN users. Through the powerful X.400 messaging system, Open Server integrates existing PC LAN e-mail systems with mainframes, minicomputers, and public mail networks into a single, unified mail network. Now you can use your favorite e-mail system to communicate to virtually anyone, anywhere. Open Server extends the reach of your mail system by tying it to other messaging systems as well as public and private mail networks. Open Server runs on a PC and uses the robust X.400 protocols for efficient and reliable transportation of the message.

Suggested Readings

A Guide to Developing Client/Server SQL Applications, Setrah Khoshafian, Arvola Chan, Anna Wong, Harry K. T. Wong, Morgan Kaufman Publishers, Inc., 1992.

Application Development for Distributed Environments, Dawna Travis Dewire, McGraw-Hill, 1993.

APPC: Introduction to LU6.2, Alex Berson, McGraw-Hill, 1990.

Client/Server Application Development, James Martin, Prentice Hall, 1993.

Client/Server Architecture, Alex Berson, McGraw-Hill, 1992.

Client/Server Computing, Dawna Travis Dewire, McGraw-Hill, 1993.

Client/Server Computing, Pat Smith and Mitchell Shutts, Howard W. Sams & Co., 1992.

Developing Client/Server Applications in an Architected Environment, William H. Inmon, QEDInfoSci, 1991.

Distributed Computing Environments, Dan Ceruti, McGraw-Hill, 1993.

Downsizing to Client/Server Architectures, Gary Gagliardi, Four-Gen Software Technologies, Inc., 1992.

Enterprise Computing, Alan R. Simon, Bantam Books, 1992.

Implementing Client/Server Computing: A Strategic Perspective, Bernard H. Boar, McGraw-Hill, 1993.

Introduction to Client/Server Systems: A Practical Guide for Systems Professionals, Paul E. Renaud, John Wiley & Sons, 1993.

Open Client/Server Computing, Martin Butler, Prentice Hall, 1993.

Open Systems Handbook, Tom Wheeler, Bantam Books, 1992.

SAA/LU6.2: Distributed Networks and Applications, J. J. Edmunds, McGraw-Hill, 1993.

Glossary

Advanced Peer-to-Peer Networking (APPN) Data communications support that routes data in a network between two or more APPC systems.

Advanced Program-to-Program Communications (APPC) Data communications support that allows programs on one system to communicate with programs on other systems having compatible communications support. APPC utilizes the SNA LU session type 6.2 protocol.

AIX An IBM UNIX operating system.

American National Standard Code for Information Interchange (ASCII) The code developed by American National Standards Institute for information exchange among data processing systems, data communications systems, and associated equipment.

American National Standards Institute (ANSI) The principal standards development body supported by more than 1,000 trade organizations, professional societies, and companies. This is the U.S.'s member body to ISO (International Standards Organization).

Application Programming Interface (API) A set of interfaces through which application programs can communicate with various types of services. APIs are used primarily in client/server computing to allow applications to interact with each other.

AS/400 IBM midrange computer system.

asynchronous transmission Transmission in which the time of occurrence of the start of each character, or block of characters, is arbitrary. Also known as start–stop transmission.

bps Bits per second.

bridge Hardware and software used to interconnect local area networks.

byte A binary element string functioning as a unit. Eight-bit bytes are most common. Also called a "character."

Carrier Sense Multiple Access with Collision Detection (CSMA/CD) A system used in networks where the interface unit listens for the presence of a carrier before attempting to send and detects the presence of a collision by monitoring for a distorted pulse.

CASE (computer-aided software engineering) Automated tools used to aid in the software development process.

Central Processing Unit (CPU) The main processor used to execute instructions in a computer.

channel-attached Devices that are directly attached to a controlling unit by cables, rather than by telecommunications lines.

cluster controller A device than can control the input/output operations of more than one device connected to it, for example, an IBM 3174.

COBOL (common business-oriented language) A high-level programming language, based on English, that is used primarily for commercial data processing.

common user access (CUA) The user interface portion of IBM's SAA enterprise architecture.

communication controller A type of communication control unit whose operations are controlled by one or more programs stored and executed in the unit. It manages the details of line control and routing of data through a network. for example, an IBM 3745.

communication protocol The rules governing the exchange of information between devices on a data link.

controller A device that coordinates and controls the operation of one or more input/output devices (such as workstations) and synchronizes the operation of such devices with the operation as a whole.

Customer Information Control System for Virtual Storage (CICS/VS) A licensed program that operates on a host system, such as System/370, 30xx, or 43xx, which can be used in a communications network.

database A collection of interrelated or independent data items to serve one or more applications.

DBMS (Database Management System) A structured software component designed to coordinate and facilitate management of data for multiple applications. DBMS products usually conform to one of several models (hierarchical, network, relational, or object oriented).

DB2   An IBM relational DBMS.

dial-up terminal   A terminal on a switched line.

DOS   See **MS-DOS**.

downloading   The process of sending software or data from a central source to remote stations.

dumb terminal   Terminals that are connected to a central processor and do not possess any processing capability.

emulation   The imitation of a computer system, performed by a combination of hardware and software, that allows a workstation to act as a terminal or other device attached to a host system.

enterprise computing   The goal of seamless integration of applications, data, user interfaces, and other computing resources among distributed heterogeneous systems of all sizes.

Ethernet   A bus local area network developed by Digital Equipment Corporation, Intel, and Xerox. Ethernet formed the basis for the IEEE 802.3 standard.

extended binary-coded decimal interchange code (EBCDIC)   A coded character set of 256 eight-bit characters used primarily in IBM environments.

front-end processor   A processor that can relieve a host computer of certain processing tasks, such as line control, message handling, code conversion, error control, and application functions.

gateway   Hardware and software used to interconnect local area networks to other systems, usually midrange or mainframe computers.

giga   Ten to the ninth power, 1,000,000,000 in decimal notation.

Graphical User Interface (GUI)   A user interface for a terminal or personal computer built around menus, windows, and pointing devices.

hierarchical network   A network in which processing and control functions are performed at several levels by computers specially suited for the functions performed.

high-level language (HHL)   A programming language, such as RPG, CL, BASIC, PL/I, Pascal, and COBOL, that translates computer programs in this language into several different machine codes.

IEEE (Institute of Electrical and Electronic Engineers)   An international professional society that issues its own standards and is a member of ANSI and ISO.

Information Warehouse   An IBM distributed database management architecture under SAA.

input/output (I/O)   Pertaining to a device or to a channel that may be involved in an input process and, at a different time, in an output process.

International Standards Organization (ISO)   An organization established to promote the development of standards to facilitate the international exchange of goods and services, and to develop mutual cooperation in areas of intellectual, scientific, technological, and economic activity.

kilo (K)   Thousand.

leased circuit   A service whereby a circuit, or circuits, of the public telephone network are made available to a user or group of users for their exclusive use; a nonswitched line.

leased line   A telephone reserved for the exclusive use of leasing customers. Also called a private line.

local area network (LAN)   A data communications system confined to a limited geographic area with moderate to high data rates (100 Kbps to 100 Mbps). The area served may consist of a single building, a cluster of buildings, or a campus-type arrangement. The network uses some type of switching technology and does not use common carrier circuits, although it may have gateways or bridges to other public or private networks.

logical unit (LU)   One of three types of network addressable units that serve as a port through which a user accesses the communications network.

log-off   The procedure by which a user ends a terminal session.

log-on   The procedure by which a user begins a terminal session.

mainframe   A large-scale, centralized, computer system.

mega (M)   Ten to the sixth power, 1,000,000 in decimal notation.

megahertz (MHz)   A unit of measure of frequency. 1 MHz = 1,000,000 hertz.

MIPS   Million Instructions Per Second.

modem   A functional unit that modulates and demodulates signals. One of the functions of a modem is to enable digital data to be transmitted over analog transmission facilities or common telephone lines.

MS-DOS   An operating system from Microsoft that has been the dominant operating system among IBM personal computers and compatibles.

MS Windows   Microsoft Windows, a GUI environment for desktop PCs.

MVS   An IBM operating system.

OfficeVision   IBM office information system that operates under SAA.

Open Systems Interconnection (OSI)   The use of standardized procedures to enable the interconnection of data processing systems in networks.

operating system   Software that controls the execution of programs; an operating system may provide services such as resource allocation, scheduling, input/output control, and data management.

OS/2   An IBM PC operating system and graphical user interface.

OS/400   An IBM operating system for the AS/400 computer.

OS/400-ICF file   A device file that allows a program on one system to communicate with a program on another system. There can be one or more sessions communicating at the same time with the same or different communication devices.

password   A unique string of characters that a program, computer operator, or user must supply to meet security requirements before gaining access to data.

peer   In network architecture, any functional unit that is in the same layer as another entity.

peer-to-peer networking   A network in which nodes communicate with each other as peers rather than in a hierarchical relationship.

physical device   A physical connection between devices on a network.

PROFS (Professional Office System)   IBM office information system product.

program device   A symbolic device that a program uses instead of a real device (identified by the device name). When the program uses a program device, the system redirects the operation to the appropriate real device.

protocol   A specification for the format and relative timing of information exchanged between communicating parties.

RISC (Reduced Instruction Set Computing/Computer)   RISC is an architecture style under which various processors have been developed.

session (SNA) A logical connection between two network locations that can be started, tailored to provide various connection protocols, and stopped, as requested.

SNA LU session type 6.2 protocol SNA application protocol for communications between peer systems.

SNA network The part of the user application network that conforms to the formats and protocols of systems network architecture. The SNA network consists of network addressable units, boundary function components, and the path control network.

source program The program that starts a session with a remote system.

source system The system that issues a request to establish communications with another system.

SQL (Structured Query Language) The standard, widely accepted relational database management language, developed by IBM, that is used in varying forms by most vendors of relational DBMS products.

synchronous A method of transmitting data over a network where the sending and receiving terminals are kept in synchronism with each other by a clock signal embedded in the data.

synchronous data link control (SDLC) A form of communications line control that uses commands to control the transfer of data over a communications line.

synchronous transmission Transmission in which data bits are sent at a fixed rate, with the transmitter and receiver synchronized. Synchronized transmission eliminates the need for start and stop bits.

Systems Network Architecture (SNA) The description of the logical structure, formats, protocols, and operational sequences for transmitting information units through, and controlling the configuration and operation of, networks.

target The program or system to which a request for processing is sent.

target program The program that is started on the remote system at the request of the source system.

TCP/IP (Transmission Control Protocol/Internet Protocol) A protocol set, originally developed for U.S. Department of Defense environments, used for specific layers of a multiple-layer communication protocol suite.

terminal A device in a system or network at which data can be either entered or displayed.

time-sharing A method that allows several interactive terminals to use one computer.

token-ring network A local area network that sends data in one direction throughout a specified number of locations by using the symbol of authority for control of the transmission line, called a token, to allow any sending station in the network (ring) to send data when the token arrives at that location.

transaction In systems with time-sharing, an exchange between a terminal and another device that accomplishes a particular action or result, for example, the entry of a customer's deposit and the updating of the customer's balance.

UNIX An operating system developed by AT&T that has become a de facto standard in the computer industry. Multiple variants are available from various consortia and vendors.

user Anyone who requires the services of a computing system.

user identification (user ID) The name used to associate the user profile with a user when a user signs on the system.

user password A unique string of characters that a system user must enter to identify him/herself to the system, if the system resources are secured.

WAN (wide area network) A communications network similar to a local area network, covering a larger geographical area.

Windows See **MS Windows**.

Windows NT A 32-bit operating system and graphical user interface.

workstation A device used to transmit information to or receive information from a computer, for example, a display station or printer.

3GL Third generation language: COBOL, FORTRAN, C, or any one of a number of other procedural languages.

4GL Fourth generation language—an "advanced" language usually found in vendor-specific environments. 4GLs usually feature reporting and querying facilities, advanced file and data management, and other capabilities that traditionally must be created by developers in 3GL environments.

Index